CAMBRIDGE ENGLISH PROSE TEXTS

*Science and Religion in
the Nineteenth Century*

s

CAMBRIDGE ENGLISH PROSE TEXTS

General editor: GRAHAM STOREY

OTHER BOOKS IN THE SERIES
The Evangelical and Oxford Movements, edited by Elisabeth Jay
Revolutionary Prose of the English Civil War,
. edited by Howard Erskine-Hill and Graham Storey

FORTHCOMING
Romantic Critical Essays, edited by David Bromwich
Burke, Godwin, Paine and the Revolution Controversy,
edited by Marilyn Butler
American Colonial Prose: John Smith to Thomas Jefferson,
edited by Mary Ann Radzinowicz
Victorian Criticism of the Novel,
edited by Edwin Eigner and George Worth

Science and Religion in the Nineteenth Century

edited by
TESS COSSLETT

CAMBRIDGE UNIVERSITY PRESS

Cambridge
London   New York   New Rochelle
Melbourne   Sydney

Published by the Press Syndicate of the University of Cambridge
The Pitt Building, Trumpington Street, Cambridge CB2 IRP
32 East 57th Street, New York, NY 10022, USA
296 Beaconsfield Parade, Middle Park, Melbourne 3206, Australia

First published 1984

Printed in Great Britain at The Pitman Press, Bath

Library of Congress catalogue card number: 83-7507

British Library Cataloguing in Publication Data

Science and religion in the nineteenth century—
  (Cambridge English prose texts)
  1. Religion and science
  I. Cosslett, Tess
  215 BL240.2

ISBN 0 521 24402 1 hard covers
ISBN 0 521 28668 9 paperback

Contents

Editorial note

Each extract has been taken from the first edition of the particular work. Authorial footnotes, when retained, have been included in the endnotes; editorial footnotes are indicated by letter and endnotes by number. In bibliographical references the place of publication is London, unless otherwise stated.

Introductory essay

In his *Autobiography* (1889), T. H. Huxley, the Victorian biologist, agnostic (he invented the word), and leading populariser of science, tells us of his 'untiring opposition to that ecclesiastical spirit, that clericalism, which in England, as everywhere else, and to whatever denomination it may belong, is the deadly enemy of science'[1] – an opposition that was one of the chief motivating forces of his life's work. Huxley's image of a necessary conflict between two deadly enemies became the received account of the relations between science and religion in the nineteenth century. In this 'battle', the turning-point is supposed to have come when Huxley confronted and routed Bishop Wilberforce, the opponent of evolution, at the British Association meeting in Oxford in 1860. From a twentieth-century perspective, perhaps coloured by the recent 'Creationist' controversies in America, it is easy to assume that Wilberforce was a Bible-thumping Fundamentalist totally opposed to scientific methods of investigation. It comes as a surprise to find that Wilberforce's objections to Darwin's theory were mainly scientific, that he had many leading scientists on his side, that he skilfully picked out all the weak points in Darwin's theory, and that his basic assumption was that science and religion were necessarily in harmony, a harmony which Darwin's theory threatened to disrupt.[2] His review of Darwin's *Origin of Species* in the *Quarterly Review* finally comes round to considering the opposition between the theory of evolution and the Creation story in the Bible, but this is not the main ground of his attack on Darwin. Evolution threatens not so much the revealed theology of the Bible, as the *natural theology* taught by science:

To oppose facts in the natural world because they seem to oppose Revelation, or to humour them so as to compel them to speak in its voice, is . . . but another form of the ever-ready feeble-minded dishonesty of lying for God, and trying by fraud or falsehood to do the work of the God of truth. It is with another and a nobler spirit that the true believer walks among the works of nature. The words graven on the everlasting rocks are the words of God, and they are graven by His hand. No more could they contradict His Word written in His book, than could the words of the old covenant graven by His hand on the stony tables contradict the writings of His hand in the volume of the new dispensation.[3]

Introductory essay

'Natural theology' means using the evidence of nature to prove God's existence and His goodness. Up to about 1860, most scientists and clergymen in England assumed that natural theology guaranteed a productive harmony between science and religion. The discoveries of the scientists provided religion with ever-more complex demonstrations of the design and order of God's universe; in this light, science was a religious pursuit. Here is an example of this reverent attitude on the part of the geologist Hugh Miller, describing a sea-urchin, in an early article: 'I am confident that there is not half the ingenuity, or half the mathematical knowledge, displayed in the dome of St Paul's at London, that we find exhibited in the construction of this simple shell.'[4]

In stark contrast, here is Darwin's opinion of such 'evidence' of God's 'design': 'We can no longer argue that, for instance, the beautiful hinge of a bivalve shell must have been made by an intelligent being. There seems to be no more design in the variability of organic beings and in the action of natural selection, than in the course which the wind blows.'[5]

It was the random, chance element in Darwin's theory that seemed to some thinkers to undermine the ordered beauty of the old 'design' argument, which had been so conclusively put by William Paley in his classic *Natural Theology* (1802). Because of the importance of natural theology to the Victorian debate, I have included an extract from Paley.[6]

Thus several modern historians have seen the Victorian 'conflict' as not between science and religion, but between 'religious science and irreligious science';[7] that is, between a science pursued in the interests of natural theology, that relates its findings to moral and religious values, and a new, professional, 'value-free' science. The triumph of this 'new' science in the modern world explains why we have been so ready to accept the science-versus-religion myth of its partisans, such as Huxley.

Significantly, natural theology began to be important in England at the same time as the rise of empirical science, in the late seventeenth century. It has been pointed out that both fitted in with the empirical, literal-minded approach of Puritanism.[8] Important early works on natural theology were John Ray's *The Wisdom of God as Manifested in the Works of the Creation* (1691), and William Derham's *Physico-Theology: or, a Demonstration of the Being and Attributes of God, from his Works of Creation* (1713). The scientists Robert Boyle and Isaac Newton were natural theologians. The tradition of natural theology was carried on in the 1830s in the eight *Bridgewater*

Treatises, in which scientists, four of them clergymen, demonstrated endlessly 'the Power, Wisdom, and Goodness of God, as manifested in the Creation'. Some natural theologians concentrated on evidence of order and design in the planetary system and in the laws of physics, as revealed by Newton. Others favoured the biological evidence of design in the organic world, the many beautiful and intricate adaptations of creatures to their surroundings. This is the type of evidence most favoured by Paley, who was something of an amateur naturalist himself.

In fact, natural history, and later geology, were eminently respectable pursuits for a clergyman to follow. Wilberforce was an amateur ornithologist, and, ironically, Darwin was at one point intended to become a clergyman. When his father opposed his plan to travel as naturalist on the *Beagle*, his uncle supported him, commenting that 'the pursuit of Natural History, though certainly not professional, is very suitable to a clergyman'.[9] This sort of duplication of roles means it is not easy to separate out individuals into two warring camps of scientists versus theologians, as James Moore has pointed out in his book *The Post-Darwinian Controversies*, which contains an important modern argument against the 'warfare' model of the history of science and religion in the Victorian period. For instance, if we look at some of the immediate reactions to Darwin's *Origin of Species*, from those to whom Darwin sent copies of the book, we find a negative response from the Rev Adam Sedgwick, geologist and clergyman, who chides Darwin for trying to break the essential link between the 'physical' and 'moral or metaphysical' parts of nature. On the other hand, we find a positive response from the Rev Charles Kingsley, clergyman and naturalist, who sees a noble new natural theology in the idea of an original Creation of self-developing forms.[10] Interestingly, both these clergymen/scientists are still taking natural theological ground in their responses to a new scientific theory; and from Kingsley's response we can also see that Darwin's theory did not necessarily strike the death-blow for natural theology.

What was it about Darwin's theory then that did seem, to some, to threaten the existing alliance between science and religion? To understand Sedgwick's response, we must understand the developments in geology in the first half of the nineteenth century, and the ways in which geology had been 'reconciled' with natural *and* revealed theology by scientists like Sedgwick, in a synthesis which evolutionary theory seemed to threaten. Again, the conflict centres on two kinds of science. At first sight, the geological discoveries would seem to be disruptive of natural theology as practised by Paley, and contradictory of revealed religion as set forth in Genesis. Geology showed that the earth was vastly older than had been assumed: the chronology of Archbishop Ussher (1581–1656), who dated the Creation at 4004 BC, was still officially accepted by the Church. Fossil evidence revealed that there had not just been one creation: species had been made extinct, and new ones created, over vast ages. Extinction could be seen as evidence of imperfection and wastefulness in God's design. Paley's 'design' argument had assumed a *fixed* creation, a once-and-for-all master plan for a perfectly adjusted machine. Geology revealed that the machine had had a history, during which it had changed, or been changed. The fossils seemed to show a 'progress' from lower to higher species: had species perhaps 'developed' of their own accord, and adapted *themselves* to changing surroundings? The French naturalist Lamarck had already suggested such a theory of development, at the beginning of the century. In that case, adaptation could not be evidence of God's direct workmanship, as it was for Paley, who seems to see God as a sort of Divine Engineer.

None of this was a problem for the Scriptural geologists such as Sedgwick, William Buckland, Thomas Chalmers, and Hugh Miller. The fossil evidence, with the absence of missing links, seemed to argue against Lamarck's theory. Instead, they saw in the rocks the evidence of a *series* of Divine Creations, each perfectly adapted, ascending progressively to the last and final Creation which included man, the culmination of the whole series. Thus they preserved the religious idea of man's recent and special separate creation by God. Miller writes mystically of the fossils of earlier creations as 'geologic prophecies' of man's creation.[11] This new scheme actually had advantages over Paley's natural theology: there was evidence not only of God's original creation of the world, but also of his direct and drastic intervention to change and improve His Creation at intervals. This geological theory of several Creations was known as 'catastrophism' – some of its proponents held that the most recent 'catastrophe' was Noah's Flood as described in the Bible. The catastrophists also had various other ingenious methods of 'reconciling' their discoveries with the Biblical narrative. (These are analysed in detail, and dismissed, by Charles Goodwin in extract 5.) For instance, the six 'days' of Creation in Genesis were read as six vast geological eras; or a long interval was held to have elapsed between the original creation of the world, and the 'six days' that followed, during which all the geological changes had occurred.

The strangest, and the most ingenious of these attempts to 'reconcile' Genesis and geology, was *Omphalos* (1857), by Philip Gosse, in which he argues that the fossils in the rocks are false evidence of a history of development, just as Adam's navel would be false evidence suggesting his previous embryonic development inside a natural mother.[12] But Gosse, a member of the literalist Plymouth Brethren, was outside the main stream of these geological 'reconcilers', who were mostly Broad Church Anglicans, apart from Hugh Miller and Thomas Chalmers, who were Scottish Evangelicals.

The catastrophists are not to be laughed at. They were eminent and productive scientists, whose theories were in line with the available facts. They attacked any theories of species 'evolution' on religious *and* on scientific grounds. The first nineteenth-century expression of an evolutionary theory in English, Robert Chambers' anonymous *Vestiges of the Natural History of Creation*,[13] played into their hands by being crude and unscientific in the extreme. It was easy for Sedgwick and Miller to shoot it down on scientific grounds, as well as expressing their moral and religious outrage. In particular, Chambers' theory of an animal ancestry for man shocked them: it degraded man from his special status as a rational, moral and spiritual creature.[14] Miller especially points out the difficulties for a belief in man's immortal soul entailed by a belief in his gradual evolution from lower species.[15] Chambers' theory of evolution also removes the direct creative intervention in which the catastrophists believed – God becomes a remote Creator, who ages ago impressed his evolutionary laws on matter,[16] and now leaves the whole development to proceed on its own, perhaps towards 'higher races' than mankind.

This Creator, as envisaged by Chambers, in fact resembles the Creator that Kingsley still finds implied by Darwin's theory. It is interesting that the reviled theories of earlier evolutionists were later taken up by the Church in the post-Darwinian effort to reconcile evolution and religion. Thus we will find Frederick Temple, later to become Archbishop of Canterbury, arguing in 1885 for just such a Creator, who 'impressed' the original laws on matter, as part of an attempt to show that Darwinism is not inconsistent with natural theology.[17] Similarly, earlier 'vitalist' theories of evolution were taken up by religious opponents of Darwin, such as the Catholic biologist St George Mivart,[18] who could accept 'guided' evolution, but not the random process of natural selection. Once again, it is necessary to point out that Mivart also had good scientific reasons for discounting natural selection as an adequate mechanism for bringing about evolution.

Introductory essay

Chambers' evolutionary theory was to some extent 'vitalist', in that it is caused by a mysterious 'law of development', which could almost be just another name for God's original plan. *Vestiges* is not in fact an irreligious book: it too is conceived in the spirit of natural theology, and aims first to show the universality of Law in God's Creation – the Law of Development is seen as a parallel to Newton's Law of Gravitation. Unity and plan are thus found everywhere. Like Paley's *Natural Theology*, the book ends by demonstrating the goodness of God, shown in the over-balance of pleasure as against pain in the Creation. Unavoidable individual pain will be compensated for by a scheme of 'mercy and redress' in the next world. *Vestiges* is the work of an old-fashioned amateur scientist, concerned to place his findings in a moral and religious perspective. 'Evolution' appears more as a philosophical notion than as a scientific theory.

The catastrophists were, however, under attack from a different, more scientifically respectable direction. From 1830 to 1833, Charles Lyell was publishing his *Principles of Geology*, in which he put forward his rival 'uniformitarian' theory. According to Lyell, all the past geological changes in the earth's surface could be explained by the gradual action of ordinary causes, such as erosion and deposition, which were still acting now. There was no need to invoke miraculous catastrophes: all had been accomplished by natural causes. Lyell was in fact developing an approach originally put forward by James Hutton, in his *Theory of the Earth* (1795). Hutton had said that, in the evidence of geology, 'We find no vestige of a beginning, – no prospect of an end',[19] and he had refused to speculate about questions of *origin*. This sounds dangerously like the atheistical 'infinity' theory that Paley and later Miller are at pains to refute:[20] if the world is infinite in duration, there is no need for an original Creator. But, as Hutton's defender Playfair pointed out, he had only meant that there was no evidence in *Nature* of a beginning:[21] for this we must go to Revelation. Nevertheless, this approach totally undercuts natural theology. Lyell too insists that he will keep away from all questions about 'cosmology'. Though he could be natural-theological on occasion, the *Principles* are dependent on an entirely different preconception from that which underlies the work of the catastrophists. Lyell assumes gradualism and natural causation,[22] and then amasses facts that fit his preconception. The catastrophists assumed divine intervention and design, and found the facts that fitted their preconception. Lyell is trying, as much as possible, to pursue science without regard to religious considerations – this is what makes him more modern, though not

6

necessarily more correct, than the catastrophists. In this he anticipates Darwin, even though he demolishes Lamarck's theory of development in the *Principles*, and even though his 'uniformitarian' approach hardly allows for the 'evolution' of anything *new*.[23]

From the point of view of the catastrophists, Darwin's *Origin of Species* (1859) must have seemed to unite the most dangerous elements of evolutionary and uniformitarian thought. Like Chambers, Darwin proposed an evolutionary origin for species, but unlike Chambers he provided a causal mechanism, natural selection, to bring it about. Unlike Chambers too, his main aim was not a religious or philosophical one: like Lyell, he largely avoided dealing with the religious implications of his theory – to some extent, his nervousness about these implications had delayed his publication of his theory for twenty years.[24] Darwin's aim, like Lyell's, is to explain what was previously thought to be miraculous, in terms of gradualism and natural causation. Natural selection, or the survival of the fittest, was the ordinary cause now in operation that could account for the whole of evolution, given a sufficiently long timespan. While it might be possible for Kingsley and Temple to argue that Darwin's theory still presupposed an original Creator who set the whole process off, the effect of Darwin's argument is to push the Creator out of areas which He had previously occupied, and substitute self-sufficient natural causes for Divine power. The eighteenth-century geologist Hutton might refuse to discuss ultimate questions about 'origins' – but the very title of Darwin's book, *The Origin of Species*, suggests that he will have to deal with such questions, and sensitive areas so far assigned to the Divine Creator. By definition, his theory of evolution of course disposes of the 'interventionist' theory of the catastrophists: it also disposes of Chambers' idea of a Creator who had planned and pre-programmed the whole development from the start, because of the *random* element in natural selection, by which any chance variation that happens to be useful to its possessor in the environment where it happens to be, is preserved.[25] Darwin's theory also highlighted the enormous amount of necessary waste and suffering in Nature, in the ruthless struggle for existence through which the 'fittest' are selected. At the end of the *Origin*, Darwin does try to argue, briefly, that the results of all this suffering are in the end 'good' – all the variations selected work for the good of their possessors, and further evolutionary 'progress' is certain.[26] But this has none of the conviction of Paley's belief in the predominant 'happiness' of Nature, and Darwin's private belief was that the evidence of imperfection, waste and suffering in Nature made against any belief in a benevolent Creator: 'I cannot persuade myself that a beneficent and omnipotent God would have designedly created the Ichneumonidae with the express intention of their feeding within the live bodies of Caterpillars, or that a cat should play with mice'.[27] Darwin's theory seems to stress *un*design rather than design: adaptations, by no means perfect, slowly and painfully built up by a process of trial and error.

It is thus clear why Sedgwick felt that Darwin was trying to break the necessary 'link' between the 'physical' and 'moral or metaphysical' parts of Nature. The essence of the conflict was between the old, religious, natural-theological science, and the new, irreligious, purely naturalistic science. In many ways, the factual evidence for Darwin's theory was not very strong: as Tyndall points out in the Belfast Address,[28] 'evolution' is hardly susceptible of proof – it is an imaginative reconstruction of past history from slender evidence – but its strength as a theory lies in its general 'harmony' with 'the method of nature'. That is, it depends on a faith in natural causation, and in 'the continuity of nature' – the same faith that in the Address leads Tyndall to extend Darwin's theory and cross 'the boundary of the experimental evidence' to imagine that life itself has originated naturally from unliving matter. Here Tyndall is using Darwin's theory as part of a near-complete 'materialistic' explanation of all phenomena, which is designed to take over from religion in the area of 'cosmogony'. It is this scientific frame of mind, this attitude to the external world, that constitutes the real threat to natural theology, rather than any particular factual evidence. Religion is being aggressively driven out of areas where it was previously in secure possession.

Darwin himself had not pushed his theory so far as to include the ultimate origin of life itself; and in the *Origin* he had also cautiously not pursued it so far in the other direction as to include the origin of *man*.[29] This was obviously another sensitive religious issue, and Darwin, unlike Tyndall or Huxley, had no interest in attacking religion directly. But popularly Darwin was immediately assumed to be suggesting that man was descended from the apes – this is what the exchange between Huxley and Wilberforce turned on at Oxford.[30] Obviously, such a descent made difficulties for the Christian conception of man as the only creature endowed with rationality, with moral responsibility, and with spiritual immortality. Darwin did eventually extend his theory to include man in *The Descent of Man* in 1871; and his attempts to explain the evolution of man's 'higher' faculties, including even his religious propensities, from simple animal instincts, seemed to many to be reductive, insulting and irreligious. Darwin's explanations of the origin of man were also not very scientifically convincing – and he was attacked on both scientific and religious grounds by the Catholic biologist, St George Mivart.[31] Mivart is cited by James Moore as another example of an individual hard to categorise on the assumption of a 'battle' between theologians on one side, and scientists on the other.[32] Though the issue between Darwin and Mivart was not centred on natural theology, it was still a dispute between two kinds of science – that which relates its findings to moral and religious issues, and that which does not. In fact, Darwin's approach tended to explain away moral and religious attitudes themselves as being only evolved animal instincts, with no universal validity. The psychological theories of Herbert Spencer, cited by Tyndall,[33] also tended to reduce human mental processes to the level of other organic and inorganic processes, from which they had evolved.

It has been pointed out that if there was a 'conflict' between science and religion after the publication of the *Origin of Species*, it was scientists like Huxley and Tyndall, rather than theologians, who were the aggressors.[34] We have seen how Tyndall claimed ground from religion, and how Huxley imaged his life's work as a battle against clericalism. In their retrospective historical accounts of the progress of science, they stressed examples of scientific martyrs, such as Bruno or Galileo, and of ecclesiastical bigotry and repression. For this version of history they were partly indebted to John William Draper's *History of the Intellectual Development of Europe*,[35] a book which is one of the sources of the influential 'warfare' model of the relations between religion and science. Huxley and Tyndall were not only concerned to 'free' science from the shackles of religion, they were also keen to extend scientific ways of thinking into other areas of life. Another of Huxley's aims in life was

to promote the increase of natural knowledge and to forward the application of scientific methods of investigation to all the problems of life, in the conviction . . . that there is no alleviation for the sufferings of mankind except veracity of thought and of action, and the resolute facing of the world as it is, when the garment of makebelieve, by which pious hands have hidden its uglier features is stripped off.[36]

Here Huxley sees his scientific mission as the removal of the outdated 'supernaturalist' approach of religion to life's problems. Similarly, Tyndall was involved in a campaign against the custom of 'special prayers' that were said in the churches at times of national emergency or disaster – again, he sees this custom as an outdated and even wicked application of ineffectual 'supernatural' remedies to natural disasters.[37] Both Huxley and Tyndall were engaged in conflicts and controversies about the necessity for scientific education.[38]

But why were Huxley and Tyndall so aggressively anti-clerical? It has been suggested that the real question here involves the professionalisation of science, and their social and political status as the new professional scientists.[39] Both of them were 'outsiders', self-made men who had not been educated through traditional English establishment channels. Huxley pursued a medical education in London, and Tyndall gained his scientific education in Germany. The cultural and educational establishment in England was dominated by the clergy, so it was natural for these scientific outsiders to see the Church as their enemy. In their bid to take over the cultural leadership of the country, they constructed a complete 'scientific' world-view to rival and supplant the world-view of Christianity; and also, presumably, in order to meet their own personal religious, moral and philosophical needs. Frank M. Turner has named this world-view, or set of attitudes, 'scientific naturalism'; we could also call it 'scientific agnosticism' or 'scientific humanism'. Among other leading exponents of variants of this creed are Herbert Spencer,[40] the mathematician W. K. Clifford, and, in a later generation, Leslie Stephen and John Morley. It is hard to tell whether such people adopted a science-based world-view for political reasons, as Turner suggests, or whether they genuinely felt it to be a consolation for the loss of their Christian faith. We could include in this category the novelist George Eliot, who clearly did not have any 'professional' reasons for her scientific agnosticism. 'Agnosticism' was quite different from atheism, which had French and/or destructively anti-establishment connotations. Agnostics held that certain ultimate questions of origin and destiny, which religion had always claimed to be able to answer, were 'unknowable' mysteries, that it is futile to inquire into.[41] But all other problems, including those of morality, were to be investigated and solved by the application of scientific thinking. Morality, like Nature, operates according to laws of cause and effect: as Huxley puts it, 'the safety of morality' lies 'in a real and living belief in that fixed order of Nature which sends social disorganisation upon the track of immorality, as surely as it sends physical disease after physical trespasses'.[42] A morality based on a theory of unavoidable consequences is also central to many of George Eliot's novels. Tyndall sees the actual pursuit of science as encouraging morality:

the earnest prosecutor of science, who does not work with the idea of producing a sensation in the world, who loves the truth better than the transitory blaze of today's fame, who comes to his task with a single eye, finds in that task an indirect means of the highest moral culture.[43]

Tyndall also finds room for religious feelings in his scientific world-view: he has a semi-mystical attitude to the structure of the universe as a whole, which he images as a gigantic organism:

> The celebrated Robert Boyle regarded the universe as a machine; Mr Carlyle prefers regarding it as a tree ... A machine may be defined as an organism with life and direction outside; a tree may be defined as an organism with life and direction within. In the light of these definitions, I close with the conception of Carlyle.[44]

This 'tree' image may allow Tyndall to go in for a form of Romantic Nature-worship; but it is interesting to remember that Robert Boyle was a leading natural theologian as well as a scientist, and his 'machine' image of the universe, like Paley's 'watch', necessarily implies a Divine Mechanic who made and runs it. Tyndall's 'organic' universe, 'with life and direction within', on the other hand, is self-sufficient and runs itself without the necessity for a Creator. Tyndall's reference to Carlyle is also interesting: he was great friends with Carlyle, and both he and Huxley were much influenced by Carlyle's writings.[45] Carlyle provided them with a means of being religious without any theology. He set an example of a moral earnestness and a mystical sense of wonder that could be quite detached from any particular religious creed.

Of course, another way to see all this is that these agnostics were merely transferring their typical Victorian moral earnestness, sense of duty, religiosity, and Romanticism, from the Christian world-view in which they were brought up, into their 'scientific' world-view. On this reading, their beliefs were in no way *derived* from science: in fact, it is quite possible that Christian ideas influenced and structured the development of modern science in the first place. As James Moore puts it, describing 'the standard revisionist thesis that Christian theology has been congenial to the development of modern science', 'the Christian (and especially the Reformed) doctrine of a contingent creation, ordered and superintended by a perpetual Providence, has led to the adoption of empirical methods in science and the extension of causo-mechanical explanations of nature'.[46] We come round full circle to the beneficial effect that Protestant natural theology had on science, an effect that the scientific agnostics tried to ignore and cut themselves off from, but which nevertheless shows in their moral and religious attitudes to their *scientific* beliefs. Huxley remarks in his *Autobiography* that as a child he wanted to be a clergyman, and that a strong religious streak has been noticed in his nature.[47] It has even been argued that Darwin's true precursors are the natural theologians Paley and Malthus, who supplied him respectively with the evidence of teleology in the natural world, which underlies Darwin's emphasis on *useful* adaptations; and with the theory of surplus population, which underlies natural selection.[48] It is true that Darwin often uses semi-religious or at least anthropomorphic language to describe the power and action of natural selection in 'creating' adaptive mechanisms,[49] which strongly recalls the language with which Paley describes his Designer–Creator. Darwin's theory also, like Paley's, depends on an analogy between human and natural activity: natural 'selection' is a metaphor from the 'selection' practised by breeders of domestic animals; Paley's 'design' argument presupposes that natural organisms are 'constructed' by means analogous to human workmanship. On the other hand, as we have seen, Darwin also overturns Paley's theory by substituting impersonal natural causation at precisely the place Paley had put his purposeful Divine Creator. 'Selection' is only a metaphor, not an analogy.

The interrelations between science and religion in the nineteenth century are thus much more intricate, complex, and positive than the simplified accounts of Huxley and Tyndall would have us believe. While the main area of conflict was *within* science, between natural theologians and agnostics who were trying to detach themselves from their natural-theological heritage, outside the scientific world the theologians themselves, for various reasons, were not especially interested in science. To more advanced or enlightened theologians, the Darwinian debate was a mere side issue in a much larger debate within the Church, or was merely irrelevant to what they took to be the true direction for theology. In the first place, within the Church of England, the controversy over Biblical Criticism overshadowed the controversy over evolution. Biblical Criticism meant studying the Bible like any other historical document, in its historical context, and working on problems like multiple authorship, and inconsistencies between different accounts of the same occurrence. It meant treating the Bible as a collection of documents written by fallible human historians, not as the directly inspired, literally true, Word of God. Those elements that were not historical were mythological. Theologians had in fact decided that this notion of direct divine 'inspiration' was not implicit in the original texts, it was a Greek idea imported by the early Church. This 'higher criticism', as it was called, had been pioneered in Germany, and was mostly done in a reverent and Christian spirit – there was no intention of debunking or destroying religion. It was also done within an 'evolutionary' model of history, derived from G. E. Lessing's *Education of the Human Race* (1780). Lessing saw God's revelation to man as *progressive* – the Old Testament was addressed to the childhood of the race, the New Testament was a further stage in our education; now perhaps new and higher forms of divine communication are possible. Thus, paradoxically, theology became 'evolutionary' before science did – 'progressive' and 'evolutionary' ways of thinking were everywhere: in history, in theology, in the Romantic interest in the psychological development of the individual. In this sense, theology and science were in harmony with each other and with the intellectual trends of the age.

It was possible, of course, for Biblical Criticism to lead away from Christianity towards humanism. George Eliot was influenced by this way of thought, and she translated David Strauss's *The Life of Jesus Critically Examined* (1835–36) in 1846, and Ludwig Feuerbach's *The Essence of Christianity* (1841) in 1854. Strauss argued that the truths of Christianity were still *philosophically* true; Feuerbach went further, and saw Christian belief as merely a projection of human needs and emotions. In her novels, George Eliot often seems to be trying to rediscover all the old religious values and emotions in a purely human context. But other thinkers did not see Biblical Criticism as necessarily destructive of Christianity. A moral and spiritual 'essence' of Christianity remained, despite the imperfection of the records through which it had been transmitted; moreover, this essence was located in our inner experience of its truth, not in external evidences of Revelation *or* of Nature. Coleridge was often quoted in this context: 'Evidences of Christianity! I am weary of the word: make a man feel the want of it . . . and you may safely trust it to its own evidence'.[50] Here we find also an impatience with the very *external* emphasis of natural theology – nineteenth-century theologians of all denominations, in different ways, were concerned to revive a more inward, spiritual, emotional type of religion, to replace the rather frigid, rationalistic, semi-deistic natural theology of the eighteenth century. Since most of the science-and-religion debate took place on natural-theological ground, it was not that interesting or relevant to progressive theologians.

Biblical Criticism first found favour in England with a group of liberal Anglicans centred on Thomas Arnold, Matthew Arnold's father. Interestingly, natural-theological *scientists*, like Sedgwick and Henslow, were also part of this group.[51] But the ideas of Biblical Criticism, as held within the Church of England, did not burst upon the British public at large until the publication of *Essays and Reviews* in 1860.[52] The controversy over *Essays and Reviews* eclipsed the smaller controversy over Darwin's *Origin*, published in the previous year. Bishop Wilberforce was again prominent on the conservative side, denouncing the Essayists, and urging them to give up their positions as clergymen: 'We see more danger in the shape of widespread suspicion and distrust likely to arise from their continuance as teachers of that Church, whilst clearly disbelieving her doctrines, than from their lucubrations themselves.'[53] Here Wilberforce represents opposition to new theological ideas, just as in his debate with Huxley he represents opposition to new scientific ideas. From his point of view, the Church was being assailed from two directions at once. German Biblical Criticism was undermining belief in revealed theology, while evolutionary science was undermining belief in natural theology. Here, the Bishop represented the views of most of the public: as Alvar Ellegård has demonstrated, in his invaluable book *Darwin and the General Reader*, the general Victorian readership believed literally in the Creation story in Genesis, and took the main point of Darwin's *Origin* to be the hateful 'ape theory'.[54] Samuel Butler parodies this literal-mindedness in *The Way of All Flesh*, from the more enlightened perspective of the 1870s and 1880s:

in those days people believed with a simple downrightness which I do not observe among educated men and women now. It had never so much as crossed Theobald's mind to doubt the literal accuracy of any syllable in the Bible. He had never seen any book in which this was disputed, nor met with anyone who doubted it. True, there was just a little scare about geology, but there was nothing in it. If it was said that God made the world in six days, why He did make it in six days, neither in more nor less; if it was said that He put Adam to sleep, took out one of his ribs and made a woman of it, why, it was so as a matter of course. He, Adam, went to sleep as it might be himself, Theobald Pontifex, in a garden, as it might be the garden at Crampsford Rectory during the summer months when it was so pretty, only that it was larger, and had some tame wild animals in it. Then God came up to him, as it might be Mr. Allaby or his father, dexterously took out one of his ribs without waking him, and miraculously healed the wound so that no trace of the operation remained. Finally, God had taken the rib perhaps into the greenhouse, and had turned it into just such another young woman as Christina. That was how it was done; there was neither difficulty nor shadow of difficulty about the matter. Could not God do anything He liked, and had He not in His own inspired Book told us that He had done this?

This was the average attitude of fairly educated young men and women towards the Mosaic cosmogony fifty, forty, or even twenty years ago.[55]

It is no wonder that such people found the account of the 'Mosaic Cosmogony' in *Essays and Reviews*[56] shocking, with its analysis of the erroneous science of the 'Hebrew records', which had been written by some aspiring but mistaken 'Hebrew Descartes or Newton'. The ideas of the Essayists eventually triumphed within the Church when Frederick Temple, one of their number, became Archbishop of Canterbury in 1896;[57] but we have to deal here with a time-lag in the acceptance of new ideas by the general public, including most of the clergy. Whether we see a 'conflict' or not between science and religion in the Victorian period depends to some extent at what *level* we observe the debate. On the level of popular reaction, *Essays and Reviews* was linked with Darwinism in a joint attack on the foundations of Christian belief. But from the more enlightened, and religious, perspective of the Essayists and their supporters, their approach made possible a closer *harmony* between science and religion. If the Church were not committed to a literalist interpretation of the Bible, it need fear nothing from any scientific theory that seemed to contradict the Bible. Thus one of the Essayists, the Rev Baden Powell, Professor of Geometry at Oxford, in his contribution 'On the Study of the Evidences of Christianity', praised Darwin's 'masterly volume which must soon bring about an entire revolution of opinion in favour of the grand principle of the self-evolving powers of nature'.[58] This sounds very like Tyndall's image of the independent cosmic tree, and is exactly the kind of idea that natural theologians and catastrophists had vigorously combatted in the past, because of its exclusion of God from an independent, self-developing Nature. Interestingly, Baden Powell had also been a supporter of *Vestiges*. In his contribution to *Essays and Reviews*, he is arguing for a separation of the areas of science and faith, and against miracle; though he still retains a vestigial natural theology, as does Charles Goodwin,[59] through his belief in designed Law in Nature.

The aim of the Essayists was thus to harmonise Christianity with contemporary intellectual developments: as Benjamin Jowett, one of the leading contributors, put it, 'The Christian religion is in a false position when all the tendencies of knowledge are opposed to it. Such a position cannot be long maintained, or can only end in the withdrawal of the educated class from the influences of religion.'[60] It is interesting that, on the whole, the scientific agnostics were of the same party as the Essayists. There was an extreme 'scientific' attack on *Essays and Reviews* from the positivist, Frederic Harrison,[61] who approved of their approach to the Bible, but, like Wilberforce, urged them to give up the pretence of being Christians at all. Influenced by the French positivist philosopher, Auguste Comte, Harrison saw the debate in terms of a conflict between outmoded 'theological' beliefs and the new 'positivist' (i.e. objective and scientific) beliefs. This may sound a bit like the 'conflict' myth of Huxley and Tyndall, but in fact the scientific agnostics had very little time for positivism. In his lecture 'On the Physical Basis of Life' (1868), Huxley maintains that 'in so far as my study of what specially characterises the Positive Philosophy has led me, I find therein little or nothing of any scientific value, and a great deal which is as thoroughly antagonistic to the very essence of science as anything in ultramontane Catholicism'.[62] Huxley is here referring to Comte's efforts to construct a religion in which the worship of Humanity would be substituted for the worship of God. This authoritarianism was quite opposed to Huxley's 'agnosticism', and to the 'liberal' theology of the Broad Church party who had produced *Essays and Reviews*. In fact, Huxley was a friend of Baden Powell, and when the Essayists were attacked and threatened with prosecution, he was one of the subscribers to a *Memorial to the Rev. Dr. Temple*, which declared that 'Feeling as we do that the discoveries in science, and the general progress of thought, have necessitated some modifications of the views generally held on Theological matters, we welcome these attempts to establish religious teaching on a firmer and broader foundation'.[63] Tyndall was a close friend of Dean Stanley, a supporter of the Essayists, who became his personal pastor. Huxley's support for the teaching of the Bible in schools is famous. The scientific agnostics only attacked what they saw as clerical repression of science, or invasion of the territory of science: any liberal tendencies within the Church were welcomed by them.

The Essayists' aim of reconciling Christianity and knowledge was eventually fulfilled, as far as the Darwinian theory of evolution was concerned, in Frederick Temple's Bampton Lectures of 1884, on 'The Relations between Religion and Science'.[64] The lectures, unlike the earlier *Essays and Reviews*, met with general approval, and Temple, as Bishop of Exeter, openly accepted Darwin's theory as true, though he did point out some gaps in it, where he still saw room for miracle. Temple also still sees room for a Darwinian natural theology, just as Charles Kingsley and Darwin's friend the scientist Asa Gray had done.[65] But he is not basing his faith on natural theology, he is merely showing that Paleyism is not incompatible with Darwinism. He is more interested in basing faith on inner spiritual conviction. As far as theology was concerned, natural theology faded out because it was felt to be old-fashioned and nonessential. It is within science that there was a 'battle' to remove a natural theological outlook that had been both useful and productive. With both sides giving up the natural theological ground, there was no need for a conflict any more. The two concluding extracts in this collection, by the scientific agnostic Tyndall, and the Anglican Bishop Temple, both present arguments for a 'reconciliation' of science and religion. But both also first define science and religion as belonging to quite separate spheres, the external and the internal worlds respectively. Tyndall banishes religion from 'the entire domain of cosmological theory', but nevertheless pays homage to the strength of the 'religious sentiment' in mankind, which he wishes to confine to the subjective areas of 'poetry and emotion'. Temple bases religion on inward experience, though he does still argue for *some* 'supernatural' intervention in Nature. But on the whole, religion is giving up its traditional claim to provide objective knowledge about the natural world, either through revealed theology or through natural theology. Rather than a 'conflict' between religion and science, we have a splitting apart, a compartmentalisation, of two ways of knowing which were once in harmony. As one religious periodical said of Darwin's *Origin*, 'It's publication is a mistake . . . at this time of day, when science has walked in calm majesty out from mists of prejudice and been accepted as a sister by sound theology'.[66] This splitting apart may mark the 'emancipation' of modern science from theology, but whether the human race as a whole has gained from the pursuit of 'value-free' science is an open question.

While Temple's Lectures may mark the acceptance of Darwinism by the Broad Church party, what of other parties and denominations? Some Evangelicals, prone to literalist interpretation of the Bible, did make head-on attacks on science. For instance, Dean Cockburn of York, at the British Association meeting in 1844, attacked the 'reconcilers' of Genesis and geology, especially Adam Sedgwick and William Buckland. Here is how his attack is described in *The Life and Letters of Sedgwick*:[67]

The Very Reverend William Cockburn, DD was at that time Dean of York. He was a Cambridge man of some distinction, having been twelfth wrangler in 1795, Fellow of St John's College, and Christian Advocate from 1803 to 1810. It might therefore have been expected that his Cambridge training would have taught him at least the rudiments of scientific methods; and that he would not have propounded crude theories upon a subject in which he was a mere beginner. For some years, however, he had become possessed with the notion that the cause of biblical truth was being emperilled by the theories of the geologists in general, and of Dr Buckland in particular; and in 1838 he had testified against the Association by warning the Duke of Northumberland, then President, against what he then called, *The Dangers of Peripatetic Philosophy*. The York meeting therefore was a golden opportunity. Under the shadow of his own Cathedral he would confute his special opponent, and in his person discredit the whole body of assembled philosophers. He obtained leave to read in the Geological Section a paper entitled: *Critical Remarks on certain Passages in Dr. Buckland's Bridgewater Treatise.* A writer in Chambers's *Edinburgh Journal* has left a description of the scene: The whimsicality of the attempt would have caused the Section to reject such paper from any man of inferior note; but the local importance of its author, and dread of being accused of fear to meet such an opponent, determined them to give it a hearing. When this was known on the morning of Friday, a vast multitude flocked to the section, and thus gave additional importance to what was at best a kind of indecent oddity in the course of the proceedings. In due time the Dean, a tall and venerable figure, with an air of imperturbable composure, walked through the crowd, and took his place by invitation beside the President on the platform. His paper, which he read with a firm voice, was briefly and elegantly expressed, but otherwise was a most extraordinary production. To the mind of the writer, the whole of those collections of facts and illustrations which the geologists have made during forty years, seemed to have existed in vain. He first presented a set of objections against the view of the earth's early history given by Dr Buckland in his *Bridgewater Treatise*; and then proceeded to develop a theory of his own, accounting for all the phenomena in a manner designed to reduce them within a very brief space of time. The theory was a wilder dream than any of Burnet's or Woodward's, and such as could not be listened to with gravity by any one acquainted with the science; yet, amidst the laughter which hailed it, the author went on in an unfaltering manner to the end, when he quietly sat down beside Mr Warburton.

The Dean attempted to explain the Mosaic cosmogony literally. Marine volcanoes, he thought, together with the supernatural rain of the Flood, had deposited all the strata, as we see them now, in the course of a few days; and the embedded fossils represent the remains of animals that were so obliging as to die in the definite and regular order in which their shells and bones are now deposited.

The task of replying to this attack was confided to Sedgwick, who, the same writer tells us, 'enchained the audience for an hour and a half, alternately charming them by his vast learning, and throwing them off their gravity by the most amusing and grotesque illustrations'. He began by pointing out at some length that the proper business of the Association was to collect facts, not to propound theories, and that such a discussion as the present would never, he hoped, be permitted again. Then he was at pains to follow the Dean through his 'irrational guesses and absurd hypotheses', as though he were dealing with an opponent worthy of his steel. His speech, as reported in *The Athenaeum*, is severe; but we have been told by one who was present that as delivered it was remarkable for a scornful bitterness beyond the power of any reporter to reproduce.

A castigation so thorough would have reduced most antagonists to silence. Not so Dean Cockburn. He demanded a second discussion; and, when this was refused, he published his paper with a new title: *The Bible defended against the British Association.* Moreover for some time he continued to harass Sedgwick with long letters, in which he not only questioned him on particular points, but entreated him to formulate a precise theory of creation. These letters the Dean published as soon as they were written; but Sedgwick wisely declined to allow him to pursue a similar course with his answers.

At the present time even the most devout and the most orthodox have abandoned those unprofitable attempts to give a literal interpretation to the figurative language of Scripture which were indulged in fifty years ago. Hence it is almost impossible to realise the alarm excited by the earlier results of geological research; and the hysterical denunciations of science and its professors which were then so common can hardly be read without a smile. Ignorant and foolish as Dean Cockburn was, it is easy to see, from the number of editions of his pamphlet published in the course of a few weeks, that he represented the feelings of a large majority of his countrymen.

I have quoted this account at length, since this collection does not contain any such examples of direct, all-out clerical attacks on science. As we can see here, such attacks were treated with incredulity and ridicule by the more informed and educated, and especially by clerical scientists like Sedgwick. But, on the other hand, as the writer here points out, Dean Cockburn's views did represent those of most of the public at large. Again, the problem is at what *level* to take the controversy. For instance, Ellegård's book furnishes many examples of direct religious attacks on Darwin's theory, such as this, from the *Methodist Recorder* of 1866: 'We regard this theory, which seeks to eliminate from the universe the immediate, ever-present, all-pervasive action of a living and personal God, which excludes the possibility of the supernatural and the miraculous . . . as practically destructive of the authority of divine revelation, and subversive of the foundation of both religion and morality'.[68] But to return to Dean Cockburn: against the popularity of his views, can be set the enormous equivalent popularity of *Vestiges*, which came out in the same year as the meeting just described.[69] If the public were hungry for 'fundamentalist' religion, they were also hungry for evolutionary theories. Dean Cockburn's views were not necessarily typical of Evangelicals: the Scottish Evangelical Hugh Miller was an immensely popular Scriptural geologist,[70] and his biographer comments,

His Evangelical Religion was of that early and vigorous type, which, having complete faith in truth, had no fear that there might turn out to be heresy in science. He belonged to the great old Evangelical school, and was perhaps its last representative to whom the title great can be accorded. . . . Hugh Miller saw with grief inexpressible that the Evangelical party in England, with its *Record* newspaper and its Dean Cockburns, was taking the fatally wrong turn in the matter of science and religion.[71]

A final interesting point about the British Association meeting in York is that in its tone and outcome it was very like the modern popular idea of the Oxford meeting of 1860 – that is, ignorant clerical opposition, based on the Bible, meeting scientific defeat. But the issues which divided Dean Cockburn on the one hand, from Adam Sedgwick on the other were quite different, and less central, than those which divided Bishop Wilberforce, Sedgwick and Owen from Darwin and Huxley.

Where were the Anglo-Catholics and the Catholics in this controversy? Charles Gillispie remarks that in the Oxford of the 1830s, the leaders of the Tractarian movement were hostile to science, and moreover 'the religious issue they raised tended to absorb the attention of the more intellectual members of the university'.[72] These issues had nothing to do with natural theology or science – theology was taking a quite different direction. But James Moore points out that, later on, in 1871,

H. P. Liddon, a canon of St Paul's, and a very orthodox Anglo-Catholic, could provide for belief in an original act of creation and the recognition of design in nature 'even if a doctrine of evolution should in time be accepted as scientifically, and so as theologically certain'. Evolution, he stated, 'from a Theistic point of view, is merely our way of describing what we can observe of God's continuous action upon the physical world'. Elsewhere in the same year, in a sermon preached at St Mary's, Oxford, Liddon went out of his way to cite approvingly a passage from Peter Lombard's *Sententiae* respecting the creative activity of God, a passage which, said Liddon, 'employs terms which almost read like a tentative anticipation of Dr Darwin's doctrine of the origin of species'. Even Liddon's master, the aged leader of the High Church Party which came to bear his name, the Reverend E. B. Pusey, eventually allowed for the truth of evolution, provided that it did not entail 'belief in our apedom'.[73]

Owen Chadwick also remarks that Pusey and Liddon were unexpectedly non-aggressive towards science, while their main hostility was directed towards Biblical Criticism.[74]

Roman Catholicism was in fact less vulnerable to scientific discoveries than was Protestantism, with its dependence on the Bible and on natural theology. In contrast, the Roman Catholics based their faith on the dogmatic authority of the Church. This attitude, and its consequences for physical science, are clearly set out in Cardinal Newman's *Idea of a University*.[75] Newman insists that science and theology pursue entirely different and separate methods of investigation:

Induction is the instrument of Physics, and deduction only is the instrument of Theology. There the simple question is, What is revealed? all doctrinal knowledge flows from one fountain head. If we are able to enlarge our views and multiply our propositions, it must be merely by the comparison and adjustment of the original truths; if we would solve new questions, it must be by consulting old answers. The notion of doctrinal knowledge absolutely novel, and of simple addition from without, is intolerable to Catholic ears, and never was entertained by any one who was even approaching to an understanding of our creed. Revelation is all in all in doctrine; the Apostles its sole depository, the inferential method its sole instrument, and ecclesiastical authority its sole sanction. The Divine Voice has spoken once for all, and the only question is about its meaning. Now this process, as far as it was reasoning, was the very mode of reasoning which, as regards physical knowledge, the school of Bacon has superseded by the inductive method: – no wonder, then, that that school should be irritated and indignant to find that a subject-matter remains still, in which their favourite instrument has no office; no wonder that they rise up against this memorial of an antiquated system, as an eyesore and an insult; and no wonder that the very force and dazzling success of their own method in its own departments should sway or bias unduly the religious sentiments of any persons who come under its influence. They assert that no new truth can be gained by deduction; Catholics assent, but add that, as regards religious truth, they have not to seek at all, for they have it already. Christian Truth is purely of revelation; that revelation we can but explain, we cannot increase, except relatively to our own apprehensions; without it we should have known nothing of its contents, with it we know just as much as its contents, and nothing more. And, as it was given by a divine act independent of man, so will it remain in spite of man. Niebuhr may revolutionise history, Lavoisier chemistry, Newton astronomy; but God himself is the author as well as the subject of theology. When Truth can change, its Revelation can change; when human reason can outreason the Omniscient, then may it supersede His work.

Holding this view of theology, Newman is highly suspicious of natural theology:

I have yet another consideration to add, not less important than any I have hitherto adduced. The physical sciences, Astronomy, Chemistry, and the rest, are doubtless engaged upon divine works, and cannot issue in untrue religious conclusions. But at the same time it must be recollected that Revelation has reference to circumstances which did not arise till after the heavens and the earth were made. They were made before the introduction of moral evil into the world: whereas the Catholic Church is the instrument of a remedial dispensation to meet that introduction. No wonder then that her teaching is simply distinct, though not divergent, from the theology which Physical Science suggests to its followers. She set before us a number of attributes and acts on the part of the Divine Being, for which the material and animal creation gives no scope; power, wisdom, goodness are the burden of the physical world, but it does not and could not speak of mercy, long-suffering, and the economy of human redemption, and but partially of the moral law and moral goodness. 'Sacred theology', says Lord Bacon, 'must be drawn from the words and oracles of God: not from the light of nature or the dictates of reason. It is written, that 'the Heavens declare the glory of God'; but we nowhere find it that the Heavens declare the will of God; which is pronounced a law and a testimony, that men should do according to it. Nor does this hold only in the great mysteries of the Godhead, of the creation, of the redemption. . . . We cannot doubt that a large part of the moral law is too sublime to be attained by the light of nature; though it is still certain that men, even with the light and law of nature, have some notions of virtue, vice, justice, wrong, good, and evil'. That the new and further manifestations of the Almighty, made by Revelation, are in perfect harmony with the teaching of the natural world, forms indeed one subject of the profound work of the Anglican Bishop Butler; but they cannot in any sense be gathered from nature, and the profound silence of nature concerning them may easily seduce the imagination, though it has no force to persuade the reason, to revolt from doctrines which have not been authenticated by facts, but are enforced by authority. In a scientific age, then, there will naturally be a parade of what is called Natural Theology, a widespread profession of the Unitarian creed, an impatience of mystery, and a scepticism about miracles.[76]

For Newman, natural theology is dangerously associated with both Protestantism and science. His conclusion is that science and theology do *not* 'correspond', they have separate territories: 'What can be more sacred than Theology? What can be more noble than the Baconian method? But these two do not correspond; they are mis-matched. The age has mistaken lock and key. It has broken the key in a lock which does not belong to it; it has ruined the wards by a key which never will fit into them.'[77] This is quite a different metaphor from Sedgwick's image of a necessary 'link' between physical and metaphysical, maintained by natural-theological science. Newman also has no difficulty with 'harmonising' the Creation story with any scientific findings, since the Church has not yet pronounced authoritatively on the interpretation of Genesis.[78]

I have quoted at such length from Newman, again because his Catholic point of view is not represented in this collection. In a sense, his argument makes science simply irrelevant to religion: there is no 'common ground upon which Theology and Physical Science may fight a battle'.[79] This does not mean that Newman is dividing up territory and conceding ground to science, as Temple seems to be doing. He is not handing over the external world to science and reserving only the internal world for theology – rather, he is saying they are two quite different methods of approaching, of knowing, the world as a whole. From a theological point of view, the 'natural' occurrences of science are 'supernatural': 'The two informations are like the distinct subjects represented by the lines of the same drawing, which, accordingly as they are read on their concave or convex side, exhibit to us now a group of trees with branches and leaves, and now human faces hid amid the leaves, or some majestic figures standing out from the branches';[80]

. . . from religious investigations, as such, physics must be excluded, and from physi-cal, as such, religion; and if we mix them, we shall spoil both. The theologian, speaking of the Divine Omnipotence, for the time simply ignores the laws of nature as existing restraints upon its exercise; and the physical philosopher, on the other hand, in his experiments upon natural phenomena, is simply ascertaining those laws, put-ting aside the question of that Omnipotence. If the theologian, in tracing the ways of Providence, were stopped with objections grounded on the impossibility of physical miracles, he would justly protest against the interruption; and were the philosopher, who was determining the motion of the heavenly bodies, to be questioned about their Final or their First Cause, he too would suffer an illogical interruption. The latter asks the cause of volcanoes, and is impatient at being told it is 'the divine vengeance'; the former asks the cause of the overthrow of the guilty cities, and is preposterously referred to the volcanic action still visible in their neighbourhood.[81]

Thus on the one hand Newman is offering no opposition to science; but on the other he is refusing to give up the 'supernatural' ground that Huxley and Tyndall were demanding from the theologians. From his point of view, theology has no need to adapt or change because of what science discovers. In fact, in 1864, the encyclical *Quanta Cura* condemned the idea that 'the Roman Pontiff can and ought to reconcile and harmonise himself with progress, with liberalism, and with modern civilisation'.[82] It was partly this intransigent attitude on the part of the contemporary Roman Catholic Church that influenced John Draper in the construction of his 'warfare' model of the relations between religion and science, which he consolidated in his *History of the Conflict between Religion and Science* in 1874. On the other hand, as James Moore points out, Draper was almost certainly over-reacting to what was not a real threat.[83]

So was there a conflict or not, and between whom? The answer seems to depend on the myth one chooses to adopt, the point of view one takes. From Sedgwick's or Miller's viewpoint, the conflict was between religious and irreligious science, and only arose if science falsely tried to detach itself from its productive harmony with natural theology. But from Newman's point of view, the unreal conflict only arose in the first place just because Protestantism had sold out to natural theology. According to Draper, Huxley and Tyndall, there was and always had been a conflict between the obscurantist and superstitious Catholic Church, and the light-bearing forces of science; but according to Tyndall, Huxley, Temple and the other Essayists, there need be no conflict between scientific naturalism and the enlightened, Biblical-critical, Broad Church. Darwin himself was simply not interested in religious questions, and lost his faith early and easily. But Alfred Russell Wallace, the co-discoverer of natural selection, ended by rejecting the claims of naturalistic science to explain everything, and became a spiritualist.[84] From the point of view of the general public, scientific materialism may have seemed to be trying to take over from religion as an explanation of the world, reducing all to mechanism and natural causes. But, from another angle, as Huxley profoundly remarked in his account of 'The Reception of the *Origin of Species*',

There is a great deal of talk and not a little lamentation about the so-called religious difficulties which physical science has created. In theological science, as a matter of fact, it has created none. Not a solitary problem presents itself to the philosophical Theist, at the present day, which has not existed from the time that philosophers began to think out the logical grounds and the logical consequences of Theism. All the real or imaginary perplexities which flow from the conception of the universe as a deterministic mechanism, are equally involved in the assumption of an Eternal, Omnipotent and Omniscient Deity. The theological equivalent of the scientific conception of order is Providence; and the doctrine of determinism follows as surely

Introductory essay

from the attributes of foreknowledge assumed by the theologian, as from the universality of natural causation assumed by the man of science.[85]

Likewise the problem of suffering, and the idea of a 'fallen', imperfect Nature, were not new to theology, nor were they first created by Darwin's theory; they had just been temporarily obscured by the optimistic natural theology of the eighteenth century. The theological view of the world was by no means irrelevant to the discoveries of Darwinian science: the new science merely showed up the inadequacies of natural theology, and forced those theologians who had not done so already to rethink their faith in a more profound, spiritual, and sometimes traditional, way.

1. *William Paley,*
Natural Theology; or, Evidences of
the Existence and Attributes of the
Deity, Collected from the
Appearances of Nature (1802)

Chapters 1–3, pp. 1–44

The Rev William Paley taught at Cambridge from 1768 to 1776, and became Archdeacon of Carlisle in 1782. This extract from his *Natural Theology* gives the framework within which much of the succeeding debate will be conducted; and it also introduces some of the complexities in the relation between science and religion in the nineteenth century. Paley is attempting to prove the existence of God from the evidence of Nature, and in particular he is using the argument from Design: that is, that the evidence of design, in the sense of purposeful contrivance, in Nature, leads us to infer a Divine Designer as its Creator. His argument is not original (both his 'watch' analogy, and the example of the eye, had been used before), but it lucidly sums up a theological approach that had been enormously influential in the eighteenth century. Paley's work became a classic, and continued its influence throughout the nineteenth century, becoming a set book for examination at Cambridge. We will find Hugh Miller referring to and extending Paley's 'watch' analogy in 1855 (see pp. 68–9), and Frederick Temple still not abandoning the design argument in 1885 (see p. 191).

It is significant that the growth of natural theology coincides with the rise of modern science in the late seventeenth century. Like that science, natural theology was supposed to be based on an empirical approach to natural evidences, and a mechanical model of the universe. Thus neither empiricism nor mechanism were seen as threats to religion – instead, both were used to strengthen religious belief. So Paley amasses empirical evidences of God's existence from biological facts, and happily reduces organic beings to feats of mechanical engineering in his efforts to prove the existence of an originating Mechanic. The nineteenth century begins with science and religion not just in harmony, but mutually interdependent. Not only did theologians use scientific evidence, but scientists investigated Nature with a religious reverence for the wonders of Divine design. Science was thus seen as a religious pursuit, providing ever more evidence for God's existence. Paley himself writes not just as a theologian, but as a scientist – he was a keen amateur naturalist, and many of his careful descriptions of organic structures and adaptations could well have been written by Darwin. This is not just coincidence: in fact, Darwin had read Paley at Cambridge. As he wrote later, 'I do not think I hardly ever admired a book more than Paley's "Natural Theology". I could almost formerly have said it by heart' (Letter of 1859, *Life and Letters* (1887), vol. 2, p. 219). It is possible to see Paley's influence in Darwin's observations of intricate biological adaptations in *The Origin of Species*: but

William Paley (1734–1805)

of course Darwin uses these observations as 'evidences' not of God's existence but of the operations of the purely mechanical process of natural selection. As Darwin said in his *Autobiography*:

> The old argument from design in nature, as given by Paley, which formerly seemed to me so conclusive, fails, now that the law of natural selection has been discovered. We can no longer argue that, for instance, the beautiful hinge of a bivalve shell must have been made by an intelligent being. There seems to be no more design in the variability of organic beings and in the action of natural selection, than in the course which the wind blows. (ed. Gavin de Beer (1974), pp. 50–1)

If we understand the background in natural theology, we can see how devastating Darwin's argument was to the widely accepted relationship between science and religion. Not only did the theory of natural selection explain functional adaptations without recourse to a Designer, but it also used the very same evidences that Paley had used, to a vastly different end. What had been the prop of religion was now turned against it. We can see that the emphasis on natural theology, as opposed to revealed religion, which had originally allowed a harmony between science and religion, eventually and inevitably produced a deep and painful rift, as mechanical explanations were extended into areas of 'origin' and 'creation' that had previously been reserved for God. As Leslie Stephen says of Paley,

> ... his God exists in space and time. A scientific induction, as he seems to imagine, would prove that at some time or other, a being of indefinite power took rude lumps of matter in his hands, rolled them into balls, and sent them spinning through space. So tremendous a catastrophe requires to be moved to as great a distance as possible; but it is not to be removed altogether out of time. Place your creative impulse at any distance you please, at six thousand or sixty million years, and Paley's God stands for the aggregate of the preceding forces. Since that date, the field is open as widely as possible to the researches of science; before it everything is hid in a mystery, which we call God. Paley is content, so long as we admit that it happened some time or other; and would allow men of science to push it as far off as possible. This curious compromise, therefore, admits for a brief period of reconciliation between science and theology. God, indeed, has almost become an object of scientific investigation; had we but a sixth sense, we might expect actually to detect him in the act of creating; and yet science may investigate the working of the machinery, instead of its original construction, without risk of meeting the supernatural. The man of science may examine the functions, though he cannot enquire into the origin of the organs ... (*History of English Thought in the Eighteenth Century* (1876; 3rd ed. 1902), vol. I, pp. 413–14)

But once 'the man of science' did inquire into the 'origin', Paley's remote God could easily be dispensed with. On the other hand, it is only fair to point out that Paley intended his natural theology to complement revealed religion, not to supersede it or stand alone. His finite and remote God was supplemented by the omnipotent and loving God of Revelation. Paley was not a deist, though some of his arguments had been used by deists.

In order to persuade his readers of the irrefutability and self-evidence of his arguments, Paley adopts a patient, almost school-masterly, expository style, using simple, repetitive or cumulative sentence structures. All the questions and doubts that might occur to his audience are carefully articulated and exhaustively answered. He spends two whole chapters establishing the first term of his watch analogy, demolishing all objections to the watch as evidence of design, before he springs its full meaning and implications on us, as an analogy of the universe. His tone is that of a simple, plain, honest, down-to-earth inquirer, painstakingly examining the empirical evidence, and drawing the obvious logical deductions from it. By contrast, his opponents are made to look both irrational and supersubtle. Atheism is an absurdity that ignores the manifest evidence. But despite the appearance of logical deduction, the crux of his argument depends on the questionable design = Designer equation: here Paley resorts to frequent repetition of the formulae 'design ... Designer', 'contrivance ... Contriver', the obvious relation between the words making the logical relation seem self-evident and irrefutable. Paley's many analogies between the natural and the man-made (the watch, the chair, the mill, the telescope) have a strange, grotesque charm, rather like the imagery of the metaphysical poets: every logical intricacy of the analogy is pursued and elaborated, as when Paley imagines a watch reproducing itself by subtle mechanisms; or describes the eyebrow as a 'thatched penthouse' and the tear-duct as a 'waste-pipe'. The absurdity of the comparison, and our delight in the ingenuity with which it is made, are of course not effects intended by Paley. Rather he intended to evoke a childlike delight at *God's* ingenuity and intricate workmanship.

Chapter I

State of the Argument

In crossing a heath, suppose I pitched my foot against a *stone*, and were asked how the stone came to be there, I might possibly answer, that, for any thing I knew to the contrary, it had lain there for ever; nor would it perhaps be very easy to show the absurdity of this answer. But suppose I had found a *watch*[1] upon the ground, and it should be enquired how the watch happened to be in that place, I should hardly think of the answer which I had before given, that, for any thing I knew, the watch might have always been there. Yet why should not this answer serve for the watch, as well as for the stone? Why is it not as admissible in the second case, as in the first? For this reason, and for no other, viz. that, when we come to inspect the watch, we perceive (what we could not discover in the stone) that its several parts are framed and put together for a purpose, e.g. that they are so formed and adjusted as to produce motion, and that motion so regulated as to point out the hour of the day; that, if the several parts had been differently shaped from what they are, of a different size from what they are, or placed after any other manner, or in any other order than that in which they are placed, either no motion at all would have been carried on in the machine, or none which would have answered the use, that is now served by it. To reckon up a few of the plainest of these parts, and of their offices, all tending to one result:- We see a cylindrical box containing a coiled elastic spring, which, by its endeavor to relax itself, turns round the box. We next observe a flexible chain (artificially wrought for the sake of flexure) communicating the action of the spring from the box to the fusee. We then find a series of wheels, the teeth of which catch in, and apply to, each other, conducting the motion from the fusee to the balance, and from the balance to the pointer; and at the same time, by the size and shape of those wheels, so regulating that motion, as to terminate in causing an index, by an equable and measured progression, to pass over a given space in a given time. We take notice that the wheels are made of brass, in order to keep them from rust; the springs of steel, no other metal being so elastic; that over the face of the watch there is placed a glass, a material employed in no other part of the work, but, in the room of which, if there had been any other than a transparent substance, the hour could not be seen without opening the case. This mechanism being observed (it requires indeed an examination of the instrument, and perhaps some previous knowledge of the subject, to perceive and understand it; but being once, as we have said, observed and understood), the inference, we think, is inevitable; that the watch must have had a maker; that there must have existed, at some time and at some place or other, an artificer or artificers who formed it for the purpose which we find it actually to answer; who comprehended its construction, and designed its use.

I. Nor would it, I apprehend, weaken the conclusion, that we had never seen a watch made; that we had never known an artist capable of making one; that we were altogether incapable of executing such a piece of workmanship ourselves, or of understanding in what manner it was performed: all this being no more than what is true of some remains of ancient art, of some lost arts, and, to the generality of mankind, of the more curious productions of modern manufacture. Does one man in a million know how oval frames are turned? Ignorance of this kind exalts our opinion of the unseen and unknown artist's skill, if he be unseen and unknown, but raises no doubt in our minds of the existence and agency of such an artist, at some former time, and in some place or other. Nor can I perceive that it varies at all the inference, whether the question arise concerning a human agent, or concerning an agent of a different species, or an agent possessing in some respects a different nature.

II. Neither, secondly, would it invalidate our conclusion, that the watch sometimes went wrong, or that it seldom went exactly right. The purpose of the machinery, the design, and the designer might be evident, and in the case supposed would be evident, in whatever way we accounted for the irregularity of the movement, or whether we could account for it or not. It is not necessary that a machine be perfect, in order to show with what design it was made: still less necessary, where the only question is, whether it were made with any design at all.

III. Nor, thirdly, would it bring any uncertainty into the argument, if there were a few parts of the watch, concerning which we could not discover, or had not yet discovered, in what manner they conduced to the general effect; or even some parts, concerning which we could not ascertain whether they conduced to that effect in any manner whatever. For, as to the first branch of the case; if by the loss, or disorder, or decay of the parts in question, the movement of the watch were found in fact to be stopped, or disturbed, or retarded, no doubt would remain in our minds as to the utility or intention of these parts, although we should be unable to investigate the manner according to which, or the connection by which, the ultimate effect depended upon their action or assistance; and the more complex the machine, the more likely is this obscurity to arise. Then, as to the second thing supposed, namely, that there were parts which might be spared without prejudice to the movement of the watch, and that we had proved this by experiment, – these superfluous parts, even if we were completely assured that they were such, would not vacate the reasoning which we had instituted concerning other parts. The indication of contrivance remained, with respect to them, nearly as it was before.

IV. Nor, fourthly, would any man in his senses think the existence of the watch, with its various machinery, accounted for, by being told that it was one out of possible combinations of material forms; that whatever he had found in the place where he found the watch, must have contained some internal configuration or other; and that this configuration might be the structure now exhibited, viz. of the works of a watch, as well as a different structure.

V. Nor, fifthly, would it yield his inquiry more satisfaction, to be answered that there existed in things a principle of order, which had disposed the parts of the watch into their present form and situation. He never knew a watch made by the principle of order; nor can he even form to himself an idea of what is meant by a principle of order, distinct from the intelligence of the watch-maker.

VI. Sixthly, he would be surprised to hear that the mechanism of the watch was no proof of contrivance, only a motive to induce the mind to think so:

VII. And not less surprised to be informed, that the watch in his hand was nothing more than the result of the laws of *metallic* nature.

It is a perversion of language to assign any law as the efficient, operative, cause of any thing. A law presupposes an agent; for it is only the mode, according to which an agent proceeds: it implies a power; for it is the order, according to which that power acts. Without this agent, without this power, which are both distinct from itself, the *law* does nothing; is nothing. The expression, 'the law of metallic nature,' may sound strange and harsh to a philosophic ear, but it seems quite as justifiable as some others which are more familiar to him, such as 'the law of vegetable nature' – 'the law of animal nature,' or indeed as 'the law of nature' in general, when assigned as the cause of phaenomena, in exclusion of agency and power, or when it is substituted into the place of these.[2]

VIII. Neither, lastly, would our observer be driven out of his conclusion, or from his confidence in its truth, by being told that he knew nothing at all about the matter. He knows enough for his argument. He knows the utility of the end: he knows the subserviency and adaptation of the means to the end. These points being known, his ignorance of other points, his doubts concerning other points, affect not the certainty of his reasoning. The consciousness of knowing little need not beget a distrust of that which he does know.

Chapter II

State of the Argument continued

Suppose, in the next place, that the person, who found the watch, should, after some time, discover, that, in addition to all the properties which he had hitherto observed in it, it possessed the unexpected property of producing, in the course of its movement, another watch like itself;[3] (the thing is conceivable;) that it contained within it a mechanism, a system of parts, a mould for instance, or a complex adjustment of laths, files, and other tools, evidently and separately calculated for this purpose; let us enquire what effect ought such a discovery to have upon his former conclusion?

I. The first effect would be to increase his admiration of the contrivance, and his conviction of the consummate skill of the contriver. Whether he regarded the object of the contrivance, the distinct apparatus, the intricate, yet in many parts intelligible, mechanism by which it was carried on, he would perceive, in this new observation, nothing but an additional reason for doing what he had already done; for referring the construction of the watch to design and to supreme art. If that construction *without* this property, or, which is the same thing, before this property had been noticed, proved intention and art to have been employed about it; still more strong would the proof appear, when he came to the knowledge of this further property, the crown and perfection of all the rest.

II. He would reflect, that though the watch before him were, *in some sense*, the maker of the watch, which was fabricated in the course of its movements, yet it was in a very different sense from that, in which a carpenter, for instance, is the maker of a chair; the author of its contrivance, the cause of the relation of its parts to their use. With respect to these, the first watch was no cause at all to the second; in no such sense as this was it the author of the constitution and order, either of the parts which the new watch contained, or of the parts by the aid and instrumentality of which it was produced. We might possibly say, but with great latitude of expression, that a stream of water ground corn: but no latitude of expression would allow us to say, no stretch of conjecture could lead us to think, that the stream of water built the mill, though it were too ancient for us to know who the builder was. What the stream of water does in the affair is neither more nor less than this: by the application of an unintelligent impulse to a mechanism previously arranged, arranged independently of it and arranged by intelligence, an effect is produced, viz. the corn is ground. But the effect results from the arrangement. The force of the stream cannot be said to be the cause or the author of the effect, still less of the arrangement. Understanding and plan in the formation of the mill were not the less necessary, for any share which the water has in grinding the corn: yet is this share the same, as that which the watch would have contributed to the production of the new watch, upon the supposition assumed in the last section. Therefore,

III. Though it be now no longer probable, that the individual watch which our observer had found, was made immediately by the hand of an artificer, yet doth not this alteration in anywise affect the inference, that an artificer had been originally employed and concerned in the production. The argument from design remains as it was. Marks of design and contrivance are no more accounted for now, than they were before. In the same thing, we may ask for the cause of different properties. We may ask for the cause of the colour of a body, of its hardness, of its heat; and these causes may be all different. We are now asking for the cause of that subserviency to an use, that relation to an end, which we have remarked in the watch before us. No answer is given to this question by telling us that a preceding watch produced it. There cannot be design without a designer; contrivance without a contriver; order without choice; arrangement, without any thing capable of arranging; subserviency and relation to a purpose, without that which could intend a purpose; means suitable to an end, and executing their office in accomplishing that end, without the end ever having been contemplated, or the means accommodated to it. Arrangement, disposition of parts, subserviency of means to an end, relation of instruments to an use, imply the presence of intelligence and mind. No one, therefore, can rationally believe that the insensible, inanimate watch, from which the watch before us issued, was the proper cause of the mechanism we so much admire in it; could be truly said to have constructed the instrument, disposed its parts, assigned their office, determined their order, action, and mutual dependency, combined their several motions into one result, and that also a result connected with the utilities of other beings. All these properties, therefore, are as much unaccounted for as they were before.

IV. Nor is any thing gained by running the difficulty farther back, i.e. by supposing the watch before us to have been produced from another watch, that from a former, and so on indefinitely. Our going back ever so far brings us no nearer to the least degree of satisfaction upon the subject. Contrivance is still unaccounted for. We still want a contriver. A designing mind is neither supplied by this supposition, nor dispensed with. If the difficulty were diminished the further we went back, by going back indefinitely we might exhaust it. And this is the only case to which this sort of reasoning applies. Where there is a tendency, or, as we increase the number of terms, a continual approach towards a limit, *there*, by supposing the number of terms to be what is called infinite, we may conceive the limit to be attained: but where there is no such tendency or approach, nothing is effected by lengthening the series. There is no difference as to the point in question (whatever there may be as to many points) between one series and another; between a series which is finite, and a series which is infinite. A chain, composed of an infinite number of links can no more support itself, than a chain composed of a finite number of links. And of this we are assured (though we never *can* have tried the experiment) because, by increasing the number of links, from ten for instance to a hundred, from a hundred to a thousand, &c. we make not the smallest approach, we observe not the smallest tendency, towards self support.[4] There is no difference in this respect (yet there may be a great difference in several respects) between a chain of a greater or less length, between one chain and another, between one that is finite and one that is infinite. This very much resembles the case before us. The machine, which we are inspecting, demonstrates, by its construction, contrivance and design. Contrivance must have had a contriver; design a designer; whether the machine immediately proceeded from another machine, or not. That circumstance alters not the case. That other machine may, in like manner, have proceeded from a former machine: nor does that alter the case: the contrivance must have had a contriver. That former one from one preceding it: no alteration still: a contriver is still necessary. No tendency is perceived, no approach towards a diminution of this necessity. It is the same with any and every succession of these machines; a succession of ten, of a hundred, of a thousand; with one series as with another; a series which is finite, as with a series which is infinite. In whatever other respects they may differ, in this they do not. In all equally, contrivance and design are unaccounted for.

The question is not simply, How came the first watch into existence? which question, it may be pretended, is done away by supposing the series of watches thus produced from one another to have been infinite, and consequently to have had no such *first*, for which it was necessary to provide a cause. This, perhaps, would have been nearly the state of the question, if nothing had been before us but an unorganised, unmechanised, substance, without mark or indication of contrivance. It might be difficult to show that such substance could not have existed from eternity, either in succession (if it were possible, which I think it is not, for unorganised bodies to spring from one another), or by individual perpetuity. But that is not the question now. To suppose it to be so, is to suppose that it made no difference whether he had found a watch or a stone. As it is, the metaphysics of that question have no place; for, in the watch which we are examining, are seen contrivance, design; an end, a purpose; means for the end, adaptation to the purpose. And the question, which irresistibly presses upon our thoughts, is, whence this contrivance and design. The thing required is the intending mind, the adapting hand, the intelligence by which that hand was directed. This question, this demand, is not shaken off by increasing a number or succession of substances destitute of these properties; nor the more, by increasing that number to infinity. If it be said, that, upon the supposition of one watch being produced from another in the course of that other's movements, and by means of the mechanism within it, we have a cause for the watch in my hand, viz.

the watch from which it proceeded, I deny, that for the design, the contrivance, the suitableness of means to an end, the adaptation of instruments to an use (all of which we discover in the watch), we have any cause whatever. It is in vain, therefore, to assign a series of such causes, or to alledge that a series may be carried back to infinity; for I do not admit that we have yet any cause at all of the phaenomena, still less any series of causes either finite or infinite. Here is contrivance, but no contriver: proofs of design, but no designer.

v. Our observer would further also reflect, that the maker of the watch before him, was, in truth and reality, the maker of every watch produced from it; there being no difference (except that the latter manifests a more exquisite skill) between the making of another watch with his own hands by the mediation of files, laths, chisels, &c. and the disposing, fixing, and inserting of these instruments, or of others equivalent to them, in the body of the watch already made, in such a manner, as to form a new watch in the course of the movements which he had given to the old one. It is only working by one set of tools, instead of another.

The conclusion which the *first* examination of the watch, of its works, construction, and movement suggested, was, that it must have had, for cause and author of that construction, an artificer, who understood its mechanism, and designed its use. This conclusion is invincible. A *second* examination presents us with a new discovery. The watch is found, in the course of its movement, to produce another watch, similar, to itself: and not only so, but we perceive in it a system of organization separately calculated for that purpose. What effect would this discovery have, or ought it to have, upon our former inference? What, as hath already been said, but to increase beyond measure our admiration of the skill, which had been employed in the formation of such a machine? Or shall it, instead of this, all at once turn us round to an opposite conclusion, viz. that no art or skill whatever has been concerned in the business, although all other evidences of art and skill remain as they were, and this last and supreme piece of art be now added to the rest? Can this be maintained without absurdity? Yet this is atheism.

Chapter III

Application of the Argument

This is atheism: for every indication of contrivance, every manifestation of design, which existed in the watch, exists in the works of nature;[5] with the difference, on the side of nature, of being greater and more, and that in a degree which exceeds all computation. I mean that the contrivances of nature surpass the contrivances of art, in the complexity, subtlety, and curiosity of the mechanism; and still more, if possible, do they go beyond them in number and variety: yet, in a multitude of cases, are not less evidently mechanical, not less evidently contrivances, not less evidently accommodated to their end, or suited to their office, than are the most perfect productions of human ingenuity.

I know no better method of introducing so large a subject, than that of comparing a single thing with a single thing; an eye, for example, with a telescope.[6] As far as the examination of the instrument goes, there is precisely the same proof that the eye was made for vision, as there is that the telescope was made for assisting it. They are made upon the same principles; both being adjusted to the laws by which the transmission and refraction of rays of light are regulated. I speak not of the origin of the laws themselves; but, such laws being fixed, the construction, in both cases, is adapted to them. For instance; these laws require, in order to produce the same effect, that the rays of light, in passing from water into the eye, should be refracted by a more convex surface than when it passes out of air into the eye. Accordingly we find, that the eye of a fish, in that part of it called the crystalline lense, is much rounder than the eye of terrestrial animals. What plainer manifestation of design can there be than this difference? What could a mathematical instrument-maker have done more, to show his knowledge of his principle, his application of that knowledge, his suiting of his means to his end; I will not say to display the compass or excellence of his skill and art, for in these all comparison is indecorous, but to testify counsel, choice, consideration, purpose?

To some it may appear a difference sufficient to destroy all similitude between the eye and the telescope, that the one is a perceiving organ, the other an unperceiving instrument. The fact is, that they are both instruments. And, as to the mechanism, at least as to mechanism being employed, and even as to the kind of it, this circumstance varies not the analogy at all. For observe, what the constitution of the eye is. It is necessary, in order to produce distinct vision, that an image or picture of the object be formed at the bottom of the eye. Whence this necessity arises, or how the picture is connected with the sensation, or contributes to it, it may be difficult, nay we will confess, if you please, impossible for us to search out. But the present question is not concerned in the inquiry. It may be true, that, in this, and in other instances, we trace mechanical contrivance a certain way; and that then we come to something which is not mechanical, or which is inscrutable. But this affects not the certainty of our investigation, as far as we have gone. The difference between an animal and an automatic statue, consists in this, – that in the animal we trace the mechanism to a certain point, and then we are stopped; either the mechanism being too subtile for our discernment, or something else besides the known laws of mechanism taking place; whereas, in the automaton, for the comparatively few motions of which it is capable, we trace the mechanism throughout. But, up to the limit, the reasoning is as clear and certain in the one case as in the other. In the example before us, it is a matter of certainty, because it is a matter which experience and observation demonstrate, that the formation of an image at the bottom of the eye is necessary to perfect vision. The image itself can be shown. Whatever affects the distinctness of the image, affects the distinctness of the vision. The formation then of such an image being necessary (no matter how), to the sense of sight, and to the exercise of that sense, the apparatus by which it is formed is constructed and put together, not only with infinitely more art, but upon the selfsame principles of art, as in the telescope or the camera obscura. The perception arising from the image may be laid out of the question: for the production of the image, these are instruments of the same kind. The end is the same; the means are the same. The purpose in both is alike; the contrivance for accomplishing that purpose is in both alike. The lenses of the telescope and the humors of the eye bear a complete resemblance to one another, in their figure, their position, and in their power over the rays of light, viz. in bringing each pencil to a point at the right distance from the lense; namely, in the eye, at the exact place where the membrane is spread to receive it. How is it possible, under circumstances of such close affinity, and under the operation of equal evidence, to exclude contrivance from the one, yet to acknowledge the proof of contrivance having been employed, as the plainest and clearest of all propositions in the other?

The resemblance between the two cases is still more accurate, and obtains in more points than we have yet represented, or than we are, on the first view of the subject, aware of. In dioptric telescopes there is an imperfection of this nature. Pencils of light, in passing through glass lenses, are separated into different colours, thereby tingeing the object, especially the edges of it, as if it were viewed through a prism. To correct this inconvenience had been long a desideratum in the art. At last it came into the mind of a sagacious optician, to inquire how this matter was managed in the eye; in which there was exactly the same difficulty to contend with, as in the telescope. His observation taught him, that, in the eye, the evil was cured by combining lenses composed of different substances, i.e. of substances which possessed different refracting powers. Our artist borrowed from thence his hint; and produced a correction of the defect by imitating, in glasses made from different materials, the effects of the different humors through which the rays of light pass before they reach the bottom of the eye. Could this be in the eye without purpose, which suggested to the optician the only effectual means of attaining that purpose?

But further; there are other points, not so much perhaps of strict resemblance between the two, as of superiority of the eye over the telescope; yet, of a superiority, which being founded in the laws that regulate both, may furnish topics of fair and just comparison. Two things were wanted to the eye, which were not wanted, at least in the same degree, to the telescope; and these were, the adaptation of the organ, first, to different degrees of light; and, secondly, to the vast diversity of distance at which objects are viewed by the naked eye, viz. from a few inches to as many miles. These difficulties present not themselves to the maker of the telescope. He wants all the light he can get; and he never directs his instrument to objects near at hand. In the eye, both these cases were to be provided for; and for the purpose of providing for them, a subtile and appropriate mechanism is introduced.

I. In order to exclude excess of light, when it is excessive, and to render objects visible under obscurer degrees of it, when no more can be had; the hole or aperture in the eye, through which the light enters, is so formed, as to contract or dilate itself for the purpose of admitting a greater or less number of rays at the same time. The chamber of the eye is a camera obscura, which, when the light is too small, can enlarge its opening; when too strong, can again contract it; and that without any other assistance than that of its own exquisite machinery. It is further also, in the human subject, to be observed, that this hole in the eye, which we call the pupil, under all its different dimensions, retains its exact circular shape. This is a structure extremely artificial. Let an artist only try to execute the same. He will find that his threads and strings must be disposed with great consideration and contrivance, to make a circle which shall continually change its diameter yet preserve its form. This is done in the eye by an application of fibres, i.e. of strings, similar, in their position and action, to what an artist would and must employ, if he had the same piece of workmanship to perform.

II. The second difficulty which has been stated, was the suiting of the same organ to the perception of objects that lie near at hand, within a few inches, we will suppose, of the eye, and of objects which were placed at a considerable distance from it, that, for example, of as many furlongs (I speak in both cases of the distance at which distinct vision can be exercised). Now, this, according to the principles of optics, that is, according to the laws by which the transmission of light is regulated, (and these laws are fixed,) could not be done without the organ itself undergoing an alteration, and receiving an adjustment, that might correspond with the exigency of the case, that is to say, with the different inclination to one another under which the rays of light reached it. Rays issuing from points placed at a small distance from the eye, and which consequently must enter the eye in a spreading or diverging order, cannot, by the same optical instrument in the same state, be brought to a point, i.e. be made to form an image, in the same place with rays proceeding from objects situated at a much greater distance, and which rays arrive at the eye in directions nearly, and physically speaking, parallel. It requires a rounder lense to do it. The point of concourse behind the lense must fall critically upon the retina, or the vision is confused; yet, this point, by the immutable properties of light, is carried further back, when the rays proceed from a near object, than when they are sent from one that is remote. A person, who was using an optical instrument, would manage this matter by changing, as the occasion required, his lense or his telescope; or by adjusting the distance of his glasses with his hand or his screw: but how is it to be managed in the eye? What the alteration was, or in what part of the eye it took place, or by what means it was effected (for, if the known laws which govern the refraction of light be maintained, some alteration in the state of the organ there must be), had long formed a subject of inquiry and conjecture. The change, though sufficient for the purpose, is so minute as to elude ordinary observation. Some very late discoveries, deduced from a laborious and most accurate inspection of the structure and operation of the organ, seem at length to have ascertained the mechanical alteration which the parts of the eye undergo. It is found, that by the action of certain muscles, called the straight muscles, and which action is the most advantageous that could be imagined for the purpose, – it is found, I say, that, whenever the eye is directed to a near object, three changes are produced in it at the same time, all severally contributing to the adjustment required. The cornea, or outermost coat of the eye, is rendered more round and prominent; the crystalline lense underneath is pushed forwards; and the axis of vision, as the depth of the eye is called, is elongated. These changes in the eye vary its power over the rays of light in such a manner and degree as to produce exactly the effect which is wanted, viz. the formation of an image *upon the retina*, whether the rays come to the eye in a state of divergency, which is the case when the object is near to the eye, or come parallel to one another, which is the case when the object is placed at a distance. Can any thing be more decisive of contrivance than this is? The most secret laws of optics must have been known to the author of a structure endowed with such a capacity of change. It is, as though an optician, when he had a nearer object to view, should *rectify* his instrument by putting in another glass, at the same time drawing out also his tube to a different length.

Observe a new-born child first lifting up its eyelids. What does the opening of the curtain discover? The anterior part of two pellucid globes, which, when they come to be examined, are found to be constructed upon strict optical principles; the self-same principles upon which we ourselves construct optical instruments. We find them perfect for the purpose of forming an image by refraction; composed of parts executing different offices; one part having fulfilled its office upon the pencil of light, delivering it over to the action of another part; that to a third, and so onward: the progressive action depending for its success upon the nicest, and minutest adjustment of the parts concerned; yet, these parts so in fact adjusted, as to produce, not by a simple action or effect, but by a combination of actions and effects, the result which is ultimately wanted. And forasmuch as this organ would have to operate under different circumstances, with strong degrees of light and with weak degrees, upon near objects, and upon remote ones, and these differences demanded, according to the laws by which the transmission of light is regulated, a corresponding diversity of structure; that the aperture, for example, through which the light passes, should be larger or less; the lenses rounder or flatter, or that their distance from the tablet, upon which the picture is delineated, should be shortened or lengthened: this, I say, being the case and the difficulty, to which the eye was to be adapted, we find its several parts capable of being occasionally changed, and a most artificial apparatus provided to produce that change. This is far beyond the common regulator of a watch, which requires the touch of a foreign hand to set it; but it is not altogether unlike Harrison's contrivance[7] for making a watch regulate itself, by inserting within it a machinery, which, by the artful use of the different expansion of metals, preserves the equability of the motion under all the various temperatures of heat and cold in which the instrument may happen to be placed. The ingenuity of this last contrivance has been justly praised. Shall, therefore, a structure which differs from it, chiefly by surpassing it, be accounted no contrivance at all? or, if it be a contrivance, that it is without a contriver?

But this, though much, is not the whole: by different species of animals the faculty we are describing is possessed, in degrees suited to the different range of vision which their mode of life, and of procuring their food, requires.[8] Birds, for instance, in general, procure their food by means of their beak; and the distance between the eye and the point of the beak being small, it becomes necessary that they should have the power of seeing very near objects distinctly. On the other hand, from being often elevated much above the ground, living in the air, and moving through it with great velocity, they require, for their safety, as well as for assisting them in descrying their prey, a power of seeing at a great distance; a power, of which, in birds of rapine, surprising examples are given. The fact accordingly is, that two peculiarities are found in the eyes of birds, both tending to facilitate the change upon which the adjustment of the eye to different distances depends. The one is a bony, yet, in most species, a flexible rim or hoop, surrounding the broadest part of the eye; which confining the action of the muscles to that part, increases the effect of their lateral pressure upon the orb, by which pressure its axis is elongated for the purpose of looking at very near objects. The other is, an additional muscle called the marsupium, to draw, upon occasion, the crystalline lens *back*, and so fit the same eye for the viewing of very distant objects. By these means the eyes of birds can pass from one extreme to another of their scale of adjustment, with more ease and readiness than the eyes of other animals.

The eyes of fishes also, compared with those of terrestrial animals, exhibit certain distinctions of structure, adapted to their state and element. We have already observed upon the figure of the crystalline compensating by its roundness the density of the medium through which their light passes. To which we have to add, that the eyes of fish, in their natural and indolent state, appear to be adjusted to near objects, in this respect differing from the human eye, as well as those of quadrupeds and birds. The ordinary shape of the fish's eye being in a much higher degree convex than that of land animals, a corresponding difference attends its muscular conformation, viz. that it is throughout calculated for *flattening* the eye.

The iris also in the eyes of fish does not admit of contraction. This is a great difference, of which the probable reason is, that the diminished light in water is never too strong for the retina.

In the eel, which has to work its head through sand and gravel, the roughest and harshest substances, there is placed before the eye, and at some distance from it, a transparent, horny, convex case or covering, which, without obstructing the sight, defends the organ. To such an animal could any thing be more wanted or more useful?

Thus, in comparing the eyes of different kinds of animals, we see, in their resemblances and distinctions, one general plan laid down, and that plan varied with the varying exigencies to which it is to be applied.

There is one property, however, common, I believe, to all eyes, at least to all which have been examined, namely, that the optic nerve enters the bottom of the eye, not in the centre or middle, but a little on one side; not in the point where the axis of the eye meets the retina, but between that point and the nose. – The difference which this makes is, that no part of an object is unperceived by both eyes at the same time.

In considering vision as achieved by the means of an image formed at the bottom of the eye, we can never reflect without wonder upon the smallness, yet correctness, of the picture, the subtilty of the touch, the fineness of the lines. A landscape of five or six square leagues is brought into a space of half an inch diameter; yet the multitude of objects which it contains are all preserved, are all discriminated in their magnitudes, positions, figures, colours. The prospect from Hampstead-hill is compressed into the compass of a sixpence, yet circumstantially represented. A stage coach travelling at its ordinary speed for half an hour, passes, in the eye, only over one-twelfth of an inch, yet is this change of place in the image distinctly perceived throughout its whole progress; for it is only by means of that perception that the motion of the coach itself is made sensible to the eye. If any thing can abate our admiration of the smallness of the visual tablet compared with the extent of vision, it is a reflection, which the view of nature leads us, every hour, to make, viz. that, in the hands of the Creator, great and little are nothing.

Sturmius[9] held, that the examination of the eye was a cure for atheism. Beside that conformity to optical principles which its internal constitution displays, and which alone amounts to a manifestation of intelligence having been exerted in its structure; besides this, which forms, no doubt, the leading character of the organ, there is to be seen, in every thing belonging to it and about it, an extraordinary degree of care, an anxiety for its preservation, due, if we may so speak, to its value and its tenderness. It is lodged in a strong, deep, bony socket, composed by the junction of seven different bones, hollowed out at their edges. In some few species, as that of the coatimondi, the orbit is not bony throughout; but whenever this is the case, the upper, which is the deficient part, is supplied by a cartilaginous ligament; a substitution which shows the same care. Within this socket it is embedded in fat, of all animal substances the best adapted both to its repose and motion. It is sheltered by the eyebrows, an arch of hair, which, like a thatched penthouse, prevents the sweat and moisture of the forehead from running down into it.

But it is still better protected by its *lid*. Of the superficial parts of the animal frame, I know none which, in its office and structure, is more deserving of attention than the eyelid. It defends the eye; it wipes it; it closes it in sleep. Are there in any work of art whatever, purposes more evident than those which this organ fulfils; or an apparatus for executing those purposes more intelligible, more appropriate, or more mechanical? If it be overlooked by the observer of nature, it can only be because it is obvious and familiar. This is a tendency to be guarded against. We pass by the plainest instances, whilst we are exploring those which are rare and curious; by which conduct of the understanding, we sometimes neglect the strongest observations, being taken up with others, which, though more recondite and scientific, are, as solid arguments, entitled to much less consideration.

In order to keep the eye moist and clean, which qualities are necessary to its brightness and its use, a wash is constantly supplied by a secretion for the purpose; and the superfluous brine is conveyed to the nose through a perforation in the bone as large as a goose-quill. When once the fluid has entered the nose, it spreads itself upon the inside of the nostril, and is evaporated by the current of warm air which, in the course of respiration, is continually passing over it. Can any pipe or outlet for carrying off the waste liquor from a dye-house or a distillery, be more mechanical than this is? It is easily perceived that the eye must want moisture; but could the want of the eye generate the gland which produces the tear, or bore the hole by which it is discharged – a hole through a bone?

It is observable that this provision is not found in fish, the element in which they live supplying a constant lotion to the eye.

It were, however, injustice to dismiss the eye as a piece of mechanism, without noticing that most exquisite of all contrivances, the nictitating membrane, which is found in the eyes of birds and of many quadrupeds. Its use is to sweep the eye, which it does in an instant; to spread over it the lachrymal humor; to defend it also from sudden injuries; yet not totally, when drawn upon the pupil, to shut out the light. The commodiousness with which it lies folded up in the inner corner of the eye, ready for use and action, and the quickness with which it executes its purpose, are properties known and obvious to every observer; but, what is equally admirable, though not quite so obvious, is the combination of two different kinds of substance, muscular and elastic, and of two different kinds of action, by which the motion of this membrane is performed. It is not, as in ordinary cases, by the action of two antagonist muscles, one pulling forward and the other backward, that a reciprocal change is effected; but it is thus: the membrane itself is an elastic substance, capable of being drawn out by force like a piece of elastic gum, and by its own elasticity returning, when the force is removed, to its former position. Such being its nature, in order to fit it up for its office it is connected by a tendon or thread, with a muscle in the back part of the eye; this tendon or thread, though strong, is so fine as not to obstruct the sight, even when it passes across it; and the muscle itself being placed in the *back* of the eye, derives from its situation the advantage, not only of being secure, but of being out of the way; which it would hardly have been in any position that could be assigned to it in the anterior part of the orb, where its function lies. When the muscle behind the eye contracts, the membrane, by means of the communicating thread, is instantly drawn over the fore part of it. When the muscular contraction (which is a positive, and, most probably, a voluntary effort,) ceases to be exerted, the elasticity alone of the membrane brings it back again to its position. Does not this, if any thing can do it, bespeak an artist, master of his work, acquainted with his materials? 'Of a thousand other things,' say the French Academicians, 'we perceive not the contrivance, because we understand them only by their effects, of which we know not the causes; but we here treat of a machine, all the parts whereof are visible; and which need only be looked upon to discover the reasons of its motion and action.'[10]

In the configuration of the muscle, which, though placed behind the eye, draws the nictitating membrane over the eye, there is, what the authors, just now quoted, deservedly call a marvellous mechanism. I suppose this structure to be found in other animals; but, in the memoirs from which this account is taken, it is anatomically demonstrated only in the cassowary. The muscle is *passed through a loop formed by another muscle*; and is there inflected as if it were round a pulley. This is a peculiarity; and observe the advantage of it. A single muscle with a straight tendon, which is the common muscular form, would have been sufficient, if it had had power to draw far enough. But the contraction, necessary to draw the membrane over the whole eye, required a longer muscle than could lie straight at the bottom of the eye. Therefore, in order to have a greater length in a less compass, the chord of the main muscle makes an angle. This, so far, answers the end; but, still further, it makes an angle, not round a fixed pivot, but round a loop formed by another muscle, which second muscle, whenever it contracts, of course twitches the first muscle at the point of inflection, and thereby assists the action designed by both.

One question may possibly have dwelt in the reader's mind during the perusal of these observations, namely, Why should not the Deity have given to the animal the faculty of vision *at once*? Why this circuitous perception; the ministry of so many means? an element provided for the purpose; reflected from opaque substances, refracted through transparent ones; and both according to precise laws: then, a complex organ, an intricate and artificial apparatus, in order, by the operation of this element, and in conformity with the restrictions of these laws, to produce an image upon a membrane communicating with the brain? Wherefore all this? Why make the difficulty in order to surmount it? If to perceive objects by some other mode than that of touch, or objects which lay out of the reach of that sense, were the thing purposed, could not a simple volition of the Creator have communicated the capacity? Why resort to contrivance, where power is omnipotent? Contrivance, by its very definition and nature, is the refuge of imperfection. To have recourse to expedients, implies difficulty, impediment, restraint, defect of power. This question belongs to the other senses, as well as to sight; to the general functions of animal life, as nutrition, secretion, respiration; to the economy of vegetables; and indeed to almost all the operations of nature. The question therefore is of very wide extent; and among other answers which may be given to it, besides reasons of which probably we are ignorant, one answer is this. It is only by the display of contrivance, that the existence, the agency, the wisdom of the Deity, *could* be testified to his rational creatures. This is the scale by which we ascend to all the knowledge of our Creator which we possess, so far as it depends upon the phaenomena, or the works of nature. Take away this, and you take away from us every subject of observation, and ground of reasoning; I mean, as our rational faculties are formed at present. Whatever is done, God could have done, without the intervention of instruments or means: but it is in the construction of instruments, in the choice and adaptation of means, that a creative intelligence is seen. It is this which constitutes the order and beauty of the universe. God, therefore, has been pleased to prescribe limits to his own power, and to work his ends within those limits. The general laws of matter have perhaps prescribed the nature of these limits; its inertia, its reaction; the laws which govern the communication of motion, the refraction and reflection of light, and the constitution of fluids non-elastic and elastic, the transmission of sound through the latter; the laws of magnetism, of electricity; and probably others yet undiscovered. These are general laws; and when a particular purpose is to be effected, it is not by making a new law, nor by the suspension of the old ones, nor by making them wind and bend and yield to the occasion (for nature with great steadiness adheres to, and supports them), but it is, as we have seen in the eye, by the interposition of an apparatus corresponding with these laws, and suited to the exigency which results from them, that the purpose is at length attained. As we have said, therefore, God prescribes limits to his power, that he may let in the exercise, and thereby exhibit demonstrations, of his wisdom. For then such laws and limitations being laid down, it is as though one Being should have fixed certain rules; and, if we may so speak, provided certain materials; and, afterwards, have committed to another Being, out of these materials, and in subordination to these rules, the task of drawing forth a creation; a supposition which evidently leaves room, and induces indeed a necessity, for contrivance. Nay, there may be many such agents, and many ranks of these. We do not advance this as a doctrine either of philosophy or of religion; but we say that the subject may safely be represented under this view, because the Deity, acting himself by general laws, will have the same consequences upon our reasoning, as if he had prescribed these laws to another. It has been said, that the problem of creation was, 'attraction and matter being given, to make a world out of them:' and, as above explained, this statement perhaps does not convey a false idea.

2. Robert Chambers,
Vestiges of the Natural History of Creation (1844), Chapter 14, 'Hypothesis of the Development of the Vegetable and Animal Kingdoms'

pp. 191–205, 212–35

Robert Chambers, a publisher and amateur geologist, brought out the *Vestiges* anonymously in 1844, and it was an immediate popular sensation, going through four editions in the first six months, and twenty editions up to 1860. *Vestiges* was the first full-length presentation of an evolutionary theory of species, in English. Lamarck's theory was known, but chiefly through Charles Lyell's refutation in *The Principles of Geology* (1830–3). Chambers' desire for anonymity shows that he knew how controversial any such theory would be, and he was fiercely attacked for irreligion and immorality. Here is an example of this reaction to *Vestiges* from the Rev Adam Sedgwick, one of its most outspoken critics:

> If the book be true, the labours of sober induction are in vain; religion is a lie; human law is a mass of folly, and a base injustice; morality is moonshine; our labours for the black people of Africa were works of madmen; and man and woman are only better beasts! (J. Clark and T. Hughes, *Life of Sedgwick* (1890), pp. 83–4)

Chambers' inclusion of man in his evolutionary scheme was seen as an especial affront, substituting descent from animal origins for direct creation by God.

But it is also important to realise that Adam Sedgwick was Professor of Geology at Cambridge, an eminent and respected scientist working in the tradition of natural theology. Geology, by revealing evidence of extinction and of progressive change in the organic world, as shown in the fossil record, had introduced some problems into natural theology as practised by Paley, who had assumed a perfect, divinely appointed, *fixed* creation. But 'catastrophist' geologists such as Sedgwick and Hugh Miller (see pp. 67–85) preserved natural theology by a theory of *successive* fixed creations. Another way round the problem was of course Chambers' idea of development according to laws initially impressed on matter by the Creator: for Chambers too, in his way, was a natural theologian. His chief aim in *Vestiges*, was not to set out a scientific theory of species development, but to demonstrate the all-pervasiveness of natural Law as the expression of God in the world. The Law of Development in the organic world paralleled the Law of Gravitation in the physical world – like Newton, Chambers saw himself as demonstrating the unity and order of God's plan. So we cannot see the controversy over *Vestiges* as a simple case of religious opposition to scientific facts: it is more of a controversy between two sorts of natural theology, that which shows God's original plans and preconceptions embodied in nature, and that which shows His continual intervention and control. On the other hand, Chambers'

God is a great deal more remote and impersonal than that of Sedgwick or Paley: 'After the primary act, according to this view, the Creator might have ceased to be – as far as the created universe was concerned', as one critic put it (see Milton Millhauser, *Just Before Darwin* (1959), p. 133).

Another complication is that *Vestiges* was also attacked on purely scientific grounds – particularly with regard to Chambers' reliance on the nebular hypothesis of Laplace (an 'evolutionary' theory of the origin of the universe), and the theory of spontaneous generation, which he used to account for the initial origin of life from inorganic matter, and supported with some very dubious evidence. Darwin was not impressed or influenced by *Vestiges*, and Huxley, later to become Darwin's most aggressive and anti-clerical advocate, attacked *Vestiges* viciously. Chambers' theory was very far from Darwin's – it relied on sudden embryological changes, brought about by changes in the environment, and following an intrinsic 'law of development'. This is how Disraeli parodied it in *Tancred* (1847):

'You must read the "Revelations"; it is all explained. But what is most interesting is the way in which man has been developed. You know, all is development. The principle is perpetually going on. First, there was nothing, then there was something; then, I forget the next, I think we were shells, then fishes; then we come, let me see, did we come next? Never mind that; we came at last. And the next change there will be something very superior to us, something with wings. Ah! that's it; we were fishes, and I believe we shall be crows.'

Here the speaker glances at a further implication that Chambers enlarges on in his final chapters: that superior species are to follow humanity, leading eventually to the 'grand crowning type'.

Chambers' only important sympathetic critic was, interestingly, the liberal theologian Baden Powell, Professor of Geometry at Oxford, and later to become a contributor to *Essays and Reviews*, where he was to argue for the separation of the spheres of science and faith, Nature and Scripture. But this is not what Chambers thought of himself as doing. He sees his theory as not contradicting Genesis:

. . . the first chapter of the Mosaic record is not only not in harmony with the ordinary ideas of mankind respecting cosmical and organic creation, but is opposed to them, and only in accordance with the views here taken. When we carefully peruse it with awakened minds, we find that all the procedure is represented primarily and pre-eminently as flowing from *commands and expressions of will, not from direct acts. (Vestiges,* p. 155)

On the other hand, having it both ways, he does also assert that 'I freely own that I do not think it right to adduce the Mosaic record, either in objection to, or support of any natural hypothesis, and this for many reasons, but particularly for this, that there is not the least appearance of an intention in that book to give philosophically exact views of nature' (p. 156). But, while Chambers may want to separate science and the Bible, his main aim is always to place scientific facts in a cosmological perspective, to relate them to religion and morality - he explicitly attacks the narrowness of scientific specialists. In this, he contrasts markedly with the exclusively scientific approach of Darwin.

Robert Chambers (1802–1871)

Chapter XIV

Hypothesis of the Development[1] of the Vegetable and Animal Kingdoms

It has been already intimated, as a general fact, that there is an obvious gradation amongst the families of both the vegetable and animal kingdoms, from the simple lichen and animalcule respectively up to the highest order of dicotyledonous trees and the mammalia. Confining our attention, in the meantime, to the animal kingdom – it does not appear that this gradation passes along one line, on which every form of animal life can be, as it were, strung; there may be branching or double lines at some places; or the whole may be in a circle composed of minor circles, as has been recently suggested. But still it is incontestable that there are general appearances of a scale beginning with the simple and advancing to the complicated. The animal kingdom was divided by Cuvier[2] into four sub-kingdoms, or divisions, and these exhibit an unequivocal gradation in the order in which they are here enumerated: – Radiata, (polypes, &c.;) mollusca, (pulpy animals;) articulata, (jointed animals;) vertebrata, (animals with internal skeleton.) The gradation can, in like manner, be clearly traced in the *classes* into which the sub-kingdoms are subdivided, as, for instance, when we take those of the vertebrata in this order – reptiles, fishes, birds, mammals.

While the external forms of all these various animals are so different, it is very remarkable that the whole are, after all, variations of a fundamental plan, which can be traced as a basis throughout the whole, the variations being merely modifications of that plan to suit the particular conditions in which each particular animal has been designed to live. Starting from the primeval germ, which, as we have seen, is the representative of a particular order of full-grown animals, we find all others to be merely advances from that type, with the extension of endowments and modification of forms which are required in each particular case; each form, also, retaining a strong affinity to that which precedes it, and tending to impress its own features on that which succeeds. This unity of structure, as it is called, becomes the more remarkable, when we observe that the organs, while preserving a resemblance, are often put to different uses. For example: the ribs become, in the serpent, organs of locomotion, and the snout is extended, in the elephant, into a prehensile instrument.

It is equally remarkable that analogous purposes are served in different animals by organs essentially different. Thus, the mammalia breathe by lungs; the fishes, by gills. These are not modifications of one organ, but distinct organs. In mammifers, the gills exist and act at an early stage of the fœtal state, but afterwards go back and appear no more; while the lungs are developed. In fishes, again, the gills only are fully developed; while the lung structure either makes no advance at all, or only appears in the rudimentary form of an air-bladder. So, also, the baleen[a] of the whale and the teeth of the land mammalia are different organs. The whale, in embryo, shews the rudiments of teeth; but these, not being wanted, are not developed, and the baleen is brought forward instead. The land animals, we may also be sure, have the rudiments of baleen in their organisation. In many instances, a particular structure is found advanced to a certain point in a particular set of animals, (for instance, feet in the serpent tribe,) although it is not there required in any degree; but the peculiarity, being carried a little farther forward, is perhaps useful in the next set of animals in the scale. Such are called rudimentary organs. With this class of phenomena are to be ranked the useless mammæ of the male human being, and the unrequired process of bone in the male opossum, which is needed in the female for supporting her pouch. Such curious features are most conspicuous in animals which form links between various classes.

As formerly stated, the marsupials, standing at the bottom of the mammalia, shew their affinity to the oviparous[b] vertebrata, by the rudiments of two canals passing from near the anus to the external surfaces of the viscera, which are fully developed in fishes, being required by them for the respiration of aerated waters, but which are not needed by the atmosphere-breathing marsupials. We have also the peculiar form of the sternum and rib-bones of the lizards *represented* in the mammalia in certain white cartilaginous lines traceable among their abdominal muscles. The struphionidæ (birds of the ostrich type) form a link between birds and mammalia, and in them we find the wings imperfectly or not at all developed, a diaphragm and urinary sac, (organs wanting in other birds,) and feathers approaching the nature of hair. Again, the ornithorynchus belongs to a class at the bottom of the mammalia, and approximating to birds, and in it behold the bill and web-feet of that order!

For further illustration, it is obvious that, various as may be the

---

a. Horny plates growing transversely on each side of whale's palate.
b. Producing young by means of eggs expelled from body before being hatched.

lengths of the upper part of the vertebral column in the mammalia, it always consists of the same parts. The giraffe has in its tall neck the same number of bones with the pig, which scarcely appears to have a neck at all. Man, again, has no tail; but the notion of a much-ridiculed philosopher of the last century is not altogether, as it happens, without foundation, for the bones of a caudal extremity exist in an undeveloped state in the *os coccygis*[a] of the human subject. The limbs of all the vertebrate animals are, in like manner, on one plan, however various they may appear. In the hind-leg of a horse, for example, the angle called the hock is the same part which in us forms the heel; and the horse, and all other quadrupeds, with almost the solitary exception of the bear, walk, in reality, upon what answers to the toes of a human being. In this and many other quadrupeds the fore part of the extremities is shrunk up in a hoof, as the tail of the human being is shrunk up in the bony mass at the bottom of the back. The bat, on the other hand, has these parts largely developed. The membrane, commonly called its wing, is framed chiefly upon bones answering precisely to those of the human hand; its extinct congener, the pterodactyle, had the same membrane extended upon the fore-finger only, which in that animal was prolonged to an extraordinary extent. In the paddles of the whale and other animals of its order, we see the same bones as in the more highly developed extremities of the land mammifers; and even the serpent tribes, which present no external appearance of such extremities, possess them in reality, but in an undeveloped or rudimental state.

The same law of development presides over the vegetable kingdom. Amongst phanerogamous[b] plants, a certain number of organs appear to be always present, either in a developed or rudimentary state; and those which are rudimentary can be developed by cultivation. The flowers which bear stamens on one stalk and pistils on another, can be caused to produce both, or to become perfect flowers, by having a sufficiency of nourishment supplied to them. So also, where a special function is required for particular circumstances, nature has provided for it, not by a new organ, but by a modification of a common one, which she has effected in development. Thus, for instance, some plants destined to live in arid situations, require to have a store of water which they may slowly

---

a. The end of the vertebral column, below the sacrum, in man and some other primates, made up of four small vertebrae fused together, representing a vestigial tail.
b. Plant having stamens and pistils.

absorb. The need is arranged for by a cup-like expansion round the stalk, in which water remains after a shower. Now the *pitcher*, as this is called, is not a new organ, but simply a metamorphose of a leaf.

These facts clearly shew how all the various organic forms of our world are bound up in one – how a fundamental unity pervades and embraces them all, collecting them, from the humblest lichen up to the highest mammifer, in one system, the whole creation of which must have depended upon one law or decree of the Almighty, though it did not all come forth at one time. After what we have seen, the idea of a separate exertion for each must appear totally inadmissible. The single fact of abortive or rudimentary organs condemns it; for these, on such a supposition, could be regarded in no other light than as blemishes or blunders – the thing of all others most irreconcilable with that idea of Almighty Perfection which a general view of nature so irresistibly conveys. On the other hand, when the organic creation is admitted to have been effected by a general law, we see nothing in these abortive parts but harmless peculiarities of development, and interesting evidences of the manner in which the Divine Author has been pleased to work.

We have yet to advert to the most interesting class of facts connected with the laws of organic development. It is only in recent times that physiologists have observed that each animal passes, in the course of its germinal history, through a series of changes resembling the *permanent forms* of the various orders of animals inferior to it in the scale.[3] Thus, for instance, an insect, standing at the head of the articulated animals, is, in the larva state, a true annelid, or worm, the annelida being the lowest in the same class. The embryo of a crab resembles the perfect animal of the inferior order myriapoda, and passes through all the forms of transition which characterize the intermediate tribes of crustacea. The frog, for some time after its birth, is a fish with external gills, and other organs fitting it for an aquatic life, all of which are changed as it advances to maturity, and becomes a land animal. The mammifer only passes through still more stages, according to its higher place in the scale. Nor is man himself exempt from this law. His first form is that which is permanent in the animalcule.[a] His organisation gradually passes through conditions generally resembling a fish, a reptile, a bird, and the lower mammalia, before it attains its specific maturity. At one of the last stages of his fœtal career, he exhibits an intermaxillary bone, which is characteristic of the perfect ape; this is suppressed, and he

a. Animal so small as only to be visible with the aid of the microscope – mainly *rotifera* and *infusoria*.

may then be said to take leave of the simial type, and become a true human creature. Even, as we shall see, the varieties of his race are represented in the progressive development of an individual of the highest, before we see the adult Caucasian, the highest point yet attained in the animal scale.

To come to particular points of the organization. The brain of man, which exceeds that of all other animals in complexity of organisation and fulness of development, is, at one early period, only 'a simple fold of nervous matter, with difficulty distinguishable into three parts, while a little tail-like prolongation towards the hinder parts, and which had been the first to appear, is the only representation of a spinal marrow. Now, in this state it perfectly resembles the brain of an adult fish, thus assuming *in transitu* the form that in the fish is permanent. In a short time, however, the structure is become more complex, the parts more distinct, the spinal marrow better marked; it is now the brain of a reptile. The change continues; by a singular motion, certain parts (*corpora quadragemina*)[a] which had hitherto appeared on the upper surface, now pass towards the lower; the former is their permanent situation in fishes and reptiles, the latter in birds and mammalia. This is another advance in the scale, but more remains yet to be done. The complication of the organ increases; cavities termed *ventricles* are formed, which do not exist in fishes, reptiles, or birds; curiously organised parts, such as the corpora straita,[b] are added; it is now the brain of the mammalia. Its last and final change alone seems wanting, that which shall render it the brain of MAN.'[4] And this change in time takes place.[5]

So also with the heart. This organ, in the mammalia, consists of four cavities, but in the reptiles of only three, and in fishes of two only, while in the articulated animals it is merely a prolonged tube. Now in the mammal fœtus, at a certain early stage, the organ has the form of a prolonged tube; and a human being may be said to have then the heart of an insect. Subsequently it is shortened and widened, and becomes divided by a contraction into two parts, a ventricle and an auricle; it is now the heart of a fish. A subdivision of the auricle afterwards makes a triple-chambered form, as in the heart of the reptile tribes; lastly, the ventricle being also subdivided, it becomes a full mammal heart.

Another illustration here presents itself with the force of the most powerful and interesting analogy. Some of the earliest fishes of our

a. In vertebrates, the basal part of the wall of each cerebral hemisphere, consisting of a mass of interwoven nerve fibre endings and nerve cells.
b. The optic lobes of the mammalian brain, transversely divided.

globe, those of the Old Red Sandstone, present, as we have seen, certain peculiarities, as the one-sided tail and an inferior position of the mouth. No fishes of the present day, in a mature state, are so characterized; but some, at a certain stage of their existence, have such peculiarities. It occurred to a geologist to inquire if the fish which existed before the Old Red Sandstone had any peculiarities assimilating them to the fœtal condition of existing fish, and particularly if they were small. The first which occur before the time of the Old Red Sandstone, are those described by Mr Murchison,[6] as belonging to the Upper Ludlow Rocks; *they are all rather small*. Still older are those detected by Mr Philips[7] in the Aymestry Limestone, being the most ancient of the class which have as yet been discovered; *these are so extremely minute as only to be distinguishable by the microscope*. Here we apparently have very close demonstrations of a parity, or rather identity, of laws presiding over the development of the animated tribes on the face of the earth, and that of the individual in embryo.

The tendency of all these illustrations is to make us look to *development* as the principle which has been immediately concerned in the peopling of this globe, a process extending over a vast space of time, but which is nevertheless connected in character with the briefer process by which an individual being is evoked from a simple germ. What mystery is there here – and how shall I proceed to enunciate the conception which I have ventured to form of what may prove to be its proper solution! It is an idea by no means calculated to impress by its greatness, or to puzzle by its profoundness. It is an idea more marked by simplicity than perhaps any other of those which have explained the great secrets of nature. But in this lies, perhaps, one of its strongest claims to the faith of mankind.

The whole train of animated beings, from the simplest and oldest up to the highest and most recent, are, then, to be regarded as a series of *advances of the principle of development*, which have depended upon external physical circumstances, to which the resulting animals are appropriate. I contemplate the whole phenomena as having been in the first place arranged in the counsels of Divine Wisdom, to take place, not only upon this sphere, but upon all the others, in space,[8] under necessary modifications, and as being carried on, from first to last, here and elsewhere, under immediate favour of the creative will or energy. The nucleated vesicle,[a] the fundamental form of all organization, we must regard as the meeting-point between the

a. The cell, recently discovered.

inorganic and the organic – the end of the mineral and beginning of the vegetable and animal kingdoms, which thence start in different directions, but in perfect parallelism and analogy. We have already seen that this nucleated vesicle is itself a type of mature and independent being in the infusory animalcules, as well as the starting point of the fœtal progress of every higher individual in creation, both animal and vegetable. We have seen that it is a form of being which electric agency will produce – though not perhaps usher into full life – in albumen, one of those compound elements of animal bodies, of which another (urea) has been made by artificial means. Remembering these things, we are drawn on to the supposition, that the first step in the creation of life upon this planet was *a chemico-electric operation, by which simple germinal vesicles were produced.* This is so much, but what were the next steps? Let a common vegetable infusion help us to an answer. There, as we have seen, simple forms are produced at first, but afterwards they become more complicated, until at length the life-producing powers of the infusion are exhausted. Are we to presume that, in this case, the simple engender the complicated? Undoubtedly, this would not be more wonderful as a natural process than one which we never think of wondering at, because familiar to us – namely, that in the gestation of the mammals, the animalcule-like ovum of a few days is the parent, in a sense, of the chick-like form of a few weeks, and that in all the subsequent stages – fish, reptile, &c. – the one may, with scarcely a metaphor, be said to be the progenitor of the other. I suggest, then, as an hypothesis already countenanced by much that is ascertained, and likely to be further sanctioned by much that remains to be known, that the first step was *an advance under favour of peculiar conditions, from the simplest forms of being, to the next more complicated, and this through the medium of the ordinary process of generation.* . . .

It has been seen that, in the reproduction of the higher animals, the new being passes through stages in which it is successively fish-like and reptile-like. But the resemblance is not to the adult fish or the adult reptile, but to the fish and reptile at a certain point in their fœtal progress; this holds true with regard to the vascular, nervous, and other systems alike. It may be illustrated by a simple diagram. The fœtus of all the four classes may be supposed to advance in an identical condition to the point A. The fish there diverges and passes along a line apart, and peculiar to itself, to its mature state at F. The reptile, bird, and mammal, go on together to C, where the reptile diverges in like manner, and advances by itself to R. The bird diverges at D, and goes on to B. The mammal then goes forward in a

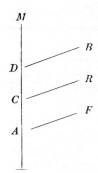

straight line to the highest point of organisation at M. This diagram shews only the main ramifications; but the reader must suppose minor ones, representing the subordinate differences of orders, tribes, families, genera, &c., if he wishes to extend his views to the whole varieties of being in the animal kingdom. Limiting ourselves at present to the outline afforded by this diagram, it is apparent that the only thing required for an advance from one type to another in the generative process is that, for example, the fish embryo should not diverge at A, but go on to C before it diverges, in which case the progeny will be, not a fish, but a reptile. To protract the *straightforward part of the gestation over a small space* – and from species to species the space would be small indeed – is all that is necessary.

This might be done by the force of certain external conditions operating upon the parturient system. The nature of these conditions we can only conjecture, for their operation, which in the geological eras was so powerful, has in its main strength been long interrupted, and is now perhaps only allowed to work in some of the lowest departments of the organic world, or under extraordinary casualties in some of the higher, and to these points the attention of science has as yet been little directed. But though this knowledge were never to be clearly attained, it need not much affect the present argument, provided it be satisfactorily shewn that there must be some such influence within the range of natural things.

To this conclusion it must be greatly conducive that the law of organic development is still daily seen at work to certain effects, only somewhat short of a transition from species to species. Sex we have seen to be a matter of development. There is an instance, in a humble department of the animal world, of arrangements being made by the animals themselves for adjusting this law to the production of a particular sex. Amongst bees, as amongst several other insect tribes, there is in each community but one true female, the queen bee, the workers being false females or neuters; that is to say, sex is carried on in them to a point where it is attended by sterility. The preparatory states of the queen bee occupy sixteen days; those of the neuters, twenty; and those of males, twenty-four. Now it is a fact, settled by innumerable observations and experiments, that the bees can so modify a worker in the larva state, that, when it emerges from the pupa, it is found to be a queen or true female. For this purpose they enlarge its cell, make a pyramidal hollow to allow of its assuming a vertical instead of a horizontal position, keep it warmer than other larvæ are kept, and feed it with a peculiar kind of food. From these simple circumstances, leading to a shortening of the embryotic condition, results a creature different in form, and also in dispositions, from what would have otherwise been produced. Some of the organs possessed by the worker are here altogether wanting. We have a creature 'destined to enjoy love, to burn with jealousy and anger, to be incited to vengeance, and to pass her time without labour,' instead of one 'zealous for the good of the community, a defender of the public rights, enjoying an immunity from the stimulus of sexual appetite and the pains of parturition; laborious, industrious, patient, ingenious, skilful; incessantly engaged in the nurture of the young, in collecting honey and pollen, in elaborating wax, in constructing cells and the like! – paying the most respectful and assiduous attention to objects which, had its ovaries been developed, it would have hated and pursued with the most vindictive fury till it had destroyed them!'[9] All these changes may be produced by a mere modification of the embryotic progress, which it is within the power of the adult animals to effect. But it is important to observe that this modification is different from working a direct change upon the embryo. It is not the different food which effects a metamorphosis. All that is done is merely to accelerate the period of the insect's perfection. By the arrangements made and the food given, the embryo becomes sooner fit for being ushered forth in its imago or perfect state. Development may be said to be thus arrested at a particular stage – that early one at which the female sex is complete. In the other circumstances, it is allowed to go on four days longer, and a stage is then reached between the two sexes, which in this species is designed to be the perfect condition of a large portion of the community. Four days more make it a perfect male. It is at the same time to be observed that there is, from the period of oviposition, a destined distinction between the sexes of the young bees. The queen lays the whole of the eggs which are designed to become workers, before she begins to lay those which become males. But probably the condition of her reproductive system governs the matter of sex, for it is remarked that when her impregnation is delayed beyond the twenty-eighth day of her entire existence, she lays only eggs which become males.

We have here, it will be admitted, a most remarkable illustration of the principle of development, although in an operation limited to the production of sex only. Let it not be said that the phenomena concerned in the generation of bees may be very different from those concerned in the reproduction of the higher animals. There is a unity throughout nature which makes the one case an instructive reflection of the other.

We shall now see an instance of development operating within the production of what approaches to the character of variety of species. It is fully established that a human family, tribe, or nation, is liable, in the course of generations, to be either advanced from a mean form to a higher one, or degraded from a higher to a lower, by the influence of the physical conditions in which it lives. The coarse features, and other structural peculiarities of the negro race only continue while these people live amidst the circumstances usually associated with barbarism. In a more temperate clime, and higher social state, the face and figure become greatly refined. The few African nations which possess any civilisation also exhibit forms approaching the European; and when the same people in the United States of America have enjoyed a within-door life for several generations, they assimilate to the whites amongst whom they live. On the other hand, there are authentic instances of a people originally well-formed and good-looking, being brought, by imperfect diet and a variety of physical hardships, to a meaner form. It is remarkable that prominence of the jaws, a recession and diminution of the cranium, and an elongation and attentuation of the limbs, are peculiarities always produced by these miserable conditions, for they indicate an unequivocal retrogression towards the type of the lower animals. Thus we see nature alike willing to go back and to go forward. Both effects are simply the result of the operation of the law of development in the generative system. Give good conditions, it advances; bad ones, it recedes. Now, perhaps, it is only because there is no longer a possibility, in the higher types of being, of giving sufficiently favourable conditions to carry on species to species, that we see the operation of the law so far limited.

Let us trace this law also in the production of certain classes of monstrosities. A human fœtus is often left with one of the most important parts of its frame imperfectly developed: the heart, for instance, goes no farther than the three-chambered form, so that it is the heart of a reptile. There are even instances of this organ being left in the two-chambered or fish form. Such defects are the result of nothing more than a failure of the power of development in the system of the mother, occasioned by weak health or misery. Here we have apparently a realisation of the converse of those conditions which carry on species to species, so far, at least, as one organ is concerned. Seeing a complete specific retrogression in this one point, how easy it is to imagine an access of favourable conditions sufficient to reverse the phenomenon, and make a fish mother develop a reptile heart, or a reptile mother develop a mammal one. It is no great boldness to surmise that a super-adequacy in the measure of this under-adequacy (and the one thing seems as natural an occurrence as the other) would suffice in a goose to give its progeny the body of a rat, and produce the ornithorynchus,[a] or might give the progeny of an ornithorynchus the mouth and feet of a true rodent, and thus complete at two stages the passage from the aves to the mammalia.

Perhaps even the transition from species to species does still take place in some of the obscurer fields of creation, or under extraordinary casualties, though science professes to have no such facts on record. It is here to be remarked, that such facts might often happen, and yet no record be taken of them, for so strong is the prepossession for the doctrine of invariable like-production, that such circumstances, on occurring, would be almost sure to be explained away on some other supposition, or, if presented, would be disbelieved and neglected. Science, therefore, has no such facts, for the very same reason that some small sects are said to have no discreditable members – namely, that they do not receive such persons, and extrude all who begin to verge upon the character. There are, nevertheless, some facts which have chanced to be reported without any reference to this hypothesis, and which it seems extremely difficult to explain satisfactorily upon any other. One of these has already been mentioned – a progression in the forms of the animalcules in a vegetable infusion from the simpler to the more complicated, a sort of microcosm, representing the whole history of the progress of animal creation as displayed by geology. Another is given in the history of the Acarus Crossii, which may be only the ultimate stage of a series of similar transformations effected by electric agency in the solution subjected to it.[10] There is, however, one direct case of a translation of species, which has been presented with a respectable amount of authority. It appears that, whenever oats sown at the usual time are kept cropped down during summer and autumn, and allowed to remain over the winter, a thin crop of rye is the harvest presented at the close of the ensuing summer. This experiment has been tried repeatedly, with but one result; invariably the *secale cereale* is the crop reaped where the *avena sativa*, a recog-

a. The duck-billed platypus.

nised different species, was sown. Now it will not satisfy a strict inquirer to be told that the seeds of the rye were latent in the ground and only superseded the dead product of the oats; for if any such fact were in the case, why should the usurping grain be always rye? Perhaps those curious facts which have been stated with regard to forests of one kind of trees, when burnt down, being succeeded (without planting) by other kinds, may yet be found most explicable, as this is, upon the hypothesis of a progression of species which take place under certain favouring conditions, now apparently of comparatively rare occurrence. The case of the oats is the more valuable, as bearing upon the suggestion as to a protraction of the gestation at a particular part of its course. Here, the generative process is, by the simple mode of cropping down, kept up for a whole year beyond its usual term. The type is thus allowed to advance, and what was oats becomes rye.

The idea, then, which I form of the progress of organic life upon the globe – and the hypothesis is applicable to all similar theatres of vital being – is, *that the simplest and most primitive type, under a law to which that of like-production is subordinate, gave birth to the type next above it, that this again produced the next higher, and so on to the very highest*, the stages of advance being in all cases very small – namely, from one species only to another; so that the phenomenon has always been of a simple and modest character. Whether the whole of any species was at once translated forward, or only a few parents were employed to give birth to the new type, must remain undetermined; but, supposing that the former was the case, we must presume that the moves along the line or lines were simultaneous, so that the place vacated by one species was immediately taken by the next in succession, and so on back to the first, for the supply of which the formation of a new germinal vesicle out of inorganic matter was alone necessary. Thus, the production of new forms, as shewn in the pages of the geological record, has never been anything more than a new stage of progress in gestation, an event as simply natural, and attended as little by any circumstances of a wonderful or startling kind, as the silent advance of an ordinary mother from one week to another of her pregnancy. Yet, be it remembered, the whole phenomena are, in another point of view, wonders of the highest kind, for in each of them we have to trace the effect of an Almighty Will which had arranged the whole in such harmony with external physical circumstances, that both were developed in parallel steps – and probably this development upon our planet is but a sample of what has taken place, through the same cause, in all the other countless theatres of being which are suspended in space.

Robert Chambers (1802–1871)

This may be the proper place at which to introduce the preceding illustrations in a form calculated to bring them more forcibly before the mind of the reader. The following table[a] was suggested to me, in consequence of seeing the scale of animated nature presented in Dr Fletcher's Rudiments of Physiology.[11] Taking that scale as its basis, it shews the wonderful parity observed in the progress of creation, as presented to our observation in the succession of fossils, and also in the fœtal progress of one of the principal human organs. This scale, it may be remarked, was not made up with a view to support such an hypothesis as the present, nor with any apparent regard to the history of fossils, but merely to express the appearance of advancement in the orders of the Cuvierian system, assuming, as the criterion of that advancement, 'an increase in the number and extent of the manifestations of life, or of the relations which an organised being bears to the external world.' Excepting in the relative situation of the annelida[b] and a few of the mammal orders, the parity is perfect; nor may even these small discrepancies appear when the order of fossils shall have been further investigated, or a more correct scale shall have been formed. Meanwhile, it is a wonderful evidence in favour of our hypothesis, that a scale formed so arbitrarily should coincide to such a nearness with our present knowledge of the succession of animal forms upon earth, and also that both of these series should harmonise so well with the view given by modern physiologists of the embryotic progress of one of the organs of the highest order of animals.

The reader has seen physical conditions several times referred to, as to be presumed to have in some way governed the progress of the development of the zoological circle. This language may seem vague, and, it may be asked, – can any particular physical condition be adduced as likely to have affected development? To this it may be answered, that air and light are probably amongst the principal agencies of this kind which operated in educing the various forms of being. Light is found to be essential to the development of the individual embryo. When tadpoles were placed in a perforated box, and that box sunk in the Seine, light being the only condition thus abstracted, they grew to a great size in their original form, but did not pass through the usual metamorphose which brings them to their mature state as frogs. The proteus, an animal of the frog kind, inhabiting the subterraneous waters of Carniola,[12] and which never acquires perfect lungs so as to become a land animal, is presumed to

a. See pp. 62–3.
b. Red-blooded worms, with bodies composed of ring-like segments.

60

be an example of arrested development, from the same cause. When, in connexion with these facts, we learn that human mothers living in dark and close cells under ground, – that is to say, with an inadequate provision of air and light, – are found to produce an unusual proportion of defective children, we can appreciate the important effects of both these physical conditions in ordinary reproduction. Now there is nothing to forbid the supposition that the earth has been at different stages of its career under different conditions, as to both air and light. On the contrary, we have seen reason for supposing that the proportion of carbonic acid gas (the element fatal to animal life) was larger at the time of the carboniferous formation than it afterwards became. We have also seen that astronomers regard the zodiacal light as a residuum of matter enveloping the sun, and which was probably at one time denser than it is now. Here we have the indications of causes for a progress in the purification of the atmosphere and in the diffusion of light during the earlier ages of the earth's history, with which the progress of organic life may have been conformable. An accession to the proportion of oxygen, and the effulgence of the central luminary, may have been the immediate prompting cause of all those advances from species to species which we have seen, upon other grounds, to be necessarily supposed as having taken place. And causes of the like nature may well be supposed to operate on other spheres of being, as well as on this. I do not indeed present these ideas as furnishing the true explanation of the progress of organic creation; they are merely thrown out as hints towards the formation of a just hypothesis, the completion of which is only to be looked for when some considerable advances shall have been made in the amount and character of our stock of knowledge.

Early in this century, M. Lamarck, a naturalist of the highest character, suggested an hypothesis of organic progress which deservedly incurred much ridicule, although it contained a glimmer of the truth. He surmised, and endeavoured, with a great deal of ingenuity, to prove, that one being advanced in the course of generations to another, in consequence merely of its experience of wants calling for the exercise of its faculties in a particular direction, by which exercise new developments of organs took place, ending in variations sufficient to constitute a new species. Thus he thought that a bird would be driven by necessity to seek its food in the water, and that, in its efforts to swim, the outstretching of its claws would lead to the expansion of the intermediate membranes, and it would thus become web-footed. Now it is possible that wants and the exercise of faculties have entered in some manner into the produc-

SCALE OF ANIMAL KINGDOM.   ORDER OF ANIMALS IN

(The numbers indicate orders:)

RADIATA (1, 2, 3, 4, 5) - - - - -
- Zoophyta - - - - - - - -
- Polypiaria - - - - - - - -

MOLLUSCA (6, 7, 8, 9, 10, 11) - - -
- Conchifera - - - - - - - -
- Double-shelled Mollusks - - - -

ARTICU-LATA
- *Annelida* (12, 13, 14) - - -
- *Crustacea* (15, 16, 17, 18, 19, 20)
- *Arachnida* & *Insecta* (21—31)

Crustacea - - - - - - - -
Annelida - - - - - - - -
Crustaceous Fishes - - - - - -

VERTE-BRATA

Pisces (32, 33, 34, 35, 36) - - True Fishes - - - - - - - -

Reptilia (37, 38, 39, 40) -
- Piscine Saurians (ichthyosaurus, &c.)
- Pterodactyles - - - - - - -
- Crocodiles - - - - - - - -
- Tortoises - - - - - - - -
- Batrachians - - - - - - - -

Aves (41, 42, 43, 44, 45, 46) - Birds - - - - - - - - - -

Mammalia

47 Cetacea
48 Ruminantia
(Bone of a marsupial animal) - - -

49 Pachydermata - Pachydermata (tapirs, horses, &c.)

50 Edentata

51 Rodentia - - Rodentia (dormouse, squirrel, &c.)

52 Marsupialia - Marsupialia (racoon, opossum, &c.)

53 Amphibia

54 Digitigrada - Digitigrada (genette, fox, wolf, &c.)

55 Plantigrada - Plantigrada (bear) - - - - -

Cetacea (lamantins, seals, whales) -

56 Insectivora - - Edentata (sloths, &c.) - - - - -

Ruminantia (oxen, deer, &c.) - -

57 Cheiroptera

58 Quadrumana - Quadrumana (monkeys) - - - -

59 Bimana - - - Bimana (man) - - - - - - -

ASCENDING SERIES OF ROCKS.	FŒTAL HUMAN BRAIN
1 Gneiss and Mica Slate system	RESEMBLES, IN
2 Clay Slate and Grawacke system	
3 Silurian system	1st month, that of an avertebrated animal ;
4 Old Red Sandstone	
5 Carboniferous formation	2nd month, that of a fish ;
6 New Red Sandstone	3rd month, that of a turtle ;
	4th month, that of a bird ;
7 Oolite	
8 Cretaceous formation	
9 Lower Eocene	5th month, that of a rodent ; 6th month, that of a ruminant ;
10 Miocene	7th month, that of a digitigrade animal ;
11 Pliocene	
12 Superficial deposits	8th month, that of the quadrumana ; 9th month, attains full human character.

63

tion of the phenomena which we have been considering; but certainly not in the way suggested by Lamarck, whose whole notion is obviously so inadequate to account for the rise of the organic kingdoms, that we only can place it with pity among the follies of the wise. Had the laws of organic development been known in his time, his theory might have been of a more imposing kind. It is upon these that the present hypothesis is mainly founded. I take existing natural means, and shew them to have been capable of producing all the existing organisms, with the simple and easily conceivable aid of a higher generative law, which we perhaps still see operating upon a limited scale. I also go beyond the French philosopher[13] to a very important point, the original Divine conception of all the forms of being which these natural laws were only instruments in working out and realising. The actuality of such a conception I hold to be strikingly demonstrated by the discoveries of Macleay, Vigors, and Swainson,[14] with respect to the affinities and analogies of animal (and by implication vegetable) organisms. Such a regularity in the *structure*, as we may call it, of the *classification of animals*, as is shewn in their systems, is totally irreconcilable with the idea of form going on to form merely as needs and wishes in the animals themselves dictated. Had such been the case, all would have been irregular, as things arbitrary necessarily are. But, lo, the whole plan of being is as symmetrical as the plan of a house, or the laying out of an old-fashioned garden! This must needs have been devised and arranged for beforehand. And what a preconception or forethought have we here! Let us only for a moment consider how various are the external physical conditions in which animals live – climate, soil, temperature, land, water, air – the peculiarities of food, and the various ways in which it is to be sought; the peculiar circumstances in which the business of reproduction and the care-taking of the young are to be attended to – all these required to be taken into account, and thousands of animals were to be formed suitable in organization and mental character for the concerns they were to have with these various conditions and circumstances – here a tooth fitted for crushing nuts; there a claw fitted to serve as a hook for suspension; here to repress teeth and develop a bony net-work instead; there to arrange for a bronchial apparatus, to last only for a certain brief time; and all these animals were to be schemed out, each as a part of a great range, which was on the whole to be rigidly regular: let us, I say, only consider these things, and we shall see that the decreeing of laws to bring the whole about was an act involving such a degree of wisdom and device as we only can attribute, adoringly, to the one Eternal and

Unchangeable. It may be asked, how does this reflection comport with that timid philosophy which would have us to draw back from the investigation of God's works, lest the knowledge of them should make us undervalue his greatness and forget his paternal character? Does it not rather appear that our ideas of the Deity can only be worthy of him in the ratio in which we advance in a knowledge of his works and ways; and that the acquisition of this knowledge is consequently an available means of our growing in a genuine reverence for him!

But the idea that any of the lower animals have been concerned in any way with the origin of man – is not this degrading? Degrading is a term, expressive of a notion of the human mind, and the human mind is liable to prejudices which prevent its notions from being invariably correct. Were we acquainted for the first time with the circumstances attending the production of an individual of our race, we might equally think them degrading, and be eager to deny them, and exclude them from the admitted truths of nature. Knowing this fact familiarly and beyond contradiction, a healthy and natural mind finds no difficulty in regarding it complacently. Creative Providence has been pleased to order that it should be so, and it must therefore be submitted to. Now the idea as to the progress of organic creation, if we become satisfied of its truth, ought to be received precisely in this spirit. It has pleased Providence to arrange that one species should give birth to another, until the second highest gave birth to man, who is the very highest: be it so, it is our part to admire and to submit. The very faintest notion of there being anything ridiculous or degrading in the theory – how absurd does it appear, when we remember that every individual amongst us actually passes through the characters of the insect, the fish, and reptile, (to speak nothing of others,) before he is permitted to breathe the breath of life! But such notions are mere emanations of false pride and ignorant prejudice. He who conceives them little reflects that they, in reality, involve the principle of a contempt for the works and ways of God, for it may be asked, if He, as appears, has chosen to employ inferior organisms as a generative medium for the production of higher ones, even including ourselves, what right have we, his humble creatures, to find fault? There is, also, in this prejudice, an element of unkindliness towards the lower animals, which is utterly out of place. These creatures are all of them part products of the Almighty Conception, as well as ourselves. All of them display wondrous evidence of his wisdom and benevolence. All of them have had assigned to them by their Great Father a part in the drama of the

Robert Chambers (1802–1871)

organic world, as well as ourselves. Why should they be held in such contempt? Let us regard them in a proper spirit, as parts of the grand plan, instead of contemplating them in the light of frivolous prejudices, and we shall be altogether at a loss to see how there should be any degradation in the idea of our race having been genealogically connected with them.[15]

3. *Hugh Miller,*
The Testimony of the Rocks, or
Geology in its Bearing on the Two
Theologies, Natural & Revealed
(1857), Lecture Fifth, 'Geology in
its Bearings on the Two Theologies'

Part I, pp. 192–218

Hugh Miller was an Evangelical Christian and self-taught geologist. He had first become interested in geology while working as a stonemason; eventually he became one of the most popular geological writers. *The Testimony of the Rocks* had sold forty-two thousand copies by the end of the century. He was famous for his lyrical descriptions of natural phenomena and for his fervent blending of science and religion. As one biographer puts it, 'Not as a mere collector of facts, or word-painter of geological landscape, would he work, but in full view and constant recollection of every momentous question relating to the nature and destiny of man on which science might touch' (Peter Bayne, *Life and Letters of Hugh Miller* (1871), vol. 2, p. 137), and in Miller's case those 'momentous questions' had Christian answers.

The Testimony of the Rocks claims to relate geology to both 'Natural and Revealed' theology. The second of these aims, Miller's 'reconciliation' of Genesis with geological evidence, is described in C. W. Goodwin's account in *Essays and Reviews* (see pp. 110–44). The lecture reproduced here, first given in 1852, concentrates on the bearing of geological evidence on *natural* theology: in the geological record, Miller finds proof of the existence of God the Creator. At the same time, he expects natural theology to provide analogies with revealed theology: so here he sees the successive Creations of geology prefiguring the final Creation of 'a new Heaven and a new earth' promised in Revelation.

Miller, like Sedgwick, was a 'catastrophist' geologist – that is, he saw the geological record as showing a number of distinct eras, each characterised by a particular landscape and set of animals and plants. The 'catastrophic' destruction of each era, and the creation of the next were brought about by Divine 'interventions' in the ordinary course of Nature. This accounted for both the extinction and the creation of species. According to Miller, each era was perfect when created, and then gradually declined; and he could produce fossil evidence to prove this and to disprove the 'development' theories of people like Lamarck or Robert Chambers. It is not fair to regard the 'catastrophists' as unscientific, or as blinded to scientific truth by their religious preconceptions. Their hypothesis of 'separate creations' was borne out by the lack of evidence of 'links' in the fossil record – a fact that was to worry Darwin. In their view, it was the developmentalists and the 'uniformitarians' like Lyell who were

67

twisting the evidence to fit their naturalistic preconceptions. Lyell's approach can be characterised by the subtitle of his *Principles of Geology* (1830–3): *Being an Attempt to Explain the Former Changes of the Earth's Surface, by Reference to Causes Now in Operation*. He was attacking the catastrophists, and arguing that present-day natural causes could account for all the transformations revealed by the rocks. All, that is, except for the creation of new species, which Lyell still referred to mysterious or supernatural causes: he also had no time for 'developmentalists' like Lamarck, whom he refuted at length. Thus Lyell's geology presents a rather depressing and destructive picture of the world – extinction is dwelt on, but not creation. Darwin was deeply indebted to Lyell, and can be seen as fulfilling Lyell's programme in extending explanation by natural 'Causes Now in Operation' to the origin of species as well, thus totally eliminating the need for the 'supernatural' interventions that catastrophists like Miller made so much of. The scientific future was to lie with the 'naturalistic' and non-theological approach of Lyell and Darwin. Though outwardly pious, Lyell's private opinion was that *Principles* aimed 'to sink the diluvialists, and in short all the theological sophists' (the diluvialists claimed to see evidence of Noah's Flood in the geological record). He identified his enemies as 'the ancient and modern physico-theologians' (Katherine M. Lyell, *Life, Letters and Journals of Sir Charles Lyell* (1881), vol. I, pp. 309–11, 271).

What is especially impressive about Miller is the way he uses his geological evidence not just to bolster up the old arguments of natural theology, but to improve and extend them. By adding a historical dimension to the Creation, geology does not destroy the argument from design, instead it provides evidence of *several* perfectly-adapted Creations. These came into existence at definite points in time – so atheists can no longer urge the 'infinity' argument against natural theology. Similarly, Miller takes on David Hume, one of the most penetrating eighteenth-century critics of natural theology, and refutes his logical objections to the design argument, from the geological record. Geology also helps Miller to criticise what he sees as the luke-warm deism of the eighteenth century, as expressed in Pope's *Essay on Man*, for demoting man from the centre of the Creation and laughing at anthropocentrism. On the contrary, the geological evidence shows a progressive creation of species leading upwards to man as the apex and goal. Man's further progression will be towards God, not towards a 'higher race' as Robert Chambers had suggested. There was as yet no geological evidence to contradict the assumption of man's *recent* appearance on the scene.

The science of the geologist seems destined to exert a marked influence on that of the natural theologian. For not only does it greatly add to the materials on which the natural theologian founds his deductions, by adding to the organisms, plant and animal, of the present creation the extinct organisms of the creations of the past, with all their extraordinary display of adaptation and design; but it affords him, besides, materials peculiar to itself, in the history which it furnishes both of the appearance of these organisms in time, and of the wonderful order in which they were chronologically arranged. Not only – to borrow from Paley's illustration[a] – does it enable him

a. See extract I, p. 27.

to argue on the old grounds, from the contrivance exhibited in the *watch* found on the moor, that the watch could not have lain upon the moor for ever; but it establishes further, on different and more direct evidence, that there was a time when absolutely the watch was not there; nay, further, so to speak, that there was a previous time in which no watches existed at all, but only water-clocks; yet further, that there was a time in which there were not even water-clocks, but only sun-dials; and further, an earlier time still in which sun-dials were not, nor any measurers of time of any kind. And this is distinct ground from that urged by Paley. For, besides holding that each of these contrivances must have had in turn an originator or contriver, it adds historic fact to philosophic inference. Geology takes up the master volume of the greatest of the natural theologians, and, after scanning its many apt instances of palpable design, drawn from the mechanism of existing plants and animals, authoritatively decides that not one of these plants or animals had begun to be in the times of the Chalk; nay, that they all date their origin from a period posterior to that of the Eocene. And the fact is, of course, corroborative of the inference. 'That well constructed edifice,' says the natural theologian, 'cannot be a mere *lusus naturæ*,[a] or chance combination of stones and wood; it must have been erected by a builder.' 'Yes,' remarks the geologist, 'it was erected some time during the last nine years. I passed the way ten years ago, and saw only a blank space where it now stands.' Nor does the established fact of an absolute beginning of organic being seem more pregnant with important consequences to the science of the natural theologian than the fact of the peculiar order in which they begin to be.

The importance of the now demonstrated fact, that all the living organisms which exist on earth had a beginning, and that a time was when they were not, will be best appreciated by those who know how much, and, it must be added, how unsuccessfully, writers on the evidences have laboured to convict of an absurdity, on this special head, the atheistic assertors of an infinite series of beings. Even Robert Hall[1] (in his famous Sermon on Modern Infidelity) could but play, when he attempted grappling with the subject, upon the words *time* and *eternity*, and strangely argue, that as each member of an infinite series must have begun in *time*, while the succession itself was *eternal*, it was palpably absurd to ask us to believe in a *succession* of beings that was thus infinitely earlier than any of the

a. Sport of Nature.

beings themselves which composed the succession. And Bentley,[2] more perversely ingenious still, could assert, that as each of the individuals in an infinite series must have consisted of many parts, – that as each man in such a series, for instance, must have had ten fingers and ten toes, – it was palpably absurd to ask us to believe in an infinity which thus comprised many infinities, – ten infinities of fingers, for example, and ten infinities of toes. The infidels had the better in this part of the argument. It was surely easy enough to show against the great preacher on the one hand, that *time* in such a question is but a mere word that means simply a certain limited or definite period which had a beginning, whereas eternity means an unlimited and undefinable period which had no beginning; – that his seeming argument was no argument, but merely a sort of verbal play on this difference of signification in the words; – further, that man could conceive of an infinite series, whether extended in infinite space or subsisting in infinite time, just as well as he could conceive of any other infinity, and in the same way; and that the only mode of disproving the possibility of such a series would be to show, what of course cannot be shown, that in conceiving of it in the progressive mode in which, according to Locke, man can alone conceive of the infinite or the eternal, there would be a point reached at which it would be impossible for him to go on adding millions on millions to the previous sum. The symbolic '*ad infinitum*' could be made as adequately representative in the case of an infinite series of men or animals in unlimited time, as of an infinite series of feet or inches in unlimited space, or of an infinite series of hours or minutes in the past eternity. And as for Bentley, on the other hand, he ought surely to have known that all infinities are not equal, seeing that Newton had expressly told him so in the second of his four famous letters; but that, on the contrary, one infinity may be not only ten times greater than another infinity, but even infinitely greater than another infinity; and that so the conception of an infinity of men possessed of ten infinities of fingers and toes is in no respect an absurdity. Of the three infinities possible in space, the second is infinitely greater than the first, and the third infinitely greater than the second. A line infinitely produced is capable of being divided into – i.e. consists of – an infinity of given parts; a plane infinitely extended is capable of being divided into an infinity of infinitely divisible lines; and a cube – i.e. a solid infinitely expanded – is capable of being divided into an infinity of infinitely divisible planes. In fine, metaphysic theology furnishes no argument against the infinite series of the atheist.[3] But geology does. Every plant and animal that now lives upon earth began to be during the great Tertiary period, and had no place among the plants and animals of the great Secondary division.[4] We can trace several of our existing quadrupeds, such as the badger, the hare, the fox, the red deer, and the wild cat, up till the earlier times of the Pleistocene;[a] and not a few of our existing shells, such as the great pecten, the edible oyster, the whelk, and the Pelican's-foot shell, up till the greatly earlier times of the Coraline Crag. But at certain definite lines in the deposits of the past, representative of certain points in the course of time, the existing mammals and molluscs cease to appear, and we find their places occupied by other mammals and molluscs. Even such of our British shells as seem to have enjoyed as species the longest term of life cannot be traced beyond the times of the Pliocene deposits. We detect their remains in a perfect state of keeping in almost every shell-bearing bed, till we reach the Red and Coraline Crags, where we find them for the last time; and, on passing into older and deeper lying beds, we see their places taken by other shells, of species altogether distinct. The very common shell *Purpura lapillus*, for instance, is found in our raised beaches, in our Clyde-beds, in our boulder-clays and mammaliferous crags, and, finally, in the Red Crag, beyond which it fails to appear. And such also is the history of the common edible mussel and common periwinkle; whereas the common edible cockle and common edible pecten (*P. opercularis*) occur not only in all these successive beds, but in the Coral Crag also. They are older by a whole deposit than their present contemporaries the mussel and periwinkle; and these, in turn, seem of older standing than shells such as *Murex erinaceus*, that has not been traced beyond the times of the mammaliferous crag, or than shells such as *Scrobicularia piperata*, that has not been detected in more ancient deposits than raised sea-beaches of the later periods, and the elevated bottoms of old estuaries and lagoons. We thus know, that in certain periods, nearer or more remote, all our existing molluscs *began* to exist, and that they had no existence during the previous periods; which were, however, richer in animals of the same great molluscan group than the present time. Our British group of recent marine shells falls somewhat short of *four* hundred species; whereas the group characteristic of the older Miocene deposits, largely developed in those districts of France which border on the Bay of Biscay, and more sparingly in the south of England, near Yarmouth, comprises more than *six* hundred species. Nearly an equal number of still older shells

a. For glosses on all geological terms mentioned by Miller in the next two pages see endnote 4.

have been detected in a single deposit of the Paris basin, – the *Calcaire grossier*; and a good many more in a more ancient formation still, the London Clay. On entering the Chalk, we find a yet older group of shells, wholly unlike any of the preceding ones; and in the Oolite and Lias yet other and different groups. And thus group preceded group throughout all the Tertiary, Secondary, and Palæozoic periods; some of them remarkable for the number of species which they contained, others for the profuse abundance of their individual specimens, until, deep in the rocks at the base of the Silurian system, we detect what seems to be the primordial group, beneath which only a single animal organism is known to occur, – the *Oldhamia antiqua*, – a plant-like zoophyte, akin apparently to some of our recent sertulariæ.[a] Each of the extinct groups had, we find, a beginning and an end; – there is not in the wide domain of physical science a more certain fact; and every species of the group which now exists had, like all their predecessors on the scene, their beginning also. The 'infinite series' of the atheists of former times can have no place in modern science: all organic existences, recent or extinct, vegetable or animal, have had their beginning; – there was a time when they were not. The geologist can indicate that time, if not by years, at least by periods, and show what its relations were to the periods that went before and that came after; and as it is equally a recognised truth on both sides of the controversy, that as something now exists, something must have existed for ever, and as it must now be not less surely recognised, that that something was not the race of man, nor yet any other of the many races of man's predecessors or contemporaries, the question, What then was that something? comes with a point and directness which it did not possess at any former time. By what, or through whom, did these races of nicely organized plants and animals begin to be? Hitherto at least there has been but one reply to the question originated on the sceptical side. All these races, it is said, have been *developed*, in the long course of ages, into what they now are, as the young animal is developed in the womb, or the young plant is developed from the seed. Topsy, in the novel,[5] ''spected that she was not made, but growed;' and the only class of opponents which the geological theist finds in the field which his science has laid open to the world is a class that hold by the philosophy of Topsy.

Let me briefly remark regarding this development hypothesis, with which I have elsewhere dealt at considerable length,[6] that while

a. Animals of very simple structure, with body forming a cylindrical tube and mouth surrounded by a ring of tentacles.

the facts of the geologist are demonstrably such, i.e. truths capable of proof, the hypothesis is a mere dream, unsupported by a shadow of evidence. A man of a lively imagination could no doubt originate many such dreams; nay, we know that in the dark ages dreams of the kind were actually originated. The *Anser Bernicla*, or barnacle goose, a common winter visitant of our coasts, was once believed to be developed out of decaying wood long submerged in sea-water; and one of our commonest cirripedes or barnacles, *Lepas anatifera*, still bears, in its specific name of the goose-producing *lepas*, evidence that it was the creature specially recognised by our ancestors as the half-developed goose. As if in memory of this old development-legend, the bird still bears the name of the barnacle, and the barnacle of the bird; and we know further, that very intelligent men for their age, such as Gerardes the herbalist (1597), and Hector Boece the historian (1524), both examined these shells, and, knowing but little of comparative anatomy, were satisfied that the animal within was the partially developed embryo of a fowl. Such was one of the fables gravely credited as a piece of natural history in Britain about three centuries ago, and such was the kind of evidence by which it was supported. And we know that the followers of Epicurus received from their master, without apparent suspicion, fables still more extravagant, and that wanted even such a shadow of proof to support them as satisfied the herbalist and the historian. The Epicureans at least professed to believe that the earth, after spontaneously producing herbs and trees, began to produce in great numbers mushroom-like bodies, that, when they came to maturity, burst open, giving egress each to a young animal, which proved the founder of a race; and that thus, in succession, all the members of the animal kingdom were ushered into existence. But whether the dream be that of the Epicureans of classic times, or that of the naturalists of the middle ages, or that of the Lamarckians of our own days,[7] it is equally a dream, and can have no place assigned to it among either the solid facts or the sober deductions of science. Nay, the dream of the Lamarckians labours under a special disadvantage, from which the dreams of the others are free. If some modern Boece or Epicurus were to assert that at certain definite periods, removed from fifteen to fifty thousand years from the present time, all our existing animals were developed from decaying wood, or from a wonderful kind of mushrooms that the earth produced only once every ten thousand years, the assertion, if incapable of proof, would be at least equally incapable of being *dis*-proven. But when the Lamarckian affirms that all our recent species of plants and animals were

developed out of previously existing plants and animals of species
entirely different, he affirms what, if true, *would* be capable of
proof; and so, if it cannot be proven, it is only because it is not
true. The trilobites have been extinct ever since the times of the
Mountain Limestone; and yet, by series of specimens, the
individual development of certain species of this family, almost
from the extrusion of the animal from the egg until the attainment
of its full size, has been satisfactorily shown. By specimen after
specimen has every stage of growth and every degree of development been exemplified; and the Palæontologist has come as
thoroughly to know the creatures, in consequence, under their
various changes from youth to age, as if they had been his contemporaries, and had grown up under his eye. And had our existing
species, vegetable and animal, been derived from other species of
the earlier periods, it would have been equally possible to demonstrate, by a series of specimens, *their* relationship. Let us again
instance the British shells. Losing certain species in each of the
older and yet older deposits at which we successively arrive, we at
length reach the Red and Coraline Crags, where we find, mingled
with the familiar forms, a large per centage of forms now extinct;
then going on to the shells of the lower Miocene, more than six
hundred species appear, almost all of which are strange to us; and
then, passing to the Eocene shells of the *Calcaire grossier*, we find
ourselves among well nigh as large a group of yet other and older
strangers, not one of which we are able to identify with any shell
now living in the British area. There would be thus no lack of
materials for forming such a genealogy of the British shells, had
they been gradually developed out of the extinct species, as that
which M. Barrande[8] has formed of the trilobites. But no such genealogy can be formed. We cannot link on a single recent shell to a
single extinct one. *Up* to a certain point we find the recent shells
exhibiting all their present specific peculiarities, and beyond that
point they cease to appear. *Down* to a certain point the extinct
shells also exhibit all *their* specific peculiarities, and then they dis-
appear for ever. There are no intermediate species, – no connecting
links,[9] – no such connected series of specimens to be found as enables us to trace a trilobite through all its metamorphoses from
youth to age. All geologic history is full of the beginnings and the
ends of species, – of their first and their last days; but it exhibits no
genealogies of development. The Lamarckian sets himself to
grapple, in his dream, with the history of all creation: we awaken
him, and ask him to grapple, instead, with the history of but a few

individual species, – with that of the mussel or the whelk, the clam or the oyster; and we find from his helpless ignorance and incapacity what a mere pretender he is.

But while no hypothesis of development can neutralize or explain away the great geologic fact, that every true species had a beginning independently, apparently, of every preceding species, there was demonstrably a general progress, in the course of creation, from lower to higher forms, which seems scarce less fraught with important consequences to the natural theologian than this fact of *beginning* itself. For while the one fact effectually disposes of the 'infinite series' of the atheist, the other fact disposes scarce less effectually of those reasonings on the sceptical side which, framed on the assumption that creation is a 'singular effect,' – an effect without duplicate, – have been employed in urging, that from that one effect only can we know aught regarding the producing cause. Knowing of the cause from but the effect, and having experience of but one effect, we cannot rationally hold, it has been argued, that the producing cause could have originated effects of a higher or more perfect kind. The creation which it produced we know; but, having no other measure of its power, we cannot regard it, it has been contended, as equal to the production of a better or nobler creation, or of course hold that it *could* originate such a state of things as that perfect future state which faith delights to contemplate. It has been well said of the author of this ingenious argument,[10] – by far the most sagacious of the sceptics, – that if we admit his premises we shall find it difficult indeed to set aside his conclusions. And how, in this case, does geology deal with his premises? By opening to us the history of the remote past of our planet, and introducing us, through the present, to former creations, it breaks down that *singularity* of effect on which he built, and for one creation gives us many. It gives us exactly that which, as he truly argued, his contemporaries had not, – an *experience* in creations. And let us mark how, applied to each of these in succession, his argument would tell.

There was a time when life, animal or vegetable, did not exist on our planet, and when all creation, from its centre to its circumference, was but a creation of dead matter. What, in that early age, would have been the effect of the argument of Hume? Simply this, – that though the producing Cause of all that appeared was competent to the formation of gases and earths, metals and minerals, it would be unphilosophic to deem Him adequate to the origination of a single plant or animal, even to that of a spore or of a monad. Ages pass by, and the Palæozoic creation is ushered in, with its tall araucarians and pines, its highly organized fishes, and its reptiles of comparatively low standing. And how now, and with what effect, does the argument apply? It is now rendered evident, that in the earlier creation the producing Cause had exerted but a portion of His power, and that He could have done greatly more than He actually did, seeing that we now find Him adequate to the origin-ation of vitality and organization in its two great kingdoms, plant and animal. But, still confining ourselves with cautious scepticism within the limits of our argument, we continue to hold that, as fishes of a high and reptiles of a low order, with trees of the cone-bearing family, are the most perfect specimens of their respective classes which the producing Cause has originated, it would be rash to hold, in the absence of proof, that He *could* originate aught higher or more perfect. And now, as yet other ages pass away, the creation of the great Secondary division takes the place of that of the vanished Palæozoic; and we find in its few dicotyledonous plants, in its rep-tiles of highest standing, in its great birds, and in its some two or three humble marsupial mammals, that in the previous, as in the earlier creation, the producing Cause had been, if I may so express myself, working greatly under His strength, and that in this third creation we have a still higher display of His potency. With some misgivings, however, we again apply our argument. And now yet another creation, – that of the Tertiary period, with its noble forests of dicotyledonous trees and its sagacious and gigantic mammals, – rises upon the scene; and as our experience in creations has now become very considerable, and as we have seen each in succession higher than that which preceded it, we find that, notwithstanding our assumed scepticism, we had, compelled by one of the most deeply-seated instincts of our nature, been secretly anticipating the advance which the new state of things actually realizes. But applying the argument once more, we at least assume to hold, that as the sagacious elephant is the highest example of animal life yet produced by the originating Cause, it would be unphilosophic to deem Him capable of producing a higher example. And, while we are thus reasoning, man appears upon creation, – a creature immeasurably superior to all the others, and whose very nature it is to make use of his experience of the past for his guidance in the future. And if that only be solid experience or just reasoning which enables us truly to anticipate the events which are to come, and so to make provision for them; and if that experience be not solid, and that reasoning not just, which would serve but to darken our discernment, and prevent us from correctly predicating the cast and complexion of coming events, what ought to be our decision regarding an argument which, had it been employed in each of the vanished creations of the past, would have had but the effect of arresting all just anticipation regarding the immediately succeeding creation, and which, thus reversing the main end and object of philosophy, would render the philosopher who clung to it less sagacious in divining the future than even the ordinary man? But, in truth, the existing premises, wholly altered by geologic science, are no longer those of Hume. The footprint on the sand – to refer to his happy illustration – does not now stand alone. Instead of one, we see many footprints, each in turn in advance of the print behind it, and on a higher level; and, founding at once on an acquaintance with the past, extended throughout all the periods of the geologist, and on that instinct of our nature whose peculiar function it is to anticipate at least one creation more, we must regard the expectation of 'new heavens and a new earth, wherein dwelleth righteousness,' as not unphilosophic, but as, on the contrary, altogether rational and according to experience.

Such is the bearing of geological science on two of the most important questions that have yet been raised in the field of natural theology. Nor does it bear much less directly on a controversy to which, during the earlier half of the last century, there was no little importance attached in Britain, and which engaged on its opposite sides some of the finest and most vigorous intellects of the age and country.

The school of infidelity represented by Bolingbroke, and, in at least his earlier writings, by Soame Jenyns,[11] and which, in a modified form, attained to much popularity through Pope's famous 'Essay,' assigned to man a comparatively inconsiderable space in the system of the universe. It regarded him as but a single link in a chain of mutual dependence, – a chain which would be no longer an entire, but a broken one, were he to be struck out of it, but as thus more important from his position than from his nature or his powers. You will remember that one of the sections of Pope's first epistle to his 'good St John' is avowedly devoted to show what he terms the 'absurdity of man's supposing himself the final cause of the creation;' and though this great master of condensed meaning and brilliant point is now less read than he was in the days of our grandfathers, you will all remember the elegant stanzas in which he states the usual claims of the species only to ridicule them. It is human pride personified that he represents as exclaiming, –

Hugh Miller (1802–1856)

'For me kind Nature wakes her genial power,
Suckles each herb, and spreads out every flower;
Annual for me the grape, the rose, renew
The juice nectarious and the balmy dew.
For me the mine a thousand treasures brings;
For me health gushes from a thousand springs;
Seas roll to waft me, suns to light me rise;
My footstool earth, my canopy the skies.'[12]

You will further remember how the poet, after thus reducing the claims and lowering the position of the species, set himself to show that man, viewed in relation to the place which he occupies, ought not to be regarded as an imperfect being. Man is, he said, as perfect as he ought to be. And, such being the case, the Author of all, looking, it would seem, very little after him, has just left him to take care of himself. A cold, unfeeling abstraction, like the gods of the old Epicurean, the Great First Cause of this school is a being

'Who sees with equal eye, as God of all,
A hero perish or a sparrow fall;
Atoms or systems into ruin hurl'd,
And now a bubble burst, and now a world.'[13]

Such, assuredly, was not that God of the New Testament whom the Saviour of mankind revealed to his disciples as caring for all his creatures of the dust, but as caring most for the highest of all. 'Are not two sparrows,' he said, 'sold for a farthing? and one of them shall not fall to the ground without your Father. Fear ye not therefore; ye are of more value than many sparrows.'

It was the error of this ingenious but very unsolid school, that it regarded the mere *order* of the universe as itself an end or final cause. It reasoned respecting creation as if it would be true philosophy to account for the origin and existence of some great city, such as the city of Washington in the United States, built, as we know, for purely political purposes, by showing that, – as it was remarkable for its order, for the rectilinear directness of its streets, and the rectangularity of its squares, – it must have been erected simply to be a perfect embodiment of regularity; and to urge further that, save in their character as component parts of a perfect whole, the House of Representatives and the mansion of the President were of no more intrinsic importance, or no more decidedly the *end* of the whole, than any low tavern or out-house in the lesser streets or lanes. The destruction of either the out-house or the House of Representatives would equally form a void in the general plan of the city, regarded as an admirably arranged whole. And it was thus with the grand scheme of creation; for,

'From nature's chain whatever link we strike,
Tenth or tenth thousand, breaks the chain alike.'[14]

Nor is it in other than due keeping with such a view of creation that its great Author should be represented as a cold abstraction, without love or regard, and equally indifferent to the man and the sparrow, to the atom and the planet. Order has respect to but the *relations* of things or of beings, – not to the things or beings themselves; order is the *figure* which, as mere etched points or strokes, they compose, – the legend which, as signs or characters, they form; and who cares anything for the component strokes or dots irrespective of the print, or for the component letters or words apart from the writing? The 'equal eye,' in such a scheme, would of necessity be an indifferent one. Against this strange doctrine, though in some measure countenanced by the glosses of Warburton in his defence of Pope, the theologians protested, – none of them, however, more vigorously than Johnson, in his famous critique on the 'Free Inquiry' of Soame Jenyns. Nor is it uninteresting to mark with what a purely instinctive feeling of the right some of the better poets, whose 'lyre,' according to Cowper, was their 'heart,' protested against it too. Poor Goldsmith, when sitting a homeless vagabond on the slopes of the Alps, could exclaim, in a greatly truer tone than that of his polished predecessor, –

'Creation's heir, the world, the world is mine!'[15]

And in Cowper himself we find all Goldsmith's intense feeling of appropriation, that 'calls the delightful scenery all its own,' associated

'With worthy thoughts of that unvaried love
That planned, and built, and still upholds, a world
So clothed with beauty, for rebellious man.'[16]

Strange to say, however, it is to the higher exponents of natural science, and in especial to the geologists, that it has been left to deal most directly with the sophistries of Bolingbroke and Pope.

Oken,[17] a man quite as far wrong in some points as either the poet or his master, was the first to remark, and this in the oracular, enigmatical style peculiar to the German, that 'man is the sum total of all the animals.' Gifted, as all allow, with a peculiarly nice eye for detecting those analogies which unite the animal world into a harmonious whole, he remarked, that in one existence or being all these analogies converge. Even the humbler students of the heavens have learned to find for themselves the star of the pole, by following the direction indicated by what are termed the two pointer stars in the Great Bear. And to the eye of Oken all the groups of the animal kingdom formed a sphere of constellations, each of which has its pointer stars, if I may so speak, turned towards man. Man occupies, as it were, the central point in the great circle of being; so that those lines which pass singly through each of the inferior animals stationed at its circumference, meet in him; and thus, as the focus in which the scattered rays unite, he imparts by his presence a unity and completeness to creation which it would not possess were he away. You will be startled, however, by the language in which the German embodies his view; though it may be not uninstructive to refer to it in evidence of the fact that a man may be *intellectually* on the very verge of truth, and yet for every moral purpose infinitely removed from it. 'Man,' he says, 'is God manifest in the flesh.' And yet it may be admitted that there is a certain loose sense in which man *is* 'God manifest in the flesh'. As may be afterwards shown, he is God's *image* manifested in the flesh; and an image or likeness *is* a manifestation or making evident of that which it represents, whether it be an image or likeness of body or of mind.

Not less extraordinary, but greatly more sound in their application, are the views of Professor Owen,[18] – supreme in his own special walk as a comparative anatomist. We find him recognising man as exemplifying in his structure the perfection of that type in which, from the earliest ages, nature had been working with reference to some future development, and as *therefore* a fore-ordained existence. 'The recognition of an ideal exemplar for the vertebrated animals proves,' he says, 'that the knowledge of such a being as man must have existed before man appeared. For the Divine mind that planned the archetype also fore-knew all its modifications. The archetypal idea was manifested in the flesh, under divers modifications, upon this planet, long prior to the existence of those animal species that actually exemplify it.'[19] So far Owen. And not less wonderful is the conclusion at which Agassiz[20] has arrived, after a survey of the geologic existences more extended and minute, in at least the ichthyic[a] department, than that of any other man. 'It is evident,' we find him saying, in the conclusion of his recent work, 'The Principles of Zoology,'[21] 'that there is a manifest progress in the succession of beings on the surface of the earth. This progress consists in an increasing similarity to the living fauna, and among the vertebrates, especially in their increasing resemblance to man.

a. Pertaining to fishes.

But this connection is not the consequence of a direct lineage between the faunas of different ages. There is nothing like parental descent connecting them. The fishes of the Palæozoic age are in no respect the ancestors of the reptiles of the Secondary age, nor does man descend from the mammals which preceded him in the Tertiary age. The link by which they are connected is of a higher and immaterial nature; and their connection is to be sought in the view of the Creator himself, whose aim in forming the earth, in allowing it to undergo the successive changes which geology has pointed out, and in creating successively all the different types of animals which have passed away, *was to introduce man upon the surface of our globe.* MAN IS THE END TOWARDS WHICH ALL THE ANIMAL CREATION HAS TENDED FROM THE FIRST APPEARANCE OF THE FIRST PALÆOZOIC FISHES.' These, surely, are extraordinary deductions. 'In thy book,' says the Psalmist, 'all my members were written, which in continuance were fashioned when as yet there was none of them.'[22] And here is natural science, by the voice of two of its most distinguished professors, saying exactly the same thing.

Of the earliest known vertebrates, – the placoidal fishes of the Upper Silurian rocks, – we possess only fragments, which, however, sufficiently indicate, from their resemblance to the corresponding parts of an existing shark, – the cestracion, – that they belonged to fishes furnished with the two pairs of fins now so generally recognised as the homologues of the fore and hinder limbs in quadrupeds. With the second earliest vertebrates, – the ganoids of the Old Red Sandstone,[a] – we are more directly acquainted, and know that they exhibited the true typical form, – a vertebral column terminating in a brain-protecting skull; and that, in at least the acanth, celacanth, and dipterian families, they had the limb-like fins. In the upper parts of the system the earliest reptiles leave the first known traces of the typical foot, with its five digits. Higher still in one of the deposits of the Trias[b] we are startled by what seems to be the impression of a human hand of an uncouth massive shape, but with the thumb apparently set in opposition, as in man, to the other fingers; we next trace the type upwards among the wonderfully developed reptiles of the Secondary periods; then among the mammals of the Tertiary ages, higher and yet higher forms appear; the mute prophecies of the coming being become with each approach clearer, fuller, more expressive, and at length receive their fulfilment in the advent of man. A double meaning attaches to the term type;[23] and hence some

a. See endnote 4.   b. See endnote 4.

ambiguity in the writings which have appeared on this curious subject. Type means a prophecy embodied in symbol; it means also what Sir Joshua Reynolds well terms 'one of the general forms of nature,' – a pattern form, from which all others in the same class or family, however numerous, are recognised as mere exceptions and aberrations. But in the geologic series both meanings converge and become one. The form or number typical as the *general* form or number is found typical also, as a *prophecy*, of the form or number that came at length to be exemplified in the deputed lord of creation. Let us in our examples take typical numbers, as more easily illustrated without diagrams than typical forms.

There are vertebrate animals of the second age of ichthyic existence, that, like the *Pterichthys* and *Coccosteus*, were furnished with but two limbs. The murænidæ[a] of recent times have no more; at least one of their number, the muræna proper, wants limbs altogether; so also do the lampreys. The snakes are equally limbless, save that the boas and pythons possess the rudiments of a single pair; and such also is the condition, among the amphibia, of all the known species of Cœcilia. And yet, notwithstanding these exceptional cases, the true typical number of limbs, as shown by a preponderating majority of the vertebrates of all ages of the world, is four. And this typical number is the human number. There is as certainly a typical number of digits too, as of the limbs which bear them. The exceptions are many. All the species of the horse genus possess but a single digit; the cattle family possess but two digits, the rhinoceros three digits, the hippopotamus four digits; many animals, such as the dog and cat, have but four digits on one pair of limbs and five on the other; whereas in some of the fishes the number of digits is singularly great, – from ten to twenty in most species, and in the rays from eighty to a hundred. And yet, as shown in the rocks, in which, however, the aberrations appear early, the true typical number is five on both the fore and hinder limbs. And such is the number in man. There is also, in at least the mammalia, a typical number of vertebræ in the neck. The three-toed sloth has nine cervical vertebræ; the manati only six; but seven is the typical number. And seven is the human number also. Man, in short, is pre-eminently what a theologian would term the antetypical existence, – the being in whom the types meet and are fulfilled. And not only do typical forms and numbers of the exemplified character meet in man, but there are not a few parts of his framework which in the inferior animals exist as but mere sym-

a. Eel family.

bols, of as little importance as dugs in the male animal, though they acquire significancy and use in him. Such, for instance, are the many-jointed but moveless and unnecessary bones of which the stiff inflexible *fin* of the dugong and the fore paw of the mole consist, and which exist in his arm as essential portions, none of which could be wanted, of an exquisitely flexible instrument. In other cases, the old types are exemplified serially in the growth and development of certain portions of his frame. Such is specially the case with that all-important portion of it, the organ of thought and feeling. The human brain is built up by a wonderful process, during which it assumes in succession the form of the brain of a fish, of a reptile, of a bird, of a mammiferous quadruped; and, finally, it takes upon it its unique character as a human brain. Hence the remark of Oken, that 'man is the sum total of all the animals;' hence, too, a recognition of type in the *history* of the successive vertebral periods of the geologist, symbolical of the history of every individual man. It is not difficult to conceive how, on a subject of such complexity, especially if approached in an irreverent spirit, grave mistakes and misconceptions should take place. Virgil knew just enough of Hebrew prophecy to misapply, in his *Pollio*, to his great patron Octavius, those ancient predictions which foretold that in that age the Messiah was to appear.[24] And I am inclined to hold, that in the more ingenious speculations of the Lamarckians we have just a similar misapplication of what, emboldened by the views of Owen and Agassiz, I shall venture to term the *Geologic Prophecies.*

The term is new, but the idea which it embodies, though it at first existed rather as a nice poetic instinct than as a scientifically based thought, is at least as old as the times of Herder[25] and Coleridge. In a passage quoted from the former writer by Dr M'Cosh, in his very masterly work on typical forms,[26] I find the profound German remarking of the strange resemblances which pervade all nature, and impart a general unity to its forms, that it would seem 'as if on all our earth the form-abounding mother had proposed to herself but one type, – one proto-plasma, – according to which, and for which, she formed them all. Know, then,' he continues, 'what this form is. It is the identical one which man also wears.' And the remark of Coleridge, in his 'Aids to Reflection', is still more definite. 'Let us carry us back in spirit,' he says, 'to the mysterious week, the teeming work-days of the Creator (*as they rose in* VISION *before the eye of the inspired historian*), of the operations of the heavens and of the earth in the day that the Lord God made the earth and the heavens. And who that watched their ways with an understanding heart could, as the

vision evolved still advanced towards him, contemplate the filial and
loyal bee, the home-building, wedded, and divorceless swallow,
and, above all, the manifoldly intelligent ant tribes, with their
commonwealths and confederacies, their warriors and miners, the
husband-folk that fold in their tiny flocks on the honey-leaf, and the
virgin sister with the holy instincts of maternal love detached and in
selfless purity, and not say in himself, Behold the shadow of approaching humanity, the sun rising from behind in the kindling
morn of creation!'[27] There is fancy here; but it is that sagacious
fancy, vouchsafed to only the true poet, which has so often proved
the pioneer of scientific discovery, and which is in reality more sober
and truthful, in the midst of its apparent extravagance, than the
gravest cogitations of ordinary men. It is surely no incredible thing,
that He who, in the dispensations of the human period, spake by
type and symbol, and who, when He walked the earth in the flesh,
taught in parable and allegory, should have also spoken in the geologic ages by prophetic figures embodied in the form and structure
of animals.[28] Nay, what the poet imagined, though in a somewhat
extreme form, the philosophers seem to be on the very eve of con-
firming. The foreknown 'archetypal idea' of Owen, – 'the
immaterial link of connection' of all the past with all the present,
which Agassiz resolves into the fore-ordained design of the Creator,
– will be yet found, I cannot doubt, to translate themselves into one
great general truth, namely, that the Palæozoic, Secondary, and
Tertiary dispensations of creation were charged, like the patriarchal
and Mosaic dispensations of grace, with the 'shadows of better
things to come.' The advent of man simply as such was the great
event prefigured during the old geologic ages. The advent of that
Divine Man 'who hath abolished death, and brought life and
immortality to light,'[29] was the great event prefigured during the
historic ages. It is these two grand events, equally portions of one
sublime scheme, originated when God took counsel with himself in
the depths of eternity, that bind together past, present, and future, –
the geologic with the Patriarchal, the Mosaic, and the Christian
ages, and all together with that new heavens and new earth, the last
of many creations, in which there shall be 'no more death nor curse,
but the throne of God and the Lamb shall be in it, and his servants
shall serve him.'[30]

'There is absurdity' said Pope 'in man's conceiting himself the
final cause of creation.'[31] Unless, however, man had the entire
scheme of creation before him, with the farther partially known
scheme of which but a part constitutes the grand theme of revel-

ation, how could he pronounce on the absurdity? The knowledge of the geologist ascends no higher than man. He sees all nature in the pre-Adamic past, pointing with prophetic finger towards him; and on even the argument of Hume, – just and solid within its proper limits, – he refuses to acquiesce in the unfounded inference of Pope. In order to prove the absurdity of 'man's conceiting himself the final cause of creation', proof of an ulterior cause, – of a higher end and aim, – must be adduced; and of aught higher than man, the geologist, as such, knows nothing. The long vista opened up by his science closes with the deputed lord of creation, – with man as he at present exists; and when, casting himself full upon revelation, the veil is drawn aside, and an infinitely grander vista stretches out before him into the future, he sees man – no longer, however, the natural, but the Divine man – occupying what is at once its terminal point and its highest apex. Such are some of the bearings of geologic science on the science of natural theology. Geology has disposed effectually and for ever of the oft-urged assumption of an infinite series; it deals as no other science could have dealt with the assertion of the sceptic, that creation is a 'singular effect;' it casts a flood of unexpected light on the somewhat obsolete plausibilities of Bolingbroke and Jenyns, that exhibits their utterly unsolid character; yet further, it exhibits in a new aspect the argument founded on design, and invests the place and standing of man in *creation* with a peculiar significancy and importance, from its relation to the future. But on this latter part of my subject – necessarily of considerable extent and multiplicity, and connected rather with revealed than with natural religion – I must not now expatiate. I shall, however, attempt laying before you on some future evening, a few thoughts on this portion of the general question, which you may at least find suggestive of others, and which, if they fail to elicit new truths, may have the effect of opening up upon an old truth or two a few fresh avenues through which to survey them. The character of man as a fellow-worker with his Creator in the material province has still to be considered in the light of geology. Man was the first, and is still the only creature of whom we know anything, who has set himself to carry on and improve the work of the world's original framer, – who is a planter of woods, a tiller of fields, and a keeper of gardens, – and who carries on his work of mechanical contrivance on obviously the same principles as those on which the Divine designer wrought of old, and on which He works still. It may not be wholly unprofitable to acquaint ourselves, through evidence furnished by the rocks, with the remarkable fact, that the Creator imparted to man the Divine image before He united to man's the Divine nature.

4. Charles Darwin,
On the Origin of Species by Means of Natural Selection, or the Preservation of Favoured Races in the Struggle for Life (1859), Chapter 14, 'Recapitulation and Conclusion'

pp. 459–90

The *Origin* was published in 1859, but Darwin sketched out his first theory of species transmutation in 1837, soon after his return from his voyage in the *Beagle*. His observations during the voyage, especially the strange pattern of species distribution and adaptation that he had seen in the Galapagos Islands, had made him begin to doubt that species were fixed. He had a copy of Lyell's *Principles of Geology* with him on the *Beagle*, and he came to see his theory as the extension of Lyell's gradualist and naturalistic approach from the inorganic to the organic world. Darwin's only example for the 'causes now in operation' was the 'selection' practised by breeders to produce varieties in domestic animals and plants. His problem was, how could this principle of selection operate under natural conditions? The answer was suggested to him in 1838, by his reading of the Rev Thomas Robert Malthus' *Essay on the Principle of Population* (1798), in which Malthus had argued that while food supply increased only arithmetically, population increased geometrically. Applying this principle to Nature, Darwin realised that the competition for survival among the surplus populations in each species would result in the preservation of any favourable variations and the elimination of unfavourable ones. But Darwin was reluctant to publish his theory – as he puts it in his *Autobiography*, 'I was so anxious to avoid prejudice, that I determined not for some time to write even the briefest sketch of it' (p. 71). By 1844, however, he had prepared the first full draft of the theory; but he still delayed publication, until it was finally forced on him by the fact that Alfred Russel Wallace had come up with the same idea, in a paper called *On the Tendency of Varieties to depart indefinitely from the Original Type*, which he sent to Darwin in 1858. Interestingly, Wallace too had been influenced by reading Malthus. To solve the problem of priority, Darwin's friends Lyell and Hooker arranged for both Darwin's work and Wallace's to be read to the Linnean Society on 1 July 1858. After this, Darwin wrote the *Origin*, which he still described as only an abstract, and which came out in the following year.

Darwin's delay in publishing can be explained by his anxiety to avoid both religious and scientific 'prejudice'; the reaction to *Vestiges* had warned him of what he might expect, and he was anxious to establish the scientific validity of his theory, and to avoid religious controversy as much as possible. In the *Origin*, unlike Chambers in *Vestiges*, he does not explicitly extend his theory to include man, and he largely avoids any

86

consideration of its religious implications. As he wrote later, 'Many years ago I was strongly advised by a friend never to introduce anything about religion in my works, if I wished to advance science in England; and this led me not to consider the mutual bearings of the two subjects' (unpublished part of letter, cited in Gertrude Himmelfarb, *Darwin and the Darwinian Revolution* (1967), p. 383). The 'friend' was Lyell, who pursued the same policy. On the other hand, the *Origin* includes references to the 'Creator' and the 'creation' of life (see p. 108) – a terminology which Darwin later came to regret: 'But I have long regretted that I truckled to public opinion, and used the Pentateuchal term of creation, by which I really meant "appeared" by some wholly unknown process' (Letter of 1863, *Life and Letters*, vol. 3, p. 18). Darwin's own belief on this matter is suggested in the section on 'Religious Beliefs' in his *Autobiography*:

> Another source of conviction in the existence of God, connected with the reason and not with the feelings, impresses me as having much more weight. This follows from the extreme difficulty or rather impossibility of conceiving this immense and wonderful universe, including man with his capacity of looking far backward and far into futurity, as the result of blind chance or necessity. When thus reflecting I feel compelled to look to a First Cause having an intelligent mind in some degree analogous to that of man; and I deserve to be called a Theist.
> This conclusion was strong in my mind about the time, as far as I can remember, when I wrote the *Origin of Species*; and it is since that time that it has very gradually with many fluctuations become weaker. (p. 54)

This remote Creator is open to the same objections raised against the Creator of *Vestiges* – except that at least Chambers' Creator planned and pre-programmed the whole development of species from the start, while, in Darwin's scheme, the process is tentative, full of mistakes, and unforeseeable. As R. H. Hutton put it, the question is 'how an omniscient mind which knows precisely what is wanted, can set Nature *groping* her way forward as if she were blind, to find the path of least resistance' ('The Materialists' Stronghold', 1874, *Aspects of Religious and Scientific Thought*, p. 48). Nevertheless, there were various attempts to reconcile Darwinism and natural theology, especially among those who misread literally Darwin's metaphor of 'natural *selection*', as if it were a conscious and voluntary process. The anthropomorphic language that Darwin often used when writing about natural selection tended to increase this confusion.

As with all our writers so far, there was no clear-cut religion-versus-science conflict over the *Origin*. One of Darwin's fiercest critics, as he had been one of Chambers', was the scientist Adam Sedgwick, with whom Darwin had worked while at Cambridge, and to whom he sent a copy of the *Origin*. Here is the centre of Sedgwick's objection:

> There is a moral or metaphysical part of Nature as well as a physical. A man who denies this is deep in the mire of folly. . . . You have ignored this link; and, if I do not mistake your meaning, you have done your best in one or two pregnant cases to break it. Were it possible (which, thank God, it is not) to break it, humanity, in my mind, would suffer a damage that might brutalise it, and sink the human race into a lower grade of degradation than any into which it has fallen since its written records tell us of its history. (Letter to Darwin, 1859, *Life and Letters of Darwin*, vol. 2, p. 249)

Here, the conflict is between religious and irreligious science. On the other hand, the clergyman Charles Kingsley responded to Darwin's gift of a copy of the *Origin* like this:

> I have gradually learnt to see that it is just as noble a conception of Deity, to

believe that He created primal forms capable of self-development into all forms needful *pro tempore* and *pro loco*, as to believe that He required a fresh act of intervention to supply the *lacunas* which He Himself had made. I question whether the former be not the loftier thought. (Letter of 1859, *Life and Letters of Darwin*, vol. 2, p. 288)

Chapter XIV

Recapitulation and Conclusion

Recapitulation of the difficulties on the theory of Natural Selection – Recapitulation of the general and special circumstances in its favour – Causes of the general belief in the immutability of species – How far the theory of natural selection may be extended – Effects of its adoption on the study of Natural history – Concluding remarks.

As this whole volume is one long argument, it may be convenient to the reader to have the leading facts and inferences briefly recapitulated.

That many and grave objections may be advanced against the theory of descent with modification through natural selection, I do not deny. I have endeavoured to give to them their full force. Nothing at first can appear more difficult to believe than that the more complex organs and instincts should have been perfected, not by means superior to, though analogous with, human reason, but by the accumulation of innumerable slight variations, each good for the individual possessor.[1] Nevertheless, this difficulty, though appearing to our imagination insuperably great, cannot be considered real if we admit the following propositions, namely, – that gradations in the perfection of any organ or instinct, which we may consider, either do now exist or could have existed, each good of its kind, – that all organs and instincts are, in ever so slight a degree, variable, – and, lastly, that there is a struggle for existence leading to the preservation of each profitable deviation of structure or instinct. The truth of these propositions cannot, I think, be disputed.

It is, no doubt, extremely difficult even to conjecture by what gradations many structures have been perfected, more especially amongst broken and failing groups of organic beings; but we see so many strange gradations in nature, as is proclaimed by the canon, 'Natura non facit saltum,'[a] that we ought to be extremely cautious in saying that any organ or instinct, or any whole being, could not have arrived at its present state by many graduated steps.[2] There are, it

a. Nature does not make a leap – i.e. proceed by large changes.

must be admitted, cases of special difficulty on the theory of natural selection; and one of the most curious of these is the existence of two or three defined castes of workers or sterile females[3] in the same community of ants; but I have attempted to show how this difficulty can be mastered.

With respect to the almost universal sterility of species when first crossed, which forms so remarkable a contrast with the almost universal fertility of varieties when crossed, I must refer the reader to the recapitulation of the facts given at the end of the eighth chapter, which seem to me conclusively to show that this sterility is no more a special endowment than is the incapacity of two trees to be grafted together; but that it is incidental on constitutional differences in the reproductive systems of the intercrossed species. We see the truth of this conclusion in the vast differences in the result, when the same two species are crossed reciprocally; that is, when one species is first used as the father and then as the mother.

The fertility of varieties when intercrossed and of their mongrel offspring cannot be considered as universal; nor is their very general fertility surprising when we remember that it is not likely that either their constitutions or their reproductive systems should have been profoundly modified. Moreover, most of the varieties which have been experimentised on have been produced under domestication; and as domestication apparently tends to eliminate sterility, we ought not to expect it also to produce sterility.

The sterility of hybrids is a very different case from that of first crosses, for their reproductive organs are more or less functionally impotent; whereas in first crosses the organs on both sides are in a perfect condition. As we continually see that organisms of all kinds are rendered in some degree sterile from their constitutions having been disturbed by slightly different and new conditions of life, we need not feel surprise at hybrids being in some degree sterile, for their constitutions can hardly fail to have been disturbed from being compounded of two distinct organisations. This parallelism is supported by another parallel, but directly opposite, class of facts; namely, that the vigour and fertility of all organic beings are increased by slight changes in their conditions of life, and that the offspring of slightly modified forms or varieties acquire from being crossed increased vigour and fertility. So that, on the one hand, considerable changes in the conditions of life and crosses between greatly modified forms, lessen fertility; and on the other hand, lesser changes in the conditions of life and crosses between less modified forms, increase fertility.

Charles Darwin (1809–1882)

Turning to geographical distribution, the difficulties encountered on the theory of descent with modification are grave enough. All the individuals of the same species, and all the species of the same genus, or even higher group, must have descended from common parents; and therefore, in however distant and isolated parts of the world they are now found, they must in the course of successive generations have passed from some one part to the others. We are often wholly unable even to conjecture how this could have been effected. Yet, as we have reason to believe that some species have retained the same specific form for very long periods, enormously long as measured by years, too much stress ought not to be laid on the occasional wide diffusion of the same species; for during very long periods of time there will always be a good chance for wide migration by many means. A broken or interrupted range may often be accounted for by the extinction of the species in the intermediate regions. It cannot be denied that we are as yet very ignorant of the full extent of the various climatal and geographical changes which have affected the earth during modern periods; and such changes will obviously have greatly facilitated migration. As an example, I have attempted to show how potent has been the influence of the Glacial period on the distribution both of the same and of representative species throughout the world. We are as yet profoundly ignorant of the many occasional means of transport. With respect to distinct species of the same genus inhabiting very distant and isolated regions, as the process of modification has necessarily been slow, all the means of migration will have been possible during a very long period; and consequently the difficulty of the wide diffusion of species of the same genus is in some degree lessened.

As on the theory of natural selection an interminable number of intermediate forms must have existed, linking together all the species in each group by gradations as fine as our present varieties, it may be asked, Why do we not see these linking forms all around us? Why are not all organic beings blended together in an inextricable chaos? With respect to existing forms, we should remember that we have no right to expect (excepting in rare cases) to discover *directly* connecting links between them, but only between each and some extinct and supplanted form. Even on a wide area, which has during a long period remained continuous, and of which the climate and other conditions of life change insensibly in going from a district occupied by one species into another district occupied by a closely allied species, we have no just right to expect often to find intermediate varieties in the intermediate zone. For we have reason to believe that only a few species are undergoing change at any one period; and all changes are slowly effected. I have also shown that the intermediate varieties which will at first probably exist in the intermediate zones, will be liable to be supplanted by the allied forms on either hand; and the latter, from existing in greater numbers, will generally be modified and improved at a quicker rate than the intermediate varieties, which exist in lesser numbers; so that the intermediate varieties will, in the long run, be supplanted and exterminated.

On this doctrine of the extermination of an infinitude of connecting links, between the living and extinct inhabitants of the world, and at each successive period between the extinct and still older species, why is not every geological formation charged with such links? Why does not every collection of fossil remains afford plain evidence of the gradation and mutation of the forms of life? We meet with no such evidence, and this is the most obvious and forcible of the many objections which may be urged against my theory. Why, again, do whole groups of allied species appear, though certainly they often falsely appear, to have come in suddenly on the several geological stages? Why do we not find great piles of strata beneath the Silurian system, stored with the remains of the progenitors of the Silurian groups of fossils? For certainly on my theory such strata must somewhere have been deposited at these ancient and utterly unknown epochs in the world's history.

I can answer these questions and grave objections only on the supposition that the geological record is far more imperfect than most geologists believe. It cannot be objected that there has not been time sufficient for any amount of organic change; for the lapse of time has been so great as to be utterly inappreciable by the human intellect. The number of specimens in all our museums is absolutely as nothing compared with the countless generations of countless species which certainly have existed. We should not be able to recognise a species as the parent of any one or more species if we were to examine them ever so closely, unless we likewise possessed many of the intermediate links between their past or parent and present states; and these many links we could hardly ever expect to discover, owing to the imperfection of the geological record. Numerous existing doubtful forms could be named which are probably varieties; but who will pretend that in future ages so many fossil links will be discovered, that naturalists will be able to decide, on the common view, whether or not these doubtful forms are varieties? As long as most of the links between any two species are unknown, if any one link or intermediate variety be discovered, it will simply be classed as another and distinct species. Only a small portion of the world has been geologically explored. Only organic beings of certain classes can be preserved in a fossil condition, at least in any great number. Widely ranging species vary most, and varieties are often at first local, – both causes rendering the discovery of inter- mediate links less likely. Local varieties will not spread into other and distant regions until they are considerably modified and improved; and when they do spread, if discovered in a geological formation, they will appear as if suddenly created there, and will be simply classed as new species. Most formations have been intermit- tent in their accumulation; and their duration, I am inclined to believe, has been shorter than the average duration of specific forms. Successive formations are separated from each other by enormous blank intervals of time; for fossiliferous formations, thick enough to resist future degradation, can be accumulated only where much sedi- ment is deposited on the subsiding bed of the sea. During the alternate periods of elevation and of stationary level the record will be blank. During these latter periods there will probably be more variability in the forms of life; during periods of subsidence, more extinction.

With respect to the absence of fossiliferous formations beneath the lowest Silurian strata, I can only recur to the hypothesis given in the ninth chapter. That the geological record is imperfect all will admit; but that it is imperfect to the degree which I require, few will be inclined to admit. If we look to long enough intervals of time, geology plainly declares that all species have changed; and they have changed in the manner which my theory requires, for they have changed slowly and in a graduated manner. We clearly see this in the fossil remains from consecutive formations invariably being much more closely related to each other, than are the fossils from forma- tions distant from each other in time.

Such is the sum of the several chief objections and difficulties which may justly be urged against my theory; and I have now briefly recapitulated the answers and explanations which can be given to them. I have felt these difficulties far too heavily during many years to doubt their weight. But it deserves especial notice that the more important objections relate to questions on which we are confess- edly ignorant; nor do we know how ignorant we are. We do not know all the possible transitional gradations between the simplest and the most perfect organs; it cannot be pretended that we know all the varied means of Distribution during the long lapse of years, or that we know how imperfect the Geological Record is. Grave as these several difficulties are, in my judgment they do not overthrow the theory of descent with modification.

Now let us turn to the other side of the argument. Under domestication we see much variability. This seems to be mainly due to the reproductive system being eminently susceptible to changes in the conditions of life; so that this system, when not rendered impotent, fails to reproduce offspring exactly like the parent-form. Variability is governed by many complex laws, – by correlation of growth,[a] by use and disuse, and by the direct action of the physical conditions of life.[4] There is much difficulty in ascertaining how much modification our domestic productions have undergone; but we may safely infer that the amount has been large, and that modifications can be inherited for long periods. As long as the conditions of life remain the same, we have reason to believe that a modification, which has already been inherited for many generations, may continue to be inherited for an almost infinite number of generations. On the other hand we have evidence that variability, when it has once come into play, does not wholly cease; for new varieties are still occasionally produced by our most anciently domesticated productions.

Man does not actually produce variability; he only unintentionally exposes organic beings to new conditions of life, and then nature acts on the organisation, and causes variability. But man can and does select the variations given to him by nature, and thus accumulates them in any desired manner. He thus adapts animals and plants for his own benefit or pleasure. He may do this methodically, or he may do it unconsciously by preserving the individuals most useful to him at the time, without any thought of altering the breed. It is certain that he can largely influence the character of a breed by selecting, in each successive generation, individual differences so slight as to be quite inappreciable by an uneducated eye. This process of selection has been the great agency in the production of the most distinct and useful domestic breeds. That many of the breeds produced by man have to a large extent the character of natural species, is shown by the inextricable doubts whether very many of them are varieties or aboriginal species.

There is no obvious reason why the principles which have acted so efficiently under domestication should not have acted under nature. In the preservation of favoured individuals and races, during the constantly-recurrent Struggle for Existence, we see the most

a. The tendency of several variations to be linked together, as with albino colouring and deafness in cats.

powerful and ever-acting means of selection. The struggle for existence inevitably follows from the high geometrical ratio of increase[5]
which is common to all organic beings. This high rate of increase is
proved by calculation, by the effects of a succession of peculiar
seasons, and by the results of naturalisation,[a] as explained in the
third chapter. More individuals are born than can possibly survive.
A grain in the balance will determine which individual shall live and
which shall die, – which variety or species shall increase in number,
and which shall decrease, or finally become extinct. As the
individuals of the same species come in all respects into the closest
competition with each other, the struggle will generally be most
severe between them; it will be almost equally severe between the
varieties of the same species, and next in severity between the species
of the same genus. But the struggle will often be very severe between
beings most remote in the scale of nature. The slightest advantage in
one being, at any age or during any season, over those with which it
comes into competition, or better adaptation in however slight a
degree to the surrounding physical conditions, will turn the balance.

With animals having separated sexes there will in most cases be a
struggle between the males for possession of the females. The most
vigorous individuals, or those which have most successfully
struggled with their conditions of life, will generally leave most
progeny. But success will often depend on having special weapons
or means of defence, or on the charms of the males; and the slightest
advantage will lead to victory.

As geology plainly proclaims that each land has undergone great
physical changes, we might have expected that organic beings would
have varied under nature, in the same way as they generally have
varied under the changed conditions of domestication. And if there
be any variability under nature, it would be an unaccountable fact if
natural selection had not come into play. It has often been asserted,
but the assertion is quite incapable of proof, that the amount of
variation under nature is a strictly limited quantity. Man, though
acting on external characters alone and often capriciously, can produce within a short period a great result by adding up mere
individual differences in his domestic productions; and every one
admits that there are at least individual differences in species under
nature. But, besides such differences, all naturalists have admitted
the existence of varieties, which they think sufficiently distinct to be

a. The introduction of animals or plants into a place where they are not indigenous. They
often multiply rapidly and take over from native species.

worthy of record in systematic works. No one can draw any clear distinction between individual differences and slight varieties; or between more plainly marked varieties and sub-species, and species. Let it be observed how naturalists differ in the rank which they assign to the many representative forms in Europe and North America.

If then we have under nature variability and a powerful agent always ready to act and select, why should we doubt that variations in any way useful to beings, under their excessively complex relations of life, would be preserved, accumulated, and inherited? Why, if man can by patience select variations most useful to himself, should nature fail in selecting variations useful, under changing conditions of life, to her living products?[6] What limit can be put to this power, acting during long ages and rigidly scrutinising the whole constitution, structure, and habits of each creature, – favouring the good and rejecting the bad? I can see no limit to this power, in slowly and beautifully adapting each form to the most complex relations of life. The theory of natural selection, even if we looked no further than this, seems to me to be in itself probable. I have already recapitulated, as fairly as I could, the opposed difficulties and objections: now let us turn to the special facts and arguments in favour of the theory.

On the view that species are only strongly marked and permanent varieties, and that each species first existed as a variety, we can see why it is that no line of demarcation can be drawn between species, commonly supposed to have been produced by special acts of creation, and varieties which are acknowledged to have been produced by secondary laws. On this same view we can understand how it is that in each region where many species of a genus have been produced, and where they now flourish, these same species should present many varieties; for where the manufactory of species has been active, we might expect, as a general rule, to find it still in action; and this is the case if varieties be incipient species. Moreover, the species of the larger genera, which afford the greater number of varieties or incipient species, retain to a certain degree the character of varieties; for they differ from each other by a less amount of difference than do the species of smaller genera. The closely allied species also of the larger genera apparently have restricted ranges, and they are clustered in little groups round other species – in which respects they resemble varieties. These are strange relations on the view of each species having been independently created, but are intelligible if all species first existed as varieties.

Charles Darwin (1809–1882)

As each species tends by its geometrical ratio of reproduction to increase inordinately in number; and as the modified descendants of each species will be enabled to increase by so much more as they become more diversified in habits and structure, so as to be enabled to seize on many and widely different places in the economy of nature, there will be a constant tendency in natural selection to preserve the most divergent offspring of any one species. Hence during a long-continued course of modification, the slight differences, characteristic of varieties of the same species, tend to be augmented into the greater differences characteristic of species of the same genus. New and improved varieties will inevitably supplant and exterminate the older, less improved and intermediate varieties; and thus species are rendered to a large extent defined and distinct objects. Dominant species belonging to the larger groups tend to give birth to new and dominant forms; so that each large group tends to become still larger, and at the same time more divergent in character. But as all groups cannot thus succeed in increasing in size, for the world would not hold them, the more dominant groups beat the less dominant. This tendency in the large groups to go on increasing in size and diverging in character, together with the almost inevitable contingency of much extinction, explains the arrangement of all the forms of life, in groups subordinate to groups, all within a few great classes, which we now see everywhere around us, and which has prevailed throughout all time. This grand fact of the grouping of all organic beings seems to me utterly inexplicable on the theory of creation.[7]

As natural selection acts solely by accumulating slight, successive, favourable variations, it can produce no great or sudden modification; it can act only by very short and slow steps. Hence the canon of 'Natura non facit saltum,' which every fresh addition to our knowledge tends to make more strictly correct, is on this theory simply intelligible. We can plainly see why nature is prodigal in variety, though niggard in innovation. But why this should be a law of nature if each species has been independently created, no man can explain.

Many other facts are, as it seems to me, explicable on this theory. How strange it is that a bird, under the form of woodpecker, should have been created to prey on insects on the ground; that upland geese, which never or rarely swim, should have been created with webbed feet; that a thrush should have been created to dive and feed on sub-aquatic insects; and that a petrel should have been created with habits and structure fitting it for the life of an auk or grebe! and so on in endless other cases. But on the view of each species constantly trying to increase in number, with natural selection always ready to adapt the slowly varying descendants of each to any unoccupied or ill-occupied place in nature, these facts cease to be strange, or perhaps might even have been anticipated.

As natural selection acts by competition, it adapts the inhabitants of each country only in relation to the degree of perfection of their associates; so that we need feel no surprise at the inhabitants of any one country, although on the ordinary view supposed to have been specially created and adapted for that country, being beaten and supplanted by the naturalised productions from another land. Nor ought we to marvel if all the contrivances in nature be not, as far as we can judge, absolutely perfect; and if some of them be abhorrent to our ideas of fitness. We need not marvel at the sting of the bee causing the bee's own death; at drones being produced in such vast numbers for one single act, and being then slaughtered by their sterile sisters; at the astonishing waste of pollen by our fir-trees; at the instinctive hatred of the queen bee for her own fertile daughters; at ichneumonidæ feeding within the live bodies of caterpillars; and at other such cases. The wonder indeed is, on the theory of natural selection, that more cases of the want of absolute perfection have not been observed.[8]

The complex and little known laws governing variation are the same, as far as we can see, with the laws which have governed the production of so-called specific forms. In both cases physical conditions seem to have produced but little direct effect; yet when varieties enter any zone, they occasionally assume some of the characters of the species proper to that zone. In both varieties and species, use and disuse seem to have produced some effect; for it is difficult to resist this conclusion when we look, for instance, at the logger-headed duck, which has wings incapable of flight, in nearly the same condition as in the domestic duck; or when we look at the burrowing tucutucu, which is occasionally blind, and then at certain moles, which are habitually blind and have their eyes covered with skin; or when we look at the blind animals inhabiting the dark caves of America and Europe. In both varieties and species correlation of growth seems to have played a most important part, so that when one part has been modified other parts are necessarily modified. In both varieties and species reversions to long-lost characters occur. How inexplicable on the theory of creation is the occasional appearance of stripes on the shoulder and legs of the several species of the horse-genus and in their hybrids! How simply is this fact explained if we believe that these species have descended from a striped progenitor, in the same manner as the several domestic breeds of pigeon have descended from the blue and barred rock-pigeon!

On the ordinary view of each species having been independently created, why should the specific characters, or those by which the species of the same genus differ from each other, be more variable than the generic characters in which they all agree? Why, for instance, should the colour of a flower be more likely to vary in any one species of a genus, if the other species, supposed to have been created independently, have differently coloured flowers, than if all the species of the genus have the same coloured flowers? If species are only well-marked varieties, of which the characters have become in a high degree permanent, we can understand this fact; for they have already varied since they branched off from a common progenitor in certain characters, by which they have come to be specifically distinct from each other; and therefore these same characters would be more likely still to be variable than the generic characters which have been inherited without change for an enormous period. It is inexplicable on the theory of creation why a part developed in a very unusual manner in any one species of a genus, and therefore, as we may naturally infer, of great importance to the species, should be eminently liable to variation; but, on my view, this part has undergone, since the several species branched off from a common progenitor, an unusual amount of variability and modification, and therefore we might expect this part generally to be still variable. But a part may be developed in the most unusual manner, like the wing of a bat, and yet not be more variable than any other structure, if the part be common to many subordinate forms, that is, if it has been inherited for a very long period; for in this case it will have been rendered constant by long-continued natural selection.

Glancing at instincts, marvellous as some are, they offer no greater difficulty than does corporeal structure on the theory of the natural selection of successive, slight, but profitable modifications. We can thus understand why nature moves by graduated steps in endowing different animals of the same class with their several instincts. I have attempted to show how much light the principle of gradation throws on the admirable architectural powers of the hive-bee. Habit no doubt sometimes comes into play in modifying instincts; but it certainly is not indispensable, as we see, in the case of neuter insects, which leave no progeny to inherit the effects of long-continued habit. On the view of all the species of the same genus having descended from a common parent, and having inherited much in common, we can understand how it is that allied species, when placed under considerably different conditions of life, yet should follow nearly the same instincts; why the thrush of South America, for instance, lines her nest with mud like our British species. On the view of instincts having been slowly acquired through natural selection we need not marvel at some instincts being apparently not perfect and liable to mistakes, and at many instincts causing other animals to suffer.

If species be only well-marked and permanent varieties, we can at once see why their crossed offspring should follow the same complex laws in their degrees and kinds of resemblance to their parents, – in being absorbed into each other by successive crosses, and in other such points, – as do the crossed offspring of acknowledged varieties. On the other hand, these would be strange facts if species have been independently created, and varieties have been produced by secondary laws.

If we admit that the geological record is imperfect in an extreme degree, then such facts as the record gives, support the theory of descent with modification. New species have come on the stage slowly and at successive intervals; and the amount of change, after equal intervals of time, is widely different in different groups. The extinction of species and of whole groups of species, which has played so conspicuous a part in the history of the organic world, almost inevitably follows on the principle of natural selection; for old forms will be supplanted by new and improved forms. Neither single species nor groups of species reappear when the chain of ordinary generation has once been broken. The gradual diffusion of dominant forms, with the slow modification of their descendants, causes the forms of life, after long intervals of time, to appear as if they had changed simultaneously throughout the world. The fact of the fossil remains of each formation being in some degree intermediate in character between the fossils in the formations above and below, is simply explained by their intermediate position in the chain of descent. The grand fact that all extinct organic beings belong to the same system with recent beings, falling either into the same or into intermediate groups, follows from the living and the extinct being the offspring of common parents. As the groups which have descended from an ancient progenitor have generally diverged in character, the progenitor with its early descendants will often be intermediate in character in comparison with its later descendants; and thus we can see why the more ancient a fossil is, the oftener it stands in some degree intermediate between existing and allied groups. Recent forms are generally looked at as being, in some vague sense, higher than ancient and extinct forms; and they are in so far higher as the later and more improved forms have conquered the older and less improved organic beings in the struggle for life. Lastly, the law of the long endurance of allied forms on the same continent, – of marsupials in Australia, of edentata in America, and other such cases, – is intelligible, for within a confined country, the recent and the extinct will naturally be allied by descent.

Looking to geographical distribution, if we admit that there has been during the long course of ages much migration from one part of the world to another, owing to former climatal and geographical changes and to the many occasional and unknown means of dispersal, then we can understand, on the theory of descent with modification, most of the great leading facts in Distribution. We can see why there should be so striking a parallelism in the distribution of organic beings throughout space, and in their geological succession throughout time; for in both cases the beings have been connected by the bond of ordinary generation, and the means of modification have been the same. We see the full meaning of the wonderful fact, which must have struck every traveller, namely, that on the same continent, under the most diverse conditions, under heat and cold, on mountain and lowland, on deserts and marshes, most of the inhabitants within each great class are plainly related; for they will generally be descendants of the same progenitors and early colonists. On this same principle of former migration, combined in most cases with modification, we can understand, by the aid of the Glacial period, the identity of some few plants, and the close alliance of many others, on the most distant mountains, under the most different climates; and likewise the close alliance of some of the inhabitants of the sea in the northern and southern temperate zones, though separated by the whole intertropical ocean. Although two areas may present the same physical conditions of life, we need feel no surprise at their inhabitants being widely different, if they have been for a long period completely separated from each other; for as the relation of organism to organism is the most important of all relations, and as the two areas will have received colonists from some third source or from each other, at various periods and in different proportions, the course of modification in the two areas will inevitably be different.

On this view of migration, with subsequent modification, we can see why oceanic islands should be inhabited by few species, but of these, that many should be peculiar. We can clearly see why those animals which cannot cross wide spaces of ocean, as frogs and terrestrial mammals, should not inhabit oceanic islands; and why, on the other hand, new and peculiar species of bats, which can traverse the ocean, should so often be found on islands far distant from any continent. Such facts as the presence of peculiar species of bats, and the absence of all other mammals, on oceanic islands, are utterly inexplicable on the theory of independent acts of creation.

The existence of closely allied or representative species in any two areas, implies, on the theory of descent with modification, that the same parents formerly inhabited both areas; and we almost invariably find that wherever many closely allied species inhabit two areas, some identical species common to both still exist. Wherever many closely allied yet distinct species occur, many doubtful forms and varieties of the same species likewise occur. It is a rule of high generality that the inhabitants of each area are related to the inhabitants of the nearest source whence immigrants might have been derived. We see this in nearly all the plants and animals of the Galapagos archipelago, of Juan Fernandez, and of the other American islands being related in the most striking manner to the plants and animals of the neighbouring American mainland;[9] and those of the Cape de Verde archipelago and other African islands to the African mainland. It must be admitted that these facts receive no explanation on the theory of creation.

The fact, as we have seen, that all past and present organic beings constitute one grand natural system, with group subordinate to group, and with extinct groups often falling in between recent groups, is intelligible on the theory of natural selection with its contingencies of extinction and divergence of character. On these same principles we see how it is, that the mutual affinities of the species and genera within each class are so complex and circuitous. We see why certain characters are far more serviceable than others for classification; – why adaptive characters, though of paramount importance to the being, are of hardly any importance in classification; why characters derived from rudimentary parts, though of no service to the being, are often of high classificatory value; and why embryological characters are the most valuable of all. The real affinities of all organic beings are due to inheritance or community of descent. The natural system is a genealogical arrangement, in which we have to discover the lines of descent by the most permanent characters, however slight their vital importance may be.

The framework of bones being the same in the hand of a man, wing of a bat, fin of the porpoise, and leg of the horse, – the same number of vertebræ forming the neck of the giraffe and of the elephant, – and innumerable other such facts, at once explain themselves on the theory of descent with slow and slight successive modifications. The similarity of pattern in the wing and leg of a bat, though used for such different purpose, – in the jaws and legs of a crab, – in the petals, stamens, and pistils of a flower, is likewise intelligible on the view of the gradual modification of parts or organs, which were alike in the early progenitor of each class. On the principle of successive variations not always supervening at an early age, and being inherited at a corresponding not early period of life, we can clearly see why the embryos of mammals, birds, reptiles, and fishes should be so closely alike, and should be so unlike the adult forms.[10] We may cease marvelling at the embryo of an air-breathing mammal or bird having branchial slits and arteries running in loops, like those in a fish which has to breathe the air dissolved in water, by the aid of well-developed branchiæ.

Disuse, aided sometimes by natural selection, will often tend to reduce an organ, when it has become useless by changed habits or under changed conditions of life; and we can clearly understand on this view the meaning of rudimentary organs. But disuse and selection will generally act on each creature, when it has come to maturity and has to play its full part in the struggle for existence, and will thus have little power of acting on an organ during early life; hence the organ will not be much reduced or rendered rudimentary at this early age. The calf, for instance, has inherited teeth, which never cut through the gums of the upper jaw, from an early progenitor having well-developed teeth; and we may believe, that the teeth in the mature animal were reduced, during successive generations, by disuse or by the tongue and palate having been fitted by natural selection to browse without their aid; whereas in the calf, the teeth have been left untouched by selection or disuse, and on the principle of inheritance at corresponding ages have been inherited from a remote period to the present day. On the view of each organic being and each separate organ having been specially created, how utterly inexplicable it is that parts, like the teeth in the embryonic calf or like the shrivelled wings under the soldered wing-covers of some beetles, should thus so frequently bear the plain stamp of inutility! Nature may be said to have taken pains to reveal, by rudimentary organs and by homologous structures, her scheme of modification, which it seems that we wilfully will not understand.

I have now recapitulated the chief facts and considerations which have thoroughly convinced me that species have changed, and are still slowly changing by the preservation and accumulation of successive slight favourable variations. Why, it may be asked, have all the most eminent living naturalists and geologists rejected this view of the mutability of species? It cannot be asserted that organic beings in a state of nature are subject to no variation; it cannot be proved that the amount of variation in the course of long ages is a limited quantity; no clear distinction has been, or can be, drawn between species and well-marked varieties. It cannot be maintained that species when intercrossed are invariably sterile, and varieties invariably fertile; or that sterility is a special endowment and sign of creation. The belief that species were immutable productions was almost unavoidable as long as the history of the world was thought to be of short duration; and now that we have acquired some idea of the lapse of time, we are too apt to assume, without proof, that the geological record is so perfect that it would have afforded us plain evidence of the mutation of species, if they had undergone mutation.

But the chief cause of our natural unwillingness to admit that one species has given birth to other and distinct species, is that we are always slow in admitting any great change of which we do not see the intermediate steps. The difficulty is the same as that felt by so many geologists, when Lyell first insisted that long lines of inland cliffs had been formed, and great valleys excavated, by the slow action of the coast-waves. The mind cannot possibly grasp the full meaning of the term of a hundred million years; it cannot add up and perceive the full effects of many slight variations, accumulated during an almost infinite number of generations.[11]

Although I am fully convinced of the truth of the views given in this volume under the form of an abstract, I by no means expect to convince experienced naturalists whose minds are stocked with a multitude of facts all viewed, during a long course of years, from a point of view directly opposite to mine. It is so easy to hide our ignorance under such expressions as the 'plan of creation,' 'unity of design,' &c.,[12] and to think that we give an explanation when we only restate a fact. Any one whose disposition leads him to attach more weight to unexplained difficulties than to the explanation of a certain number of facts will certainly reject my theory. A few naturalists, endowed with much flexibility of mind, and who have already begun to doubt on the immutability of species, may be influenced by this volume; but I look with confidence to the future, to young and rising naturalists, who will be able to view both sides of the question with impartiality. Whoever is led to believe that species are mutable will do good service by conscientiously expressing his conviction;

for only thus can the load of prejudice by which this subject is overwhelmed be removed.

Several eminent naturalists have of late published their belief that a multitude of reputed species in each genus are not real species; but that other species are real, that is, have been independently created. This seems to be a strange conclusion to arrive at. They admit that a multitude of forms, which till lately they themselves thought were special creations, and which are still thus looked at by the majority of naturalists, and which consequently have every external characteristic feature of true species, – they admit that these have been produced by variation, but they refuse to extend the same view to other and very slightly different forms. Nevertheless they do not pretend that they can define, or even conjecture, which are the created forms of life, and which are those produced by secondary laws. They admit variation as a *vera causa* in one case, they arbitrarily reject it in another, without assigning any distinction in the two cases. The day will come when this will be given as a curious illustration of the blindness of preconceived opinion. These authors seem no more startled at a miraculous act of creation than at an ordinary birth. But do they really believe that at innumerable periods in the earth's history certain elemental atoms have been commanded suddenly to flash into living tissues? Do they believe that at each supposed act of creation one individual or many were produced? Were all the infinitely numerous kinds of animals and plants created as eggs or seed, or as full grown? and in the case of mammals, were they created bearing the false marks of nourishment from the mother's womb?[13] Although naturalists very properly demand a full explanation of every difficulty from those who believe in the mutability of species, on their own side they ignore the whole subject of the first appearance of species in what they consider reverent silence.

It may be asked how far I extend the doctrine of the modification of species. The question is difficult to answer, because the more distinct the forms are which we may consider, by so much the arguments fall away in force. But some arguments of the greatest weight extend very far. All the members of whole classes can be connected together by chains of affinities, and all can be classified on the same principle, in groups subordinate to groups. Fossil remains sometimes tend to fill up very wide intervals between existing orders. Organs in a rudimentary condition plainly show that an early progenitor had the organ in a fully developed state; and this in some instances necessarily implies an enormous amount of modification in the descendants. Throughout whole classes various structures are formed on the same pattern, and at an embryonic age the species closely resemble each other. Therefore I cannot doubt that the theory of descent with modification embraces all the members of the same class. I believe that animals have descended from at most only four or five progenitors, and plants from an equal or lesser number.

Analogy would lead me one step further, namely, to the belief that all animals and plants have descended from some one prototype. But analogy may be a deceitful guide. Nevertheless all living things have much in common, in their chemical composition, their germinal vesicles,[a] their cellular structure, and their laws of growth and reproduction. We see this even in so trifling a circumstance as that the same poison often similarly affects plants and animals; or that the poison secreted by the gall-fly produces monstrous growths on the wild rose or oak-tree. Therefore I should infer from analogy that probably all the organic beings which have ever lived on this earth have descended from some one primordial form, into which life was first breathed.

When the views entertained in this volume on the origin of species, or when analogous views are generally admitted, we can dimly foresee that there will be a considerable revolution in natural history. Systematists will be able to pursue their labours as at present; but they will not be incessantly haunted by the shadowy doubt whether this or that form be in essence a species. This I feel sure, and I speak after experience, will be no slight relief. The endless disputes whether or not some fifty species of British brambles are true species will cease. Systematists will have only to decide (not that this will be easy) whether any form be sufficiently constant and distinct from other forms, to be capable of definition; and if definable, whether the differences be sufficiently important to deserve a specific name. This latter point will become a far more essential consideration than it is at present; for differences, however slight, between any two forms, if not blended by intermediate gradations, are looked at by most naturalists as sufficient to raise both forms to the rank of species. Hereafter we shall be compelled to acknowledge that the only distinction between species and well-marked varieties is, that the latter are known, or believed, to be connected at the present day by intermediate gradations, whereas species were formerly thus connected. Hence, without quite rejecting the consideration of the

a. Reproductive cells.

present existence of intermediate gradations between any two forms, we shall be led to weigh more carefully and to value higher the actual amount of difference between them. It is quite possible that forms now generally acknowledged to be merely varieties may hereafter be thought worthy of specific names, as with the primrose and cowslip; and in this case scientific and common language will come into accordance. In short, we shall have to treat species in the same manner as those naturalists treat genera, who admit that genera are merely artificial combinations made for convenience. This may not be a cheering prospect; but we shall at least be freed from the vain search for the undiscovered and undiscoverable essence of the term species.

The other and more general departments of natural history will rise greatly in interest. The terms used by naturalists of affinity, relationship, community of type, paternity, morphology, adaptive characters, rudimentary and aborted organs, &c., will cease to be metaphorical, and will have a plain signification. When we no longer look at an organic being as a savage looks at a ship, as at something wholly beyond his comprehension; when we regard every production of nature as one which has had a history; when we contemplate every complex structure and instinct as the summing up of many contrivances, each useful to the possessor, nearly in the same way as when we look at any great mechanical invention as the summing up of the labour, the experience, the reason, and even the blunders of numerous workmen; when we thus view each organic being, how far more interesting, I speak from experience, will the study of natural history become!

A grand and almost untrodden field of inquiry will be opened, on the causes and laws of variation, on correlation of growth, on the effects of use and disuse, on the direct action of external conditions, and so forth. The study of domestic productions will rise immensely in value. A new variety raised by man will be a far more important and interesting subject for study than one more species added to the infinitude of already recorded species. Our classifications will come to be, as far as they can be so made, genealogies; and will then truly give what may be called the plan of creation. The rules for classifying will no doubt become simpler when we have a definite object in view. We possess no pedigrees or armorial bearings; and we have to discover and trace the many diverging lines of descent in our natural genealogies, by characters of any kind which have long been inherited. Rudimentary organs will speak infallibly with respect to the nature of long-lost structures. Species and groups of species, which are called aberrant, and which may fancifully be called living fossils, will aid us in forming a picture of the ancient forms of life. Embryology will reveal to us the structure, in some degree obscured, of the prototypes of each great class.

When we can feel assured that all the individuals of the same species, and all the closely allied species of most genera, have within a not very remote period descended from one parent, and have migrated from some one birthplace; and when we better know the many means of migration, then, by the light which geology now throws, and will continue to throw, on former changes of climate and of the level of the land, we shall surely be enabled to trace in an admirable manner the former migrations of the inhabitants of the whole world. Even at present, by comparing the differences of the inhabitants of the sea on the opposite sides of a continent, and the nature of the various inhabitants of that continent in relation to their apparent means of immigration, some light can be thrown on ancient geography.

The noble science of Geology loses glory from the extreme imperfection of the record. The crust of the earth with its embedded remains must not be looked at as a well-filled museum, but as a poor collection made at hazard and at rare intervals. The accumulation of each great fossiliferous formation will be recognised as having depended on an unusual concurrence of circumstances, and the blank intervals between the successive stages as having been of vast duration. But we shall be able to gauge with some security the duration of these intervals by a comparison of the preceding and succeeding organic forms. We must be cautious in attempting to correlate as strictly contemporaneous two formations, which include few identical species, by the general succession of their forms of life. As species are produced and exterminated by slowly acting and still existing causes, and not by miraculous acts of creation and by catastrophes; and as the most important of all causes of organic change is one which is almost independent of altered and perhaps suddenly altered physical conditions, namely, the mutual relation of organism to organism, – the improvement of one being entailing the improvement or the extermination of others; it follows, that the amount of organic change in the fossils of consecutive formations probably serves as a fair measure of the lapse of actual time. A number of species, however, keeping in a body might remain for a long period unchanged, whilst within this same period, several of these species, by migrating into new countries and coming into competition with foreign associates, might become modified; so that we must not overrate the accuracy of organic change as a measure of time. During early periods of the earth's history, when the forms of life were probably fewer and simpler, the rate of change was probably slower; and at the first dawn of life, when very few forms of the simplest structure existed, the rate of change may have been slow in an extreme degree. The whole history of the world, as at present known, although of a length quite incomprehensible by us, will hereafter be recognised as a mere fragment of time, compared with the ages which have elapsed since the first creature, the progenitor of innumerable extinct and living descendants, was created.

In the distant future I see open fields for far more important researches. Psychology will be based on a new foundation, that of the necessary acquirement of each mental power and capacity by gradation. Light will be thrown on the origin of man and his history.[14]

Authors of the highest eminence seem to be fully satisfied with the view that each species has been independently created. To my mind it accords better with what we know of the laws impressed on matter by the Creator, that the production and extinction of the past and present inhabitants of the world should have been due to secondary causes, like those determining the birth and death of the individual. When I view all beings not as special creations, but as the lineal descendants of some few beings which lived long before the first bed of the Silurian system was deposited, they seem to me to become ennobled. Judging from the past, we may safely infer that not one living species will transmit its unaltered likeness to a distant futurity. And of the species now living very few will transmit progeny of any kind to a far distant futurity; for the manner in which all organic beings are grouped, shows that the greater number of species of each genus, and all the species of many genera, have left no descendants, but have become utterly extinct. We can so far take a prophetic glance into futurity as to foretell that it will be the common and widely-spread species, belonging to the larger and dominant groups, which will ultimately prevail and procreate new and dominant species. As all the living forms of life are the lineal descendants of those which lived long before the Silurian epoch, we may feel certain that the ordinary succession by generation has never once been broken, and that no cataclysm has desolated the whole world. Hence we may look with some confidence to a secure future of equally inappreciable length. And as natural selection works solely by and for the good of each being, all corporeal and mental endowments will tend to progress towards perfection.[15]

It is interesting to contemplate an entangled bank, clothed with many plants of many kinds, with birds singing on the bushes, with various insects flitting about, and with worms crawling through the damp earth, and to reflect that these elaborately constructed forms, so different from each other, and dependent on each other in so complex a manner, have all been produced by laws acting around us. These laws, taken in the largest sense, being Growth with Reproduction; Inheritance which is almost implied by reproduction; Variability from the indirect and direct action of the external conditions of life, and from use and disuse; a Ratio of Increase so high as to lead to a Struggle for Life, and as a consequence to Natural Selection, entailing Divergence of Character and the Extinction of less-improved forms. Thus, from the war of nature, from famine and death, the most exalted object which we are capable of conceiving, namely, the production of the higher animals, directly follows.[16] There is grandeur in this view of life, with its several powers, having been originally breathed into a few forms or into one; and that, whilst this planet has gone cycling on according to the fixed law of gravity, from so simple a beginning endless forms most beautiful and most wonderful have been, and are being, evolved.

5. Charles Goodwin, 'On the Mosaic Cosmogony', Essays and Reviews (1860)

pp. 207–53

Essays and Reviews was an immediate sensation when it came out in 1860. It was a collection of essays by seven 'liberal' Anglicans, six of them clergymen, who were vilified by their opponents as 'Septem Contra Christum' (Seven Against Christ). *Essays and Reviews* was associated in the public mind with Darwin's *Origin of Species* which had come out the year before: this is how Samuel Butler sees it in *The Way of All Flesh* (1903):

> It must be remembered that the year 1858 was the last of a term during which the peace of the Church of England was singularly unbroken ... I need hardly say that the calm was only on the surface ... the wave of scepticism which had broken over Germany was setting towards our own shores, nor was it long, indeed, before it reached them ... three works in succession arrested the attention even of those who paid least heed to theological controversy. I mean *Essays and Reviews*, Charles Darwin's *Origin of Species*, and Bishop Colenso's *Criticisms on the Pentateuch*. (Ch. 47)

The main concern of the Essayists was not, however, with science, but with German Biblical Criticism (as Butler implies), though one of them, Baden Powell, welcomed Darwin's theory in passing. Goodwin's Essay is the only one to deal with science at length. But the new Biblical Criticism was important for the relation of science to religion in two ways: first, for these liberal churchmen, the substitution of a *historical* for a *literal* reading of the Bible meant that their religion had nothing to fear from scientific discoveries that seemed to contradict the Bible. Secondly, to the general public and the more conservative churchmen it seemed, on the contrary, that the Bible was being attacked from two directions at once, being demythologised by sceptical historians, and contradicted by godless scientists.

Charles Goodwin was the only non-clerical contributor to *Essays and Reviews*: he had been elected a fellow of St Catharine's College, Cambridge, in 1850, but he did not feel he could take orders, so he resigned. He became an amateur geologist, and his essay on the Mosaic Cosmogony is an attempt to dispose of the 'Scriptural geology' of people like William Buckland and Hugh Miller. As we have seen, Miller pursued his geological investigations not only with an eye to natural theology, but also with the faith that natural theology would not contradict the revealed theology of the Bible. The same approach characterised William Buckland, the leading English 'catastrophist', who was Professor of Geology at Oxford until 1845, when he had become Dean of Westminster. In his inaugural lecture, published in 1820, with the title *Vindicae Geologicae; or, the Connexion of Geology with Religion Explained*, his aim had been 'to shew that the study of geology has a tendency to confirm the evidences of natural religion; and that the facts developed by it are consistent with the accounts of the creation and deluge recorded in the Mosaic writings'. In order to maintain this 'consistency', Buckland and Miller were forced to reinterpret the account of Creation in Genesis, into line with their geological discoveries. Buckland's interpretation was that all the great geological transformations took place *before* the 'six days' recorded in Genesis – that is, that there was a vast gap between the creation 'in the beginning', and the first of the six days of creation. Miller's interpretation was different: he read each of the 'days' as representing a vast geological epoch, which had been shown to Moses in a series of visions. Buckland had set out his theory in his *Bridgewater Treatise* in 1836. The *Bridgewater Treatises* were instituted by the will of the Earl of Bridgewater in 1829, in order to show 'The Power, Wisdom, and Goodness of God, as manifested in the Creation.' Thus they represent the continuing tradition of scientific natural theology: but Buckland had also used his to do some 'reconciling' of natural and revealed theology.

Goodwin's aim is to show that this sort of 'reconciliation' is untenable. Ironically, Buckland had already been attacked from the conservative side. Dean Cockburn of York, at the British Association meeting in 1844, had maintained that Buckland's views were not in accord with Scripture; instead, the Dean offered his own geological theory, based on a literal reading of Genesis (see pp. 17–19). Goodwin too believes that Buckland's, and Miller's, geology is at odds with Genesis – but his 'liberal' response to this is to say that Genesis is both imperfect and *erroneous* as an account of the origin of the world. He rejects the reconcilers' argument that Genesis was not intended by its writer (or writers) to teach physical truths but was only a description of 'appearances' or 'visions'. In his view, it is clearly the attempt of some 'Hebrew Descartes or Newton' to account for the origin of things according to his own limited and primitive ideas. As such it is historically interesting, though scientifically incorrect. Thus Goodwin hopes to liberate geology from the restrictions of Genesis, and to liberate Genesis from the contradictory and tortuous interpretations of Buckland and Miller.

In his attitude to the Bible, Goodwin is in line with the 'higher critical' approach of the other Essayists. The Bible must be studied as a human, historical document. He points out that there are *two* creation stories in Genesis, probably written by different writers. In the same way, Biblical Criticism pointed out problems of multi-authorship and inconsistencies in the Gospel stories. Like Frederick Temple, in his Essay on 'The Education of the World', Goodwin sees God's revelation through Scripture as a *progressive* enlightenment of the human race. The Old Testament is addressed to the less developed understanding of the race in its infancy: 'the plan of Providence for the education of man is a progressive one, and as imperfect men have been used as the agents for teaching mankind, is it not to be expected that their teachings should be partial and, to some extent, erroneous?' (p. 142). In line with German Biblical scholarship, the Essayists are all revising the idea that the Bible is the *directly* 'inspired' Word of God. The Bible may be wrong as to matters of fact: its value lies in its moral and spiritual truths. Goodwin, however, is not abandoning natural theology: the 'great truth' he sees in Genesis is also 'the highest revelation of modern enquiry – namely, the unity of design of the world, and its subordination to one sole Maker and Lawgiver' (p. 143).

Mosaic Cosmogony[a]

On the revival of science in the 16th century, some of the earliest conclusions at which philosophers arrived were found to be at

a. Theory of the origin of the universe.

variance with popular and long-established belief. The Ptolemaic[a] system of astronomy, which had then full possession of the minds of men, contemplated the whole visible universe from the earth as the immovable centre of things. Copernicus[1] changed the point of view, and placing the beholder in the sun, at once reduced the earth to an inconspicuous globule, a merely subordinate member of a family of planets, which the terrestrials had until then fondly imagined to be but pendants and ornaments of their own habitation. The Church naturally took a lively interest in the disputes which arose between the philosophers of the new school and those who adhered to the old doctrines, inasmuch as the Hebrew records, the basis of religious faith, manifestly countenanced the opinion of the earth's immobility and certain other views of the universe very incompatible with those propounded by Copernicus. Hence arose the official proceedings against Galileo,[2] in consequence of which he submitted to sign his celebrated recantation, acknowledging that 'the proposition that the sun is the centre of the world and immovable from its place is absurd, philosophically false, and formally heretical, because it is expressly contrary to the Scripture'; and that 'the proposition that the earth is not the centre of the world, nor immovable, but that it moves and also with a diurnal motion, is absurd, philosophically false, and at least erroneous in faith'.

The Romish Church, it is presumed, adheres to the old views to the present day.[3] Protestant instincts, however, in the 17th century were strongly in sympathy with the augmentation of science, and consequently Reformed Churches more easily allowed themselves to be helped over the difficulty, which, according to the views of inspiration[4] then held and which have survived to the present day, was in reality quite as formidable for them as for those of the old faith. The solution of the difficulty offered by Galileo and others was, that the object of a revelation or divine unveiling of mysteries, must be to teach man things which he is unable and must ever remain unable to find out for himself; but not physical truths, for the discovery of which he has faculties specially provided by his Creator. Hence it was not unreasonable that, in regard to matters of fact merely, the Sacred Writings should use the common language and assume the common belief of mankind, without purporting to correct errors upon points morally indifferent. So, in regard to such a text as, 'The world is established, it cannot be moved',[5] though it

---

a. Claudius Ptolemaeus of Alexandria, a first-century astronomer, originated the medieval world-picture in which the sun, moon, planets, and stars moved around the earth.

might imply the sacred penman's ignorance of the fact that the earth does move, yet it does not put forth this opinion as an indispensable point of faith. And this remark is applicable to a number of texts which present a similar difficulty.

It might be thought to have been less easy to reconcile in men's minds the Copernican view of the universe with the very plain and direct averments contained in the opening chapter of Genesis. It can scarcely be said that this chapter is not intended in part to teach and convey at least some physical truth, and taking its words in their plain sense it manifestly gives a view of the universe adverse to that of modern science. It represents the sky as a watery vault in which the sun, moon and stars are set. But the discordance of this description with facts does not appear to have been so palpable to the minds of the seventeenth century as it is to us. The mobility of the earth was a proposition startling not only to faith but to the senses. The difficulty involved in this belief having been successfully got over, other discrepancies dwindled in importance. The brilliant progress of astronomical science subdued the minds of men; the controversy between faith and knowledge gradually fell to slumber; the story of Galileo and the Inquisition became a school commonplace, the doctrine of the earth's mobility found its way into children's catechisms, and the limited views of the nature of the universe indicated in the Old Testament ceased to be felt as religious difficulties.

It would have been well if theologians had made up their minds to accept frankly the principle that those things for the discovery of which man has faculties specially provided are not fit objects of a divine revelation. Had this been unhesitatingly done, either the definition and idea of divine revelation must have been modified, and the possibility of an admixture of error have been allowed, or such parts of the Hebrew writings as were found to be repugnant to fact must have been pronounced to form no part of revelation. The first course is that which theologians have most generally adopted, but with such limitations, cautels, and equivocations as to be of little use in satisfying those who would know how and what God really has taught mankind, and whether anything beyond that which man is able and obviously intended to arrive at by the use of his natural faculties.

The difficulties and disputes which attended the first revival of science have recurred in the present century in consequence of the growth of geology. It is in truth only the old question over again – precisely the same point of theology which is involved, – although the difficulties which present themselves are fresh. The school-books of the present day, while they teach the child that the earth moves, yet assure him that it is a little less than six thousand years old,[6] and that it was made in six days. On the other hand, geologists of all religious creeds are agreed that the earth has existed for an immense series of years, – to be counted by millions rather than by thousands; and that indubitably more than six days elapsed from its first creation to the appearance of man upon its surface. By this broad discrepancy between old and new doctrine is the modern mind startled, as were the men of the sixteenth century when told that the earth moved.

When this new cause of controversy first arose, some writers more hasty than discreet, attacked the conclusions of geologists, and declared them scientifically false. This phase may now be considered past, and although school-books probably continue to teach much as they did, no well-instructed person now doubts the great antiquity of the earth any more than its motion. This being so, modern theologians, forsaking the maxim of Galileo, or only using it vaguely as an occasional make-weight, have directed their attention to the possibility of reconciling the Mosaic narrative with those geological facts which are admitted to be beyond dispute. Several modes of doing this have been proposed which have been deemed more or less satisfactory. In a text-book of theological instruction widely used,[7] we find it stated in broad terms, 'Geological investigations, it is now known, all prove the perfect harmony between scripture and geology, in reference to the history of creation.'

In truth, however, if we refer to the plans of conciliation proposed, we find them at variance with each other and mutually destructive. The conciliators are not agreed among themselves, and each holds the views of the other to be untenable and unsafe. The ground is perpetually being shifted, as the advance of geological science may require. The plain meaning of the Hebrew record is unscrupulously tampered with, and in general the pith of the whole process lies in divesting the text of all meaning whatever. We are told that Scripture not being designed to teach us natural philosophy, it is in vain to attempt to make out a cosmogony from its statements. If the first chapter of Genesis conveys to us no information concerning the origin of the world, its statements cannot indeed be contradicted by modern discovery. But it is absurd to call this harmony. Statements such as that above quoted are, we conceive, little calculated to be serviceable to the interests of theology, still less to religion and morality. Believing, as we do, that if the value of the Bible as a book of religious instruction is to be maintained, it must be not by striving to prove it scientifically exact, at the expense of every sound principle of interpretation, and in defiance of common sense, but by the frank recognition of the erroneous views of nature which it contains, we have put pen to paper to analyse some of the popular conciliation theories. The inquiry cannot be deemed a superfluous one, nor one which in the interests of theology had better be let alone. Physical science goes on unconcernedly pursuing its own paths. Theology, the science whose object is the dealing of God with man as a moral being, maintains but a shivering existence, shouldered and jostled by the sturdy growths of modern thought, and bemoaning itself for the hostility which it encounters. Why should this be, unless because theologians persist in clinging to theories of God's procedure towards man, which have long been seen to be untenable? If, relinquishing theories, they would be content to inquire from the history of man what this procedure has actually been, the so-called difficulties of theology would, for the most part, vanish of themselves.

The account which astronomy gives of the relations of our earth to the rest of the universe, and that which geology gives of its internal structure and the development of its surface, are sufficiently familiar to most readers. But it will be necessary for our purpose to go over the oft-trodden ground, which must be done with rapid steps. Nor let the reader object to be reminded of some of the most elementary facts of his knowledge. The human race has been ages in arriving at conclusions now familiar to every child.

This earth apparently so still and stedfast, lying in majestic repose beneath the ætherial vault, is a globular body of comparatively insignificant size, whirling fast through space round the sun as the centre of its orbit, and completing its revolution in the course of one year, while at the same time it revolves daily once about its own axis, thus producing the changes of day and night. The sun, which seems to leap up each morning from the east, and traversing the skyey bridge, slides down into the west, is relatively to our earth motionless. In size and weight it inconceivably surpasses it. The moon, which occupies a position in the visible heavens only second to the ṣun, and far beyond that of every other celestial body in conspicuousness, is but a subordinate globe, much smaller than our own, and revolving round the earth as its centre, while it accompanies it in yearly revolutions about the sun. Of itself it has no lustre, and is visible to us only by the reflected sunlight. Those beautiful stars which are perpetually changing their position in the heavens, and shine with a soft and moon-like light, are bodies, some much larger, some less, than our earth, and like it revolve round the sun, by the reflection of whose rays we see them. The telescope has revealed to us the fact that several of these are attended by moons of their own, and that besides those which the unassisted eye can see, there are others belonging to the same family coursing round the sun. As for the glittering dust which emblazons the nocturnal sky, there is reason to believe that each spark is a self-luminous body, perhaps of similar material to our sun, and that the very nearest of the whole tribe is at an incalculable distance from us, the very least of them of enormous size compared with our own humble globe. Thus has modern science reversed nearly all the *primâ facie* views to which our senses lead us as to the constitution of the universe; but so thoroughly are the above statements wrought into the culture of the present day, that we are apt to forget that mankind once saw these things very differently, and that but a few centuries have elapsed since such views were startling novelties.

Our earth then is but one of the lesser pendants of a body which is itself only an inconsiderable unit in the vast creation. And now if we withdraw our thoughts from the immensities of space, and look into the construction of man's obscure home, the first question is whether it has ever been in any other condition than that in which we now see it, and if so, what are the stages through which it has passed, and what was its first traceable state. Here geology steps in and successfully carries back the history of the earth's crust to a very remote period, until it arrives at a region of uncertainty, where philosophy is reduced to mere guesses and possibilities, and pronounces nothing definite. To this region belong the speculations which have been ventured upon as to the original concretion of the earth and planets out of nebular matter of which the sun may have been the nucleus.[8] But the first clear view which we obtain of the early condition of the earth, presents to us a ball of matter, fluid with intense heat, spinning on its own axis and revolving round the sun. How long it may have continued in this state is beyond calculation or surmise. It can only be believed that a prolonged period, beginning and ending we know not when, elapsed before the surface became cooled and hardened and capable of sustaining organized existences. The water which now enwraps a large portion of the face of the globe, must for ages have existed only in the shape of steam, floating above and enveloping the planet in one thick curtain of mist. When the cooling of the surface allowed it to condense and descend, then commenced the process by which the lowest stratified rocks were formed, and gradually spread out in vast layers. Rains and rivers now acted upon the scoriaceous integument,[a] grinding it to sand and carrying it down to the depths and cavities. Whether organised beings co-existed with this state of things we know not, as the early rocks have been acted upon by interior heat to an extent which must have destroyed all traces of animal and vegetable life, if any such ever existed. This period has been named by geologists the Azoic, or that in which life was not. Its duration no one presumes to define.

It is in the system of beds which overlies these primitive formations that the first records of organisms present themselves. In the so-called Silurian system we have a vast assemblage of strata of various kinds, together many thousands of feet thick, and abounding in remains of animal life. These strata were deposited at the bottom of the sea, and the remains are exclusively marine. The creatures whose exuviæ[b] have been preserved belong to those classes which are placed by naturalists the lowest with respect to organization, the mollusca, articulata, and radiata. Analogous beings exist at the present day, but not their lineal descendants, unless time can effect transmutation of species, an hypothesis not generally accepted by naturalists.[9] In the same strata with these inhabitants of the early seas are found remains of fucoid or seaweed-like plants, the lowest of the vegetable tribe, which may have been the first of this kind of existences introduced into the world. But, as little has yet been discovered to throw light upon the state of the dry land and its productions at this remote period, nothing can be asserted positively on the subject.

In the upper strata of the Silurian system is found the commencement of the race of fishes, the lowest creatures of the vertebrate type, and in the succeeding beds they become abundant. These monsters clothed in mail who must have been the terror of the seas they inhabited, have left their indestructible coats behind them as evidence of their existence.

Next come the carboniferous strata, containing the remains of a gigantic and luxuriant vegetation, and here reptiles and insects begin to make their appearance. At this point geologists make a kind of artificial break, and for the sake of distinction, denominate the whole of the foregoing period of animated existences the Palæozoic, or that of antique life.

In the next great geological section, the so-called Secondary period, in which are comprised the oolitic and cretaceous systems,

a. Outer skin or rind made of lava.   b. Animal's cast skin, shell, or covering.

the predominant creatures are different from those which figured conspicuously in the preceding. The land was inhabited by gigantic animals, half-toad, half-lizard, who hopped about, leaving often their foot-prints like those of a clumsy human hand, upon the sandy shores of the seas they frequented. The waters now abounded with monsters, half-fish, half-crocodile, the well-known saurians,[a] whose bones have been collected in abundance. Even the air had its tenantry from the same family type, for the pterodactyls were creatures, half-lizard, half-vampyre, provided with membranous appendages which must have enabled them to fly. In an early stage of this period traces of birds appear, and somewhat later those of mammals, but of the lowest class belonging to that division, namely, the marsupial or pouch-bearing animals, in which naturalists see affinities to the oviparous[b] tribes. The vegetation of this period seems to have consisted principally of the lower classes of plants, according to the scale of organisation accepted by botanists, but it was luxuriant and gigantic.

Lastly, comes the Tertiary period, in which mammalia of the highest forms enter upon the scene, while the composite growths of the Secondary period in great part disappear, and the types of creatures approach more nearly to those which now exist. During long ages this state of things continued, while the earth was the abode principally of mastodons, elephants, rhinoceroses, and their thick-hided congeners, many of them of colossal proportions, and of species which have now passed away. The remains of these creatures have been found in the frozen rivers of the north, and they appear to have roamed over regions of the globe where their more delicate representatives of the present day would be unable to live. During this era the ox, horse, and deer, and perhaps other animals, destined to be serviceable to man, became inhabitants of the earth. Lastly, the advent of man may be considered as inaugurating a new and distinct epoch, that in which we now are, and during the whole of which the physical conditions of existence cannot have been very materially different from what they are now. Thus, the reduction of the earth into the state in which we now behold it has been the slowly continued work of ages. The races of organic beings which have populated its surface have from time to time passed away, and been supplanted by others, introduced we know not certainly by what means, but evidently according to a fixed method and order, and with a gradually increasing complexity and fineness of organization,

a. Lizard-like animals.   b. Producing young by means of eggs.

until we come to man as the crowning point of all.[10] Geologically speaking, the history of his first appearance is obscure, nor does archæology do much to clear this obscurity. Science has, however, made some efforts towards tracing man to his cradle, and by patient observation and collection of facts much more may perhaps be done in this direction. As for history and tradition, they afford little upon which anything can be built. The human race, like each individual man, has forgotten its own birth, and the void of its early years has been filled up by imagination, and not from genuine recollection. Thus much is clear, that man's existence on earth is brief, compared with the ages during which unreasoning creatures were the sole possessors of the globe.

We pass to the account of the creation contained in the Hebrew record. And it must be observed that in reality two distinct accounts are given us in the book of Genesis, one being comprised in the first chapter and the first three verses of the second, the other commencing at the fourth verse of the second chapter and continuing till the end. This is so philologically certain that it were useless to ignore it. But even those who may be inclined to contest the fact that we have here the productions of two different writers, will admit that the account beginning at the first verse of the first chapter, and ending at the third verse of the second, is a complete whole in itself. And to this narrative, in order not to complicate the subject unnecessarily, we intend to confine ourselves. It will be sufficient for our purpose to enquire, whether this account can be shown to be in accordance with our astronomical and geological knowledge. And for the right under-standing of it the whole must be set out, so that the various parts may be taken in connexion with one another.

We are told that 'in the beginning God created the heaven and the earth.' It has been matter of discussion amongst theologians whether the word 'created' (Heb. *bara*) here means simply shaped or formed, or shaped or formed out of nothing. From the use of the verb *bara* in other passages, it appears that it does not necessarily mean to make out of nothing, but it certainly might impliedly mean this in a case so peculiar as the present. The phrase 'the heaven and the earth', is evidently used to signify the universe of things, inasmuch as the heaven in its proper signification has no existence until the second day. It is asserted then that God shaped the whole material universe, whether out of nothing, or out of pre-existing matter. But which sense the writer really intended is not material for our present purpose to enquire, since neither astronomical nor geological science affects to state anything concerning the first origin of matter.

Charles Goodwin (1817–1878)

In the second verse the earliest state of things is described; according to the received translation, 'the earth was without form and void'. The prophet Jeremiah[11] uses the same expression to describe the desolation of the earth's surface occasioned by God's wrath, and perhaps the words 'empty and waste' would convey to us at present something more nearly approaching the meaning of *tohu va-bohu*, than those which the translators have used.

The earth itself is supposed to be submerged under the waters of the deep, over which the breath of God – the air or wind – flutters while all is involved in darkness. The first special creative command is that which bids the light appear, whereupon daylight breaks over the two primæval elements of earth and water – the one lying still enveloped by the other; and the space of time occupied by the original darkness and the light which succeeded, is described as the first day. Thus light and the measurement of time are represented as existing before the manifestation of the sun, and this idea, although repugnant to our modern knowledge, has not in former times appeared absurd. Thus we find Ambrose[12] (*Hexaemeron* lib. 4, cap. 3) remarking: – 'We must recollect that the light of day is one thing, the light of the sun, moon, and stars another, – the sun by his rays appearing to add lustre to the daylight. For before sunrise the day dawns, but is not in full refulgence, for the midday sun adds still further to its splendour.' We quote this passage to show how a mind unsophisticated by astronomical knowledge understood the Mosaic statement; and we may boldly affirm that those for whom it was first penned could have taken it in no other sense than that light existed before and independently of the sun, nor do we misrepresent it when we affirm this to be its natural and primary meaning. How far we are entitled to give to the writer's words an enigmatical and secondary meaning, as contended by those who attempt to conciliate them with our present knowledge, must be considered further on.

The work of the second day of creation is to erect the vault of Heaven (Heb. *rakia*; Gr. στερέωμα; Lat. *firmamentum*) which is represented as supporting an ocean of water above it. The waters are said to be divided, so that some are below, some above the vault. That the Hebrews understood the sky, firmament, or heaven to be a permanent solid vault, as it appears to the ordinary observer, is evident enough from various expressions made use of concerning it. It is said to have pillars (Job xxvi. 11), foundations (2 Sam. xxii. 8), doors (Ps. lxxviii. 23), and windows (Gen. vii. 11). No quibbling about the derivation of the word *rakia*, which is literally something beaten out, can affect the explicit description of the Mosaic writer, contained in the words 'the waters that are above the firmament', or avail to show that he was aware that the sky is but transparent space.

On the third day, at the command of God, the waters which have hitherto concealed the earth are gathered together in one place – the sea, – and the dry land emerges. Upon the same day the earth brings forth grass, herb yielding seed and fruit trees, the destined food of the animals and of man (v. 29). Nothing is said of herbs and trees which are not serviceable to this purpose, and perhaps it may be contended, since there is no vegetable production which may not possibly be useful to man, or which is not preyed upon by some animal, that in this description the whole terrestrial flora is implied. We wish, however, to call the attention of the reader to the fact, that trees and plants destined for food are those which are particularly singled out here as the earliest productions of the earth, as we shall have occasion to refer to this again presently.

On the fourth day, the two great lights, the sun and moon, are *made* (Heb. *hasah*) and *set* in the firmament of heaven to give light to the earth, but more particularly to serve as the means of measuring time, and of marking out years, days, and seasons. This is the most prominent office assigned to them (v. 14–18). The formation of the stars is mentioned in the most cursory manner. It is not said out of what materials all these bodies were made, and whether the writer regarded them as already existing, and only waiting to have a proper place assigned them, may be open to question. At any rate, their allotted receptacle – the firmament – was not made until the second day, nor were they set in it until the fourth; vegetation, be it observed, having already commenced on the third, and therefore independently of the warming influence of the sun.

On the fifth day the waters are called into productive activity, and bring forth fishes and marine animals, as also the birds of the air. It is also said that God created or formed (*bara*) great whales and other creatures of the water and air. On the sixth day the earth brings forth living creatures, cattle, and reptiles, and also 'the beast of the field', that is, the wild beasts. And here also it is added that God made (*hasah*) these creatures after their several kinds. The formation of man is distinguished by a variation of the creative fiat. 'Let us make man in our image after our likeness.' Accordingly, man is made and formed (*bara*) in the image and likeness of God, a phrase which has been explained away to mean merely 'perfect, sinless', although the Pentateuch abounds in passages showing that the Hebrews contemplated the Divine being in the visible form of a man. Modern spiritualism has so entirely banished this idea, that probably many may not without an effort be able to accept the plain language of the Hebrew writer in its obvious sense in the 26th verse of the 1st chapter of Genesis, though they will have no difficulty in doing so in the 3rd verse of the 5th chapter, where the same words 'image' and 'likeness' are used. Man is said to have been created male and female, and the narrative contains nothing to show that a single pair only is intended.[13] He is commanded to increase and multiply, and to assume dominion over all the other tribes of beings. The whole of the works of creation being complete, God gives to man, beast, fowl, and creeping thing, the vegetable productions of the earth as their appointed food. And when we compare the verses Gen. i. 29, 30, with Gen. ix. 3, in which, after the Flood, animals are given to man for food in addition to the green herb, it is difficult not to come to the conclusion that in the earliest view taken of creation, men and animals were supposed to have been, in their original condition, not carnivorous. It is needless to say that this has been for the most part the construction put upon the words of the Mosaic writer, until a clear perception of the creative design which destined the tiger and lion for flesh-eaters, and latterly the geological proof of flesh-eating monsters having existed among the pre-adamite inhabitants of the globe, rendered it necessary to ignore this meaning.

The 1st, 2nd, and 3rd verses of the second chapter of Genesis, which have been most absurdly divided from their context, conclude the narrative.[14] On the seventh day God rests from His work, and blesses the day of rest, a fact which is referred to in the Commandment given from Sinai as the ground of the observance of Sabbatic rest imposed upon the Hebrews.

Remarkable as this narrative is for simple grandeur, it has nothing in it which can be properly called poetical. It bears on its face no trace of mystical or symbolical meaning. Things are called by their right names with a certain scientific exactness widely different from the imaginative cosmogonies of the Greeks, in which the powers and phenomena of nature are invested with personality, and the passions and qualities of men are represented as individual existences.

The circumstances related in the second narrative of creation are indeed such as to give at least some ground for the supposition that a mystical interpretation was intended to be given to it. But this is far from being the case with the first narrative, in which none but a professed mystifier of the school of Philo[15] could see anything but a plain statement of facts. There can be little reasonable dispute then as to the sense in which the Mosaic narrative was taken by those who first heard it, nor is it indeed disputed that for centuries, putting apart the Philonic mysticism, which after all did not exclude a primary sense, its words have been received in their genuine and natural meaning. That this meaning is *primâ facie* one wholly adverse to the present astronomical and geological views of the universe is evident enough. There is not a mere difference through deficiency. It cannot be correctly said that the Mosaic writer simply leaves out details which modern science supplies, and that, therefore, the inconsistency is not a real but only an apparent one. It is manifest that the whole account is given from a different point of view from that which we now unavoidably take; that the order of things as we now know them to be, is to a great extent reversed, although here and there we may pick out some general analogies and points of resemblance. Can we say that the Ptolemaic system of astronomy is not at variance with modern science, because it represents with a certain degree of correctness some of the apparent motions of the heavenly bodies?

The task which sundry modern writers have imposed upon themselves is to prove, that the Mosaic narrative, however apparently at variance with our knowledge, is essentially, and in fact true, although never understood properly until modern science supplied the necessary commentary and explanation.

Two modes of conciliation have been propounded which have enjoyed considerable popularity, and to these two we shall confine our attention.

The first is that originally brought into vogue by Chalmers[16] and adopted by the late Dr Buckland[a] in his Bridgewater Treatise, and which is probably still received by many as a sufficient solution of all difficulties. Dr Buckland's treatment of the case may be taken as a fair specimen of the line of argument adopted, and it shall be given in his own words. 'The word *beginning*,' he says, 'as applied by Moses in the first verse of the book of Genesis, expresses an undefined period of time which was antecedent to the last great change that affected the surface of the earth, and to the creation of its present animal and vegetable inhabitants, during which period a long series of operations may have been going on; which as they are wholly unconnected with the history of the human race, are passed over in silence by the sacred historian, whose only concern was barely to state, that the matter of the universe is not eternal and self-existent, but was originally created by the power of the Almighty.' 'The Mosaic narrative commences with a declaration that

a. See headnote.

Charles Goodwin (1817–1878)

"in the beginning God created the heaven and the earth." These few first words of Genesis may be fairly appealed to by the geologist as containing a brief statement of the creation of the material elements, at a time distinctly preceding the operations of the first day; it is nowhere affirmed that God created the heaven and the earth in the *first day*, but in the *beginning*; this beginning may have been an epoch at an unmeasured distance, followed by periods of undefined duration during which all the physical operations disclosed by geology were going on.'

'The first verse of Genesis, therefore, seems explicitly to assert the creation of the universe; the heaven, including the sidereal systems; and the earth, more especially specifying our own planet, as the subsequent scene of the operations of the six days about to be described; no information is given as to events which may have occurred upon this earth, unconnected with the history of man, between the creation of its component matter recorded in the first verse, and the era at which its history is resumed in the second verse; nor is any limit fixed to the time during which these intermediate events may have been going on: millions of millions of years may have occupied the indefinite interval, between the beginning in which God created the heaven and the earth, and the evening or commencement of the first day of the Mosaic narrative.'

'The second verse may describe the condition of the earth on the evening of this first day (for in the Jewish mode of computation used by Moses each day is reckoned from the beginning of one evening to the beginning of another evening). This first evening may be considered as the termination of the indefinite time which followed the primeval creation announced in the first verse, and as the commencement of the first of the six succeeding days in which the earth was to be filled up, and peopled in a manner fit for the reception of mankind. We have in this second verse, a distinct mention of earth and waters, as already existing and involved in darkness; their condition also is described as a state of confusion and emptiness (*tohu bohu*), words which are usually interpreted by the vague and indefinite Greek term chaos, and which may be geologically considered as designating the wreck and ruins of a former world. At this intermediate point of time the preceding undefined geological periods had terminated, a new series of events commenced, and the work of the first morning of this new creation was the calling forth of light from a temporary darkness, which had overspread the ruins of the ancient earth.'

With regard to the formation of the sun and moon, Dr Buckland observes, p. 27, 'We are not told that the substance of the sun and moon was first called into existence on the fourth day; the text may equally imply that these bodies were then prepared and appointed to certain offices, of high importance to mankind, 'to give light upon the earth, and to rule over the day, and over the night, to be for signs, and for seasons, and for days, and for years. The fact of their creation had been stated before in the first verse.'

The question of the meaning of the word *bara*, create, has been previously touched upon; it has been acknowledged by good critics that it does not of itself necessarily imply 'to make out of nothing', upon the simple ground that it is found used in cases where such a meaning would be inapplicable. But the difficulty of giving to it the interpretation contended for by Dr Buckland, and of uniting with this the assumption of a six days' creation, such as that described in Genesis, at a comparatively recent period, lies in this, that the heaven itself is distinctly said to have been formed by the division of the waters on the second day. Consequently during the indefinite ages which elapsed from the primal creation of matter until the first Mosaic day of creation, there was no sky, no local habitation for the sun, moon, and stars, even supposing those bodies to have been included in the original material. Dr Buckland does not touch this obvious difficulty, without which his argument that the sun and moon might have been contemplated as pre-existing, although they are not stated to have been set in the heaven until the fourth day, is of no value at all.

Dr Buckland appears to assume that when it is said that the heaven and the earth were created in the beginning, it is to be understood that they were created in their present form and state of completeness, the heaven raised above the earth as we see it, or seem to see it now. This is the fallacy of his argument. The circumstantial description of the framing of the heaven out of the waters, proves that the words 'heaven and earth', in the first verse, must be taken either proleptically, as a general expression for the universe, the matter of the universe in its crude and unformed shape, or else the word *bara* must mean formed, not created, the writer intending to say 'God formed the heaven and earth in manner following', in which case heaven is used in its distinct and proper sense. But these two senses cannot be united in the manner covertly assumed in Dr Buckland's argument.

Having, however, thus endeavoured to make out that the Mosaic account does not negative the idea that the sun, moon, and stars had 'been created at the indefinitely distant time designated by the word beginning', he is reduced to describe the primæval darkness of the first day as 'a temporary darkness, produced by an accumulation of dense vapours upon the face of the deep'. 'An incipient dispersion of these vapours may have readmitted light to the earth, upon the first day, whilst the exciting cause of light was obscured, and the further purification of the atmosphere upon the fourth day, may have caused the sun and moon and stars to re-appear in the firmament of heaven, to assume their new relations to the newly modified earth and to the human race.'

It is needless to discuss the scientific probability of this hypothesis, but the violence done to the grand and simple words of the Hebrew writer must strike every mind. 'And God said, Let there be light – and there was light – and God saw the light that it was good. And God divided the light from the darkness, and God called the light day, and the darkness called he night; and the evening and the morning were the first day.' Can any one sensible of the value of words suppose, that nothing more is here described, or intended to be described, than the partial clearing away of a fog? Can such a manifestation of light have been dignified by the appellation of day? Is not this reducing the noble description which has been the admiration of ages to a pitiful *caput mortuum*ᵃ of empty verbiage?

What were the *new relations* which the heavenly bodies according to Dr Buckland's view, assumed to the newly modified earth and to the human race? They had, as we well know, marked out seasons, days and years, and had given light for ages before to the earth, and to the animals which preceded man as its inhabitants, as is shown, Dr Buckland admits, by the eyes of fossil animals, optical instruments of the same construction as those of the animals of our days, and also by the existence of vegetables in the early world, to the development of which light must have been as essential then as now.

The hypothesis adopted by Dr Buckland was first promulgated at a time when the gradual and regular formation of the earth's strata was not seen or admitted so clearly as it is now.[17] Geologists were more disposed to believe in great catastrophes and sudden breaks. Buckland's theory supposes that previous to the appearance of the present races of animals and vegetables there was a great gap in the globe's history, – that the earth was completely depopulated, as well of marine as land animals; and that the creation of all existing plants and animals was coæval with that of man. This theory is by no means supported by geological phenomena, and is, we suppose, now re-

---

a. Worthless residue – an alchemical term.

jected by all geologists whose authority is valuable. Thus writes Hugh Miller in 1857 – 'I certainly did once believe with Chalmers and with Buckland that the six days were simply natural days of twenty-four hours each – that they had comprised the entire work of the existing creation – and that the latest of the geologic ages was separated by a great chaotic gap from our own. My labours at the time as a practical geologist had been very much restricted to the palæozoic and secondary rocks, more especially to the old red and carboniferous systems of the one division, and the oolitic system of the other; and the long-extinct organisms which I found in them certainly did not conflict with the view of Chalmers. All I found necessary at the time to the work of reconciliation was some scheme that would permit me to assign to the earth a high antiquity, and to regard it as the scene of many succeeding creations. During the last nine years, however, I have spent a few weeks every autumn in exploring the late formations, and acquainting myself with their particular organisms. I have traced them upwards from the raised beaches and old coast lines of the human period, to the brick clays, Clyde beds, and drift and boulder deposits of the Pleistocene era; and again from them, with the help of museums and collections, up through the mammaliferous crag of England to its red and coral crags; and the conclusion at which I have been compelled to arrive is, that for many long ages ere man was ushered into being, not a few of his humbler contemporaries of the fields and woods enjoyed life in their present haunts, and that for thousands of years anterior to even *their* appearance, many of the existing molluscs lived in our seas. That *day* during which the present creation came into being, and in which God, when he had made 'the beast of the earth after his kind, and the cattle after their kind', at length terminated the work by moulding a creature in His own image, to whom He gave dominion over them all, was not a brief period of a few hours' duration, but extended over, mayhap, millenniums of centuries. No blank chaotic gap of death and darkness separated the creation to which man belongs from that of the old extinct elephant, hippopotamus, and hyæna; for familiar animals, such as the red deer, the roe, the fox, the wild cat, and the badger, lived throughout the period which connected their time with our own; and so I have been compelled to hold that the days of creation were not natural but prophetic days, and stretched far back into the bygone eternity.'[18]

Hugh Miller will be admitted by many as a competent witness to the untenability of the theory of Chalmers and Buckland on mere geological grounds. He had, indeed, a theory of his own to propose, which we shall presently consider; but we may take his word that it was not without the compulsion of what he considered irresistible evidence that he relinquished a view which would have saved him infinite time and labour, could he have adhered to it.

But whether contemplated from a geological point of view, or whether from a philological one, that is, with reference to the value of words, the use of language, and the ordinary rules which govern writers whose object it is to make themselves understood by those to whom their works are immediately addressed, the interpretation proposed by Buckland to be given to the Mosaic description will not bear a moment's serious discussion. It is plain, from the whole tenor of the narrative, that the writer contemplated no such representation as that suggested, nor could any such idea have entered into the minds of those to whom the account was first given. Dr Buckland endeavours to make out that we have here simply a case of leaving out facts which did not particularly concern the writer's purpose, so that he gave an account true so far as it went, though imperfect. 'We may fairly ask,' he argues, 'of those persons who consider physical science a fit subject for revelation, what point they can imagine short of a communication of Omniscience at which such a revelation might have stopped without imperfections of omission, less in degree, but similar in kind, to that which they impute to the existing narrative of Moses? A revelation of so much only of astronomy as was known to Copernicus would have seemed imperfect after the discoveries of Newton; and a revelation of the science of Newton would have appeared defective to La Place: a revelation of all the chemical knowledge of the eighteenth century would have been as deficient in comparison with the information of the present day, as what is now known in this science will probably appear before the termination of another age; in the whole circle of sciences there is not one to which this argument may not be extended, until we should require from revelation a full development of all the mysterious agencies that uphold the mechanism of the material world.' Buckland's question is quite inapplicable to the real difficulty, which is, not that circumstantial details are omitted – that might reasonably be expected, – but that what is told, is told so as to convey to ordinary apprehensions an impression at variance with facts. We are indeed told that certain writers of antiquity had already anticipated the hypothesis of the geologist, and two of the Christian fathers, Augustine[19] and Episcopius,[20] are referred to as having actually held that a wide interval elapsed between the first act of creation, mentioned in the Mosaic account, and the commencement

of the six days' work.[21] If, however, they arrived at such a conclusion, it was simply because, like the modern geologist, they had
theories of their own to support, which led them to make somewhat
similar hypotheses.

'After all,' says Buckland, 'it should be recollected that the question is not respecting the correctness of the Mosaic narrative, but of
our interpretation of it,' a proposition which can hardly be
sufficiently reprobated. Such a doctrine, carried out unreservedly,
strikes at the root of critical morality. It may, indeed, be sometimes
possible to give two or three different interpretations to one and the
same passage, even in a modern and familiar tongue, in which case
this may arise from the unskilfulness of the writer or speaker who
has failed clearly to express his thought. In a dead or foreign language the difficulty may arise from our own want of familiarity with
its forms of speech, or in an ancient book we may be puzzled by
allusions and modes of thought the key to which has been lost. But it
is no part of the commentator's or interpreter's business to introduce obscurity or find difficulties where none exist, and it cannot be
pretended that, taking it as a question of the use of words to express
thoughts, there are any peculiar difficulties about understanding the
first chapter of Genesis, whether in its original Hebrew or in our
common translation, which represents the original with all necessary exactness. The difficulties arise for the first time, when we seek to
import a meaning into the language which it certainly never could
have conveyed to those to whom it was originally addressed. Unless
we go the whole length of supposing the simple account of the
Hebrew cosmogonist to be a series of awkward equivocations, in
which he attempted to give a representation widely different from
the facts, yet, without trespassing against literal truth, we can find
no difficulty in interpreting his words. Although language may be,
and often has been, used for the purpose, not of expressing, but
concealing thought, no such charge can fairly be laid against the
Hebrew writer.

'It should be borne in mind,' says Dr Buckland, 'that the object of
the account was, not to state *in what manner*, but *by whom* the world
was made.' Every one must see that this is an unfounded assertion,
inasmuch as the greater part of the narrative consists in a minute and
orderly description of the manner in which things were made. We
can know nothing as to the *object* of the account, except from the
account itself. What the writer meant to state is just that which he
has stated, for all that we can know to the contrary. Or can we
seriously believe that if appealed to by one of his Hebrew hearers or

readers as to his intention, he would have replied, My only object in what I have written is to inform you that God made the world; as to the manner of His doing it, of which I have given so exact an account, I have no intention that my words should be taken in their literal meaning.

We come then to this, that if we sift the Mosaic narrative of all definite meaning, and only allow it to be the expression of the most vague generalities, if we avow that it admits of no certain interpretation, of none that may not be shifted and altered as often as we see fit, and as the exigencies of geology may require, then may we reconcile it with what science teaches. This mode of dealing with the subject has been broadly advocated by a recent writer of mathematical eminence, who adopts the Bucklandian hypothesis, a passage from whose work we shall quote.[22]

'The Mosaic account of the six days' work is thus harmonised by some. On the first day, while the earth was "without form and void", the result of a previous convulsion in nature, "and darkness was upon the face of the deep", God commanded light to shine upon the earth. This may have been effected by such a clearing of the thick and loaded atmosphere, as to allow the light of the sun to penetrate its mass with a suffused illumination, sufficient to dispel the total darkness which had prevailed, but proceeding from a source not yet apparent on the earth. On the second day a separation took place in the thick vapoury mass which lay upon the earth, dense clouds were gathered up aloft and separated by *an expanse* from the waters and vapours below. On the third day these lower vapours, or fogs and mists which hitherto concealed the earth, were condensed and gathered with the other waters of the earth into seas, and the dry land appeared. Then grass and herbs began to grow. On the fourth day the clouds and vapours so rolled into separate masses, or were so entirely absorbed into the air itself, that the sun shone forth in all its brilliancy, the visible source of light and heat to the renovated earth, while the moon and stars gave light by night, and God appointed them henceforth for signs, and for seasons, and for days, and for years, to his creatures whom he was about to call into existence, as he afterwards set or appointed his bow in the clouds, which had appeared ages before, to be a sign to Noah and his descendants. The fifth and sixth days' work needs no comment.

'According to this explanation, the first chapter of Genesis does not pretend (as has been generally assumed) to be a cosmogony, or an account of the original creation of the material universe. The only cosmogony which it contains, in that sense at least, is confined to the sublime declaration of the first verse, "In the beginning God created the heavens and the earth." The inspired record thus stepping over an interval of indefinite ages with which man has no direct concern, proceeds at once to narrate the events preparatory to the introduction of man on the scene; employing phraseology strictly faithful to the *appearances* which would have met the eye of man, could he have been a spectator on the earth of what passed during those six days. All this has been commonly supposed to be a more detailed account of the general truth announced in the first verse, in short, a cosmogony: such was the idea of Josephus;[23] such probably was the idea of our translators; for their version, without form and void, points to the primæval chaos, out of which all things were then supposed to emerge; and these words standing *in limine*,[a] have tended, perhaps more than anything else, to foster the idea of a cosmogony in the minds of general readers to this very day.

'The foregoing explanation many have now adopted. It is sufficient for my purpose, if it be a possible explanation, and if it meet the difficulties of the case. That it is possible in itself, is plain from the fact above established, that the Scriptures wisely speak on natural things according to their *appearances* rather than their *physical realities*. It meets the difficulties of the case, because all the difficulties hitherto stated against this chapter on scientific grounds proceeded on the principle that it is a cosmogony; which this explanation repudiates, and thus disposes of the difficulties. It is therefore an explanation satisfactory to my own mind. I may be tempted to regret that I can gain no certain scientific information from Genesis regarding the process of the original creation; but I resist the temptation, remembering the great object for which the Scripture was given – to tell man of his origin and fall, and to draw his mind to his Creator and Redeemer. Scripture was not designed to teach us natural philosophy, and it is vain to attempt to make a cosmogony out of its statements. The Almighty declares himself the originator of all things, but he condescends not to describe the process or the laws by which he worked. All this he leaves for reason to decipher from the phenomena which his world displays.

'This explanation, however, I do not wish to impose on Scripture; and am fully prepared to surrender it, should further scientific discovery suggest another better fitted to meet all the requirements of the case.'

We venture to think that the world at large will continue to

a. On the threshold, at the very outset.

consider the account in the first chapter of Genesis to be a cosmogony. But as it is here admitted that it does not describe physical realities, but only outward appearances, that is, gives a description false in fact, and one which can teach us no scientific truth whatever, it seems to matter little what we call it. If its description of the events of the six days which it comprises be merely one of appearances and not of realities, it can teach us nothing regarding them.

Dissatisfied with the scheme of conciliation which has been discussed, other geologists have proposed to give an entirely mythical or enigmatical sense to the Mosaic narrative, and to consider the creative days described as vast periods of time. This plan was long ago suggested, but it has of late enjoyed a high degree of popularity, through the advocacy of the Scotch geologist Hugh Miller, an extract from whose work has been already quoted. Dr Buckland gives the following account of the first form in which this theory was propounded, and of the grounds upon which he rejected it in favour of that of Chalmers:[24] –

'A third opinion has been suggested both by learned theologians and by geologists, and on grounds independent of one another – viz., that the days of the Mosaic creation need not be understood to imply the same length of time which is now occupied by a single revolution of the globe, but successive periods each of great extent; and it has been asserted that the order of succession of the organic remains of a former world accords with the order of creation recorded in Genesis. This assertion, though to a certain degree apparently correct, is not entirely supported by geological facts, since it appears that the most ancient marine animals occur in the same division of the lowest transition strata with the earliest remains of vegetables, so that the evidence of organic remains, as far as it goes, shows the origin of plants and animals to have been contemporaneous: if any creation of vegetables preceded that of animals, no evidence of such an event has yet been discovered by the researches of geology. Still there is, I believe, no sound critical or theological objection to the interpretation of the word "day" as meaning a long period.'

Archdeacon Pratt also summarily rejects this view as untenable:[25]–

'There is one other class of interpreters, however, with whom I find it impossible to agree, – I mean those who take the six days to be six periods of unknown indefinite length. This is the principle of interpretation in a work on the *Creation and the Fall*, by the Rev D.

Macdonald;[26] also in Mr Hugh Miller's posthumous work, the *Testimony of the Rocks*, and also in an admirable treatise on the *Præ-Adamite Earth* in Dr Lardner's *Museum of Science*.[27] In this last it is the more surprising because the successive chapters are in fact an accumulation of evidence which points the other way, as a writer in the *Christian Observer*, Jan. 1858, has conclusively shown. The late M. D'Orbigny has demonstrated in his *Prodrome de Palæontologie*,[28] after an elaborate examination of vast multitudes of fossils, that there have been at least twenty-nine distinct periods of animal and vegetable existence – that is, twenty-nine creations separated one from another by catastrophes which have swept away the species existing at the time, with a very few solitary exceptions, never exceeding one and a-half per cent of the whole number discovered which have either survived the catastrophe, or have been erroneously designated. But not a single species of the preceding period survived the last of these catastrophes, and this closed the Tertiary period and ushered in the Human period. The evidence adduced by M. D'Orbigny shows that both plants and animals appeared in every one of those twenty-nine periods. The notion, therefore, that the "days" of Genesis represent periods of creation from the beginning of things is at once refuted. The parallel is destroyed both in the number of the periods (thirty, including the Azoic, instead of six), and also in the character of the things created. No argument could be more complete; and yet the writer of the *Præ-Adamite Earth*, in the last two pages, sums up his lucid sketch of M. D'Orbigny's researches by referring the account in the first chapter of Genesis to the whole creation from the beginning of all things, a *selection* of epochs being made, as he imagines, for the six days or periods.'

In this trenchant manner do theological geologists overthrow one another's theories. However, Hugh Miller was perfectly aware of the difficulty involved in his view of the question, and we shall endeavour to show the reader the manner in which he deals with it.

He begins by pointing out that the families of vegetables and animals were introduced upon earth as nearly as possible according to the great classes in which naturalists have arranged the modern flora and fauna. According to the arrangement of Lindley,[29] he observes – 'Commencing at the bottom of the scale we find the thallogens, or flowerless plants, which lack proper stems and leaves – a class which includes all the algæ. Next succeed the acrogens, or flowerless plants that possess both stems and leaves – such as the ferns and their allies. Next, omitting an inconspicuous class,

Charles Goodwin (1817–1878)

represented by but a few parasitical plants incapable of preservation as fossils, come the endogens – monocotyledonous flowering plants, that include the palms, the liliaceæ, and several other families, all characterised by the parallel venation of their leaves. Next, omitting another inconspicuous tribe, there follows a very important class, the gymnogens – polycotyledonous trees, represented by the coniferæ and cycadaceæ. And last of all come the dicotyledonous exogens – a class to which all our fruit and what are known as our forest trees belong, with a vastly preponderating majority of the herbs and flowers that impart fertility and beauty to our gardens and meadows.' The order in which fossils of these several classes appear in the strata, Hugh Miller states to be as follows: – In the Lower Silurian we find only thallogens, in the Upper Silurian acrogens are added. The gymnogens appear rather prematurely, it might be thought, in the old red sandstone, the endogens (monocotyledonous) coming after them in the carboniferous group. Dicotyledonous exogens enter at the close of the oolitic period, and come to their greatest development in the tertiary. Again, the animal tribes have been introduced in an order closely agreeing with the geological divisions established by Cuvier.[30] In the Silurian beds the invertebrate creatures, the radiata, articulata, and mollusca, appear simultaneously. At the close of the period, fishes, the lowest of the vertebrata, appear: before the old red sandstone period had passed away, reptiles had come into existence; birds, and the marsupial mammals, enter in the oolitic period; placental mammals in the tertiary; and man last of all.

Now, these facts do certainly tally to some extent with the Mosaic account, which represents fish and fowl as having been produced from the waters on the fifth day, reptiles and mammals from the earth on the sixth, and man as made last of all. The agreement, however, is far from exact, as according to geological evidence, reptiles would appear to have existed ages before birds and mammals, whereas here the creation of birds is attributed to the fifth day, that of reptiles to the sixth. There remains, moreover, the insuperable difficulty of the plants and trees being represented as made on the third day – that is, more than an age before fishes and birds; which is clearly not the case.

Although, therefore, there is a superficial resemblance in the Mosaic account to that of the geologists, it is evident that the bare theory that a 'day' means an age or immense geological period might be made to yield some rather strange results. What becomes of the evening and morning of which each day is said to have consisted?

Was each geologic age divided into two long intervals, one all darkness, the other all light? and if so, what became of the plants and trees created in the third day or period, when the evening of the fourth day (the evenings, be it observed, precede the mornings) set in? They must have passed through half a seculum[a] of total darkness, not even cheered by that dim light which the sun, not yet completely manifested, supplied on the morning of the third day. Such an ordeal would have completely destroyed the whole vegetable creation, and yet we find that it survived, and was appointed on the sixth day as the food of man and animals. In fact, we need only substitute the word 'period' for 'day' in the Mosaic narrative to make it very apparent that the writer at least had no such meaning, nor could he have conveyed any such meaning to those who first heard his account read.

'It has been held,' says Hugh Miller, 'by accomplished philologists, that the days of Mosaic creation may be regarded without doing violence to the Hebrew language, as successive periods of great extent.'[31] We do not believe that there is any ground for this doctrine. The word 'day' is certainly used occasionally in particular phrases, in an indefinite manner, not only in Hebrew, but other languages. As for instance, Gen. xxxix. 11 – 'About this time', Heb. literally, 'about this day'. But every such phrase explains itself, and not only philology but common sense disclaims the notion, that when 'day' is spoken of in terms like those in the first chapter of Genesis, and described as consisting of an evening and a morning, it can be understood to mean a seculum.

Archdeacon Pratt,[32] treating on the same subject, says (p. 41, note), 'Were there no other ground of objection to this mode of interpretation, I think the wording of the fourth commandment is clearly opposed to it. Ex. xx. 8. "Remember the Sabbath day to keep it holy. 9. Six days shalt thou labour and do all thy work. 10. But the seventh day is the Sabbath of the Lord thy God. In it thou, shalt not do any work, thou, nor thy son, nor thy daughter, thy manservant, nor thy maidservant, nor thy cattle, nor thy stranger that is within thy gates. 11. For in six days the Lord made heaven and earth, the sea and all that in them is, and rested the seventh day; wherefore the Lord blessed the Sabbath day and hallowed it."

'Is it not a harsh and forced interpretation to suppose that the six days in v. 9 do not mean the same as the six days in v. 11, but that in this last place they mean six periods? In reading through the eleventh

a. Generation, age.

135

verse, it is extremely difficult to believe that the seventh day is a long period, and the sabbath day an ordinary day, that is, that the same word day should be used in two such totally different senses in the same short sentence and without any explanation.'

Hugh Miller saw the difficulty; but he endeavours to escape the consequences of a rigorous application of the periodic theory by modifying it in a peculiar, and certainly ingenious manner. 'Waiving,' he says, 'the question as a philological one, and simply holding with Cuvier, Parkinson,[33] and Silliman,[34] that each of the *six* days of the Mosaic account in the first chapter were what is assuredly meant by the *day*[35] referred to in the second, not natural days but lengthened periods, I find myself called on, as a geologist, to account for but three out of the six. Of the period during which light was created, of the period during which a firmament was made to separate the waters from the waters, or of the period during which the two great lights of the earth, with the other heavenly bodies, became visible from the earth's surface – we need expect to find no record in the rocks. Let me, however, pause for a moment, to remark the peculiar character of the language in which we are first introduced in the Mosaic narrative, to the heavenly bodies – sun, moon, and stars. The moon, though absolutely one of the smallest lights of our system, is described as secondary and subordinate to only its greatest light, the sun. It is the apparent, then, not the actual, which we find in the passage – what *seemed* to be, not what *was*; and as it was merely what appeared to be greatest that was described as greatest, on what grounds are we to hold that it may not also have been what *appeared* at the time to be made that has been described as made? The sun, moon, and stars, may have been created long before, though it was not until this fourth day of creation that they became visible from the earth's surface.'[36]

The theory founded upon this hint is that the Hebrew writer did not state facts, but merely certain appearances, and those not of things which really happened, as assumed in the explanation adopted by Archdeacon Pratt, but of certain occurrences which were presented to him in a vision, and that this vision greatly deceived him as to what he seemed to see; and thus, in effect, the real discrepancy of the narrative with facts is admitted. He had in all, seven visions, to each of which he attributed the duration of a day, although indeed each picture presented to him the earth during seven long and distinctly marked epochs. While on the one hand this supposition admits all desirable latitude for mistakes and misrepresentations, Hugh Miller, on the other hand, endeavours to show

that a substantial agreement with the truth exists, and to give sufficient reason for the mistakes. We must let him speak for himself. 'The
geologist, in his attempts to collate the Divine with the geologic
record, has, I repeat, only three of the six periods of creation to
account for[37] – the period of plants, the period of great sea-monsters
and creeping things, and the period of cattle and beasts of the earth.
He is called on to question his systems and formations regarding the
remains of these three great periods, and of them only. And the question once fairly stated, what, I ask, is the reply? All geologists agree in
holding that the vast geological scale naturally divides into three
great parts. There are many lesser divisions – divisions into systems,
formations, deposits, beds, strata; but the master divisions, in each of
which we find a type of life so unlike that of the others, that even the
unpractised eye can detect the difference, are simply three: the
palæozoic, or oldest fossiliferous division; the secondary, or middle
fossiliferous division; and the tertiary, or latest fossiliferous division.
In the first, or palæozoic division, we find corals, crustaceans, molluscs, fishes; and in its later formations, a few reptiles. But none of
these classes give its leading character to the palæozoic; they do not
constitute its prominent feature, or render it more remarkable as a
scene of life than any of the divisions which followed. That which
chiefly distinguished the palæozoic from the secondary and tertiary
periods was its gorgeous flora. It was emphatically the period of
plants – "of herbs yielding seed after their kind". In no other age did
the world ever witness such a flora; the youth of the earth was peculiarly a green and umbrageous youth – a youth of dusk and tangled
forests, of huge pines and stately araucarians,[a] of the reed-like
calamite,[b] the tall tree-fern, the sculptured sigillaria,[c] and the hirsute
lepidodendrons.[d] Wherever dry land, or shallow lakes, or running
stream appeared, from where Melville Island now spreads out its icy
coast under the star of the pole, to where the arid plains of Australia lie
solitary beneath the bright cross of the south, a rank and luxuriant
herbage cumbered every foot-breadth of the dank and steaming soil;
and even to distant planets our earth must have shone through the
enveloping cloud with a green and delicate ray. . . . The geologic evidence is so complete as to be patent to all, that the first great period of
organised being was, as described in the Mosaic record, peculiarly a
period of herbs and trees "yielding seed after their kind".'

a. Evergreen trees, e.g. monkey-puzzles.
b. Fossil plant with jointed stem, like mare's tail.
c. Fossil tree.
d. Fossil plant.

Charles Goodwin (1817–1878)

'The middle great period of the geologist – that of the secondary division – possessed, like the earlier one, its herbs and plants, but they were of a greatly less luxuriant and conspicuous character than their predecessors, and no longer formed the prominent trait or feature of the creation to which they belonged. The period had also its corals, its crustaceans, its molluscs, its fishes, and in some one or two exceptional instances, its dwarf mammals. But the grand existences of the age – the existences in which it excelled every other creation, earlier or later – were its huge creeping things – its enormous monsters of the deep, and, as shown by the impressions of their footprints stamped upon the rocks, its gigantic birds. It was peculiarly the age of egg-bearing animals, winged and wingless. Its wonderful *whales*, not however, as now, of the mammalian, but of the reptilian class, – ichthyosaurs, plesiosaurs, and cetosaurs, must have tempested the deep; its creeping lizards and crocodiles, such as the teliosaurus, megalosaurus, and iguanodon – creatures, some of which more than rivalled the existing elephant in height, and greatly more than rivalled him in bulk – must have crowded the plains, or haunted by myriads the rivers of the period; and we know that the foot-prints of at least one of its many birds are of fully twice the size of those made by the horse or camel. We are thus prepared to demonstrate, that the second period of the geologist was peculiarly and characteristically a period of whale-like reptiles of the sea, of enormous creeping reptiles of the land, and of numerous birds, some of them of gigantic size; and in meet accordance with the fact, we find that the second Mosaic period with which the geologist is called on to deal, was a period in which God created the fowl that flieth above the earth, with moving (or creeping) creatures, both in the waters and on land, and what our translation renders great whales, but that I find rendered in the margin great sea-monsters. The tertiary period had also its prominent class of existences. Its flora seems to have been no more conspicuous than that of the present time; its reptiles occupy a very subordinate place; but its beasts of the field were by far the most wonderfully developed, both in size and numbers, that ever appeared on earth. Its mammoths and its mastodons, its rhinoceri and its hippopotami, its enormous dinotherium, and colossal megatherium, greatly more than equalled in bulk the hugest mammals of the present time, and vastly exceeded them in number. "Grand, indeed," says an English naturalist, "was the fauna of the British Islands in these early days. Tigers as large again as the biggest Asiatic species lurked in the ancient thickets; elephants of nearly twice the bulk of the largest individuals that now exist in Africa or

Ceylon roamed in herds; at least two species of rhinoceros forced their way through the primæval forest; and the lakes and rivers were tenanted by hippopotami as bulky and with as great tusks as those of Africa." The massive cave-bear and large cave-hyæna belonged to the same formidable group, with at least two species of great oxen (*Bos longifrons* and *Bos primigenius*), with a horse of smaller size, and an elk (*Megaceros Hibernicus*) that stood ten feet four inches in height. Truly this Tertiary age – this third and last of the great geologic periods – was peculiarly the age of great "beasts of the earth after their kind, and cattle after their kind".'

Thus by dropping the invertebrata, and the early fishes and rep-tiles of the Palæozoic period as inconspicuous and of little account, and bringing prominently forward the carboniferous era which succeeded them as the most characteristic feature of the first great division, by classing the great land reptiles of the secondary period with the moving creatures of the waters, (for in the Mosaic account it does not appear that any inhabitants of the land were created on the fifth day), and evading the fact that terrestrial reptiles seem to have preceded birds in their order of appearance upon earth, the geologic divisions are tolerably well assimilated to the third, fifth, and sixth Mosaic days. These things were represented, we are told, to Moses in visionary pictures, and resulted in the short and sum-mary account which he has given.

There is something in this hypothesis very near to the obvious truth, while at the same time something very remote from that truth is meant to be inferred. If it be said the Mosaic account is simply the speculation of some early Copernicus or Newton who devised a scheme of the earth's formation, as nearly as he might in accordance with his own observations of nature, and with such views of things as it was possible for an unassisted thinker in those days to take, we may admire the approximate correctness of the picture drawn, while we see that the writer, as might be expected, took everything from a different point of view from ourselves, and consequently repre-sented much quite differently from the fact. But nothing of this sort is really intended. We are asked to believe that a vision of creation was presented to him by Divine power, for the purpose of enabling him to inform the world of what he had seen, which vision in-evitably led him to give a description which has misled the world for centuries, and in which the truth can now only with difficulty be recognised. The Hebrew writer informs us that on the third day 'the earth brought forth grass, the herb yielding seed after his kind, and the tree yielding fruit, whose seed was in itself, after his kind;' and in the 29th verse, that God on the sixth day said, 'Behold, I have given you every herb bearing seed, which is upon the face of all the earth, and every tree in the which is the fruit of a tree yielding seed, to you it shall be for meat. And to every beast of the earth, and to every fowl of the air, and to everything that creepeth upon the earth, wherein there is life, I have given every green herb for meat.' Can it be disputed that the writer here conceives that grass, corn, and fruit, were created on the third day, and with a view to the future nourishment of man and beast? Yet, according to the vision hypothesis, he must have been greatly deceived; for that luxuriant vegetation which he saw on the third day, consisted not of plants destined for the food of man, but for his fuel. It was the flora of the carboniferous period which he beheld, concerning which Hugh Miller makes the following remark, p. 24: – 'The existing plants whence we derive our analogies in dealing with the vegetation of this early period, contribute but little, if at all, to the support of animal life. The ferns and their allies remain untouched by the grazing animals. Our native club-mosses, though once used in medicine, are positively deleterious; the horsetails, though harmless, so abound in silex, which wraps them round with a cuticle of stone, that they are rarely cropped by cattle; while the thickets of fern which cover our hillsides, and seem so temptingly rich and green in their season, scarce support the existence of a single creature, and remain untouched in stem and leaf from their first appearance in spring, until they droop and wither under the frosts of early winter. Even the insects that infest the herbaria of the botanist almost never injure his ferns. Nor are our resin-producing conifers, though they nourish a few beetles, favourites with the herbivorous tribes in a much greater degree. Judging from all we yet know, the earliest terrestrial flora may have covered the dry land with its mantle of cheerful green, and served its general purposes, chemical and others, in the well-balanced economy of nature; but the herb-eating animals would have fared but ill, even where it throve most luxuriantly; and it seems to harmonize with the fact of its unedible character that up to the present time we know not that a single herbivorous animal lived amongst its shades.' The Mosaic writer is, however, according to the theory, misled by the mere appearance of luxurious vegetation, to describe fruit trees and edible seed-bearing vegetables as products of the third day.

Hugh Miller's treatment of the description of the first dawn of light is not more satisfactory than that of Dr Buckland. He supposes the prophet in his dream to have heard the command 'Let there be light' enunciated, whereupon 'straightway a grey diffused light springs up in the east, and casting its *sickly gleam* over a cloud-limited expanse of steaming vaporous sea, journeys through the heavens towards the west. One heavy, sunless day is made the representative of myriads; the faint light waxes fainter, – it sinks beneath the dim, undefined horizon.'

We are then asked to imagine that a second and a third day, each representing the characteristic features of a great distinctly-marked epoch, and the latter of them marked by the appearance of a rich and luxuriant vegetation, are presented to the seer's eye; but without sun, moon, or stars as yet entering into his dream. These appear first in his fourth vision, and then for the first time we have 'a brilliant day,' and the seer, struck with the novelty, describes the heavenly bodies as being the most conspicuous objects in the picture. In reality we know that he represents them (v. 16) as having been *made* and *set* in the heavens on that day, though Hugh Miller avoids reminding us of this.

In one respect the theory of Hugh Miller agrees with that advocated by Dr Buckland and Archdeacon Pratt. Both these theories divest the Mosaic narrative of real accordance with fact; both assume that appearances only, not facts, are described, and that in riddles, which would never have been suspected to be such, had we not arrived at the truth from other sources. It would be difficult for controversialists to cede more completely the point in dispute, or to admit more explicitly that the Mosaic narrative does not represent correctly the history of the universe up to the time of man. At the same time, the upholders of each theory see insuperable objections in details to that of their allies, and do not pretend to any firm faith in their own. How can it be otherwise when the task proposed is to evade the plain meaning of language, and to introduce obscurity into one of the simplest stories ever told, for the sake of making it accord with the complex system of the universe which modern science has unfolded? The spectacle of able and, we doubt not, conscientious writers engaged in attempting the impossible is painful and humiliating. They evidently do not breathe freely over their work, but shuffle and stumble over their difficulties in a piteous manner; nor are they themselves again until they return to the pure and open fields of science.

It is refreshing to return to the often echoed remark, that it could not have been the object of a Divine revelation to instruct mankind in physical science, man having had faculties bestowed upon him to enable him to acquire this knowledge by himself. This is in fact

Charles Goodwin (1817–1878)

pretty generally admitted; but in the application of the doctrine, writers play at fast and loose with it according to circumstances. Thus an inspired writer may be permitted to allude to the phenomena of nature according to the vulgar view of such things, without impeachment of his better knowledge; but if he speaks of the same phenomena assertively, we are bound to suppose that things are as he represents them, however much our knowledge of nature may be disposed to recalcitrate. But if we find a difficulty in admitting that such misrepresentations can find a place in revelation, the difficulty lies in our having previously assumed what a Divine revelation ought to be. If God made use of imperfectly informed men to lay the foundations of that higher knowledge for which the human race was destined, is it wonderful that they should have committed themselves to assertions not in accordance with facts, although they may have believed them to be true? On what grounds has the popular notion of Divine revelation been built up? Is it not plain that the plan of Providence for the education of man is a progressive one, and as imperfect men have been used as the agents for teaching mankind, is it not to be expected that their teachings should be partial and, to some extent, erroneous? Admitted, as it is, that physical science is not what the Hebrew writers, for the most part, profess to convey, at any rate, that it is not on account of the communication of such knowledge that we attach any value to their writings, why should we hesitate to recognise their fallibility on this head?

Admitting, as is historically and in fact the case, that it was the mission of the Hebrew race to lay the foundation of religion upon the earth, and that Providence used this people specially for this purpose, is it not our business and our duty to look and see how this has really been done? not forming for ourselves theories of what a revelation ought to be, or how we, if entrusted with the task, would have made one, but enquiring how it has pleased God to do it. In all his theories of the world, man has at first deviated widely from the truth, and has only gradually come to see how far otherwise God has ordered things than the first daring speculator had supposed. It has been popularly assumed that the Bible, bearing the stamp of Divine authority, must be complete, perfect, and unimpeachable in all its parts, and a thousand difficulties and incoherent doctrines have sprung out of this theory. Men have proceeded in the matter of theology, as they did with physical science before inductive philosophy sent them to the feet of nature, and bid them learn in patience and obedience the lessons which she had to teach. Dogma and groundless assumption occupy the place of modest enquiry after truth, while at the same time the upholders of these theories claim credit for humility and submissiveness. This is exactly inverting the fact; the humble scholar of truth is not he who, taking his stand upon the traditions of rabbins, Christian fathers, or schoolmen, insists upon bending facts to his unyielding standard, but he who is willing to accept such teaching as it has pleased Divine Providence to afford, without murmuring that it has not been furnished more copiously or clearly.

The Hebrew race, their works, and their books, are great facts in the history of man; the influence of the mind of this people upon the rest of mankind has been immense and peculiar, and there can be no difficulty in recognising therein the hand of a directing Providence. But we may not make ourselves wiser than God, nor attribute to Him methods of procedure which are not His. If, then, it is plain that He has not thought it needful to communicate to the writer of the Cosmogony that knowledge which modern researches have revealed, why do we not acknowledge this, except that it conflicts with a human theory which presumes to point out how God ought to have instructed man? The treatment to which the Mosaic narrative is subjected by the theological geologists is anything but respectful. The writers of this school, as we have seen, agree in representing it as a series of elaborate equivocations – a story which 'palters with us in a double sense'. But if we regard it as the speculation of some Hebrew Descartes or Newton, promulgated in all good faith as the best and most probable account that could be then given of God's universe, it resumes the dignity and value of which the writers in question have done their utmost to deprive it. It has been sometimes felt as a difficulty to taking this view of the case, that the writer asserts so solemnly and unhesitatingly that for which he must have known that he had no authority. But this arises only from our modern habits of thought, and from the modesty of assertion which the spirit of true science has taught us. Mankind has learnt caution through repeated slips in the process of tracing out the truth.

The early speculator was harassed by no such scruples, and asserted as facts what he knew in reality only as probabilities. But we are not on that account to doubt his perfect good faith, nor need we attribute to him wilful misrepresentation, or consciousness of asserting that which he knew not to be true. He had seized one great truth, in which, indeed, he anticipated the highest revelation of modern enquiry – namely, the unity of the design of the world, and its subordination to one sole Maker and Lawgiver. With regard to details, observation failed him. He knew little of the earth's surface, or of its shape and place in the universe; the infinite varieties of organized existences which people it, the distinct floras and faunas of its different continents, were unknown to him. But he saw that all which lay within his observation had been formed for the benefit and service of man, and the goodness of the Creator to his creatures was the thought predominant in his mind. Man's closer relation to his Maker is indicated by the representation that he was formed last of all creatures, and in the visible likeness of God. For ages, this simple view of creation satisfied the wants of man, and formed a sufficient basis of theological teaching, and if modern research now shows it to be physically untenable, our respect for the narrative which has played so important a part in the culture of our race need be in nowise diminished. No one contends that it can be used as a basis of astronomical or geological teaching, and those who profess to see in it an accordance with facts, only do this *sub modo*,[a] and by processes which despoil it of its consistency and grandeur, both which may be preserved if we recognise in it, not an authentic utterance of Divine knowledge, but a human utterance, which it has pleased Providence to use in a special way for the education of mankind.[38]

a. Under certain conditions, with qualifications, within limits.

6. Leonard Huxley,
Life and Letters of Thomas Henry
Huxley (1903), vol. 1, Chapter 14,
'1859–1860'

This extract gives a description (or rather, several descriptions) of the famous encounter between T. H. Huxley and Bishop Samuel Wilberforce at the British Association in 1860. Unfortunately, no full contemporary account of the affair exists, which may indicate that at the time it was not thought so important or so decisive as it later became in the retrospective accounts of the Darwinian party. It is significant that no one seems to be able to remember exactly *what* it was that Huxley said in his famous retort to the Bishop: 'he stood before us and spoke those tremendous words – words which no one seems sure of now, nor, I think, could remember just after they were spoken, for their meaning took away our breath, though it left us in no doubt as to what it was', as one writer rather lamely puts it (see p. 152). In evaluating the significance of the incident, we must consider three main points: first, the attitudes of the contemporary press, the audience, and Wilberforce himself – did they think Huxley had scored a victory? Secondly, Wilberforce's status as a critic of Darwinism: was he really as ill-informed and unintelligent as his enemies made out, and did he have no right, as a clergyman, to speak on scientific matters? Thirdly, the aggressive nature of Huxley's defence of Darwin: what interest did he have in creating a myth of 'warfare' between science and religion?

The incident was hardly well covered by the press – but this is how the pro-Church *Athenaeum* described it:

The Bishop of Oxford came out strongly against a theory which holds it possible that a man may be descended from an ape – in which protest he is sustained by Prof. Owen, Sir Benjamin Brodie, Dr Daubeny, and the most eminent naturalists assembled at Oxford. But others, conspicuous among these, Prof. Huxley – have expressed their willingness to accept for themselves, as well as for their friends and enemies, all actual truths, even the last humiliating truth of a pedigree not registered in the Herald's College. The dispute has at least made Oxford uncommonly lively during the week. (Quoted in Alvar Ellegård, *Darwin and the General Reader* (Göteborg, 1958, pp. 68–9)

What is seen as important in this report is the opposition of distinguished *scientists* to Darwin's theory, rather than 'the open clash between Science and the Church' that Leonard Huxley describes (p. 149). The audience at the debate were not won over by Huxley, 'the majority' bestowing 'looks of bitter hatred' on Huxley and his party as they left, and the general sentiment was felt to be 'how abominably the Bishop was treated' (p. 154). Moreover, the account of the debate in Wilberforce's biography does not present it as a defeat for the Bishop (see Owen Chadwick, *The Victorian Church* (1970), vol. 2, pp. 10–12).

Though Wilberforce may have been 'crammed' by Owen, he was not ignorant about science: he was an ornithologist with an interest in geology – he represents that characteristic Victorian type, the clergyman-naturalist, who depended on the harmony that had been established between science and natural theology (see J. R. Lucas, 'Wilberforce and Huxley: a legendary encounter', *The Historical Journal*, 22, no. 2 (1979), 313–30, an important modern pro-Wilberforce assessment of the incident). It is agreed that his speech at Oxford was based on his article that was to appear in the *Quarterly Review*: the article is by no means unscientific, and most of it is devoted to refuting Darwin on scientific grounds, focusing on the weaknesses in the 'selection' analogy, and the difficulties in the accumulation of variations when the tendency to reversion is so strong. Darwin himself admitted that 'it picks out with skill all the most conjectural parts, and brings forward all the difficulties' (*Life and Letters*, vol. 2, pp. 324–5). While Wilberforce does finally point out the contradictions between Darwin's theory and Revelation, his main line of attack is the scientific one, based on his faith that natural theology cannot contradict revealed religion: 'We have no sympathy with those who object to any facts or alleged facts in nature, or to any inference logically deduced from them, because they believe them to contradict what it appears to them is taught by Revelation. We think that all such objections savour of a timidity which is really inconsistent with a firm and well-instructed faith.' Here Wilberforce quotes Sedgwick in support. He goes on: 'He who is as sure as he is of his own existence that the God of Truth is at once the God of Nature and the God of Revelation, cannot believe it to be possible that His voice in either, rightly understood, can differ, or deceive His creatures' (*Quarterly Review*, July 1860, p. 256). The Oxford debate thus appears as a confrontation between religious science, as practised by the leading scientists of the day, and the new irreligious science to be championed by Huxley and Tyndall (see pp. 172–3).

Huxley's own aggressive attitude is important too: he was known as 'Darwin's bulldog', while Darwin himself kept out of any public controversies about his theory. On reading the *Origin*, Huxley wrote to Darwin: 'You must recollect that some of your friends, at any rate, are endowed with an amount of combativeness which (though you have often and justly rebuked it) may stand you in good stead. I am sharpening my beak and claws in readiness' (*Life and Letters of Darwin*, vol. 2, p. 231). While Wilberforce may be seen to represent the old natural theological science, Huxley represents the new professional science: like Tyndall, he was a self-made man and an 'outsider', eager to secure power and influence for his profession in an establishment dominated by the Church. This may have caused him to adopt a myth of 'warfare' between theology and science, in which theology was cast as the dangerous aggressor. Huxley defined himself as an 'agnostic', a term he coined himself, and his main aim was to free science from its former attachment to religious values. On the other hand, the 'religious' streak in Huxley's own character has often been commented on, and he tended to attach moral if not religious value to his crusade on behalf of science:

> But if I may speak of the objects I have had more or less in view since I began the ascent of my hillock, they are briefly these: to promote the increase of natural knowledge and to forward the application of scientific investigation to all the problems of life to the best of my ability, in the conviction – which has grown with my growth and strengthened with my strength - that there is no alleviation for the sufferings of mankind except veracity of thought and of action, and the

resolute facing of the world as it is when the garment of makebelieve by which pious hands have hidden its uglier features, is stripped off.

It is with this intent that I have subordinated any reasonable or unreasonable ambition for scientific fame, which I may have permitted myself to entertain, to other ends; to the popularisation of science; to education; to the endless series of battles and skirmishes over evolution; and to untiring opposition to that ecclesiastical spirit, that clericalism, which in England, as everywhere else, and to whatever denomination it may belong, is the deadly enemy of science. (*Autobiography*, ed. Gavin de Beer (1974), p. 109)

A gallery of famous Victorians attended the Oxford meeting, and are referred to in Leonard Huxley's account. 'Dr Daubeny', with whom Huxley was staying, was Charles Daubeny, Professor of Chemistry, Botany and Rural Economy at Oxford. He did important research in chemistry, geology and botany, worked energetically for the British Association, and did much to end Oxford's neglect of science. Richard Owen was an anatomist, palaeontologist and geologist. In 1856, he had been made Superintendent of the natural history departments of the British Museum. Later, he was in charge of the new Natural History Museum at South Kensington. He also lectured at the Royal Institution and the School of Mines. He was influenced in his scientific ideas by Cuvier, and also by German *Naturphilosophie* (see extract 3, pp. 80–4). He was a friend of Wilberforce and an opponent of Darwin and Huxley (see endnote 4, p. 234). 'Professor Henslow' was the Rev John Henslow, Professor of Mineralogy and Botany at Cambridge. He was a friend of Adam Sedgwick, and Darwin had been one of his students. In fact, Henslow had recommended Darwin as naturalist for the *Beagle*. Henslow was a founder member of the British Association. Sir Joseph Dalton Hooker was an eminent botanist, as his father, Sir William Jackson Hooker, had been. He succeeded his father as director of Kew Gardens in 1865. He was a friend of Darwin, who had kept him informed of the progress of his thinking on species. It was Hooker, with Lyell, who persuaded Darwin and Wallace to agree to a joint presentation of their ideas to the Linnean Society. Sir John Lubbock (later Lord Avebury), while working in the family bank, worked also on entomology, anthropology and botany, with encouragement and help from Darwin. He was a convinced believer in natural selection from the beginning. Later, he applied evolutionary thought to human prehistoric remains – he coined the terms Neolithic and Palaeolithic. He was also a Liberal MP, and later a peer, and was very involved in the spread of scientific education. 'Professor Beale' was Lionel Smith Beale, Professor of Physiology at King's College, London. He pioneered the use of the microscope in pathological anatomy. He was a 'vitalist', and a strong opponent of any 'mechanistic' theory of life: in 1868, he wrote a refutation of Huxley's 'on the Physical Basis of Life'. T. H. Green, who was an undergraduate at the time, later became a famous philosopher, sympathetic to Wordsworth, Carlyle, Kant and Hegel. 'Old Sir Benjamin Brodie' was a surgeon and physiologist, and was President of the Royal Society at this time. 'Professor Brodie' was his son, also called Benjamin, who was Professor of Chemistry at Oxford. Professor Farrar was a Canon of Durham. The Rev Richard Greswell was a Tutor at Worcester College, Oxford, who played a great part in setting up the new Museum at Oxford, and was active in the sphere of public education. John Richard Green, who was present as an undergraduate, later became a famous historian. Admiral Fitzroy had been the Captain of the *Beagle* during Darwin's voyage. Sir Michael Foster was a physiologist, who was encouraged and helped in his career by Huxley. In 1883, he became the first Professor of Physiology at Cambridge, and he worked hard at reviving the study of biology at Cambridge. Like Huxley, he was keen to see the spread of scientific education. Finally, Sir William

Flower was a surgeon, who became interested in zoology. He was working on the classification of mammals, especially the primates, and was able to provide evidence to help Huxley refute Owen's distinction between human and other primate brains.

Chapter XIV

1859–1860

The famous Oxford Meeting of 1860 was of no small importance in Huxley's career. It was not merely that he helped to save a great cause from being stifled under misrepresentation and ridicule – that he helped to extort for it a fair hearing; it was now that he first made himself known in popular estimation as a dangerous adversary in debate – a personal force in the world of science which could not be neglected. From this moment he entered the front fighting line in the most exposed quarter of the field.[1]

Most unluckily, no contemporary account of his own exists of the encounter. Indeed, the same cause which prevented his writing home the story of the day's work nearly led to his absence from the scene. It was known that Bishop Wilberforce, whose first class in mathematics gave him, in popular estimation, a right to treat on scientific matters,[2] intended to 'smash Darwin'; and Huxley, expecting that the promised debate would be merely an appeal to prejudice in a mixed audience, before which the scientific arguments of the Bishop's opponents would be at the utmost disadvantage, intended to leave Oxford that very morning and join his wife at Hardwicke, near Reading, where she was staying with her sister. But in a letter, quoted below, he tells how, on the Friday afternoon, he chanced to meet Robert Chambers, the reputed author of the *Vestiges of Creation*, who begged him 'not to desert them.' Accordingly he postponed his departure; but seeing his wife next morning, had no occasion to write a letter.

Several accounts of the scene are already in existence: one in the *Life of Darwin*, another in the 1892 *Life*, a third that of *Lyell*,[3] the slight differences between them representing the difference between individual recollections of eye-witnesses. In addition to these I have been fortunate enough to secure further reminiscences from several other eye-witnesses.

Two papers in Section D, of no great importance in themselves, became historical as affording the opponents of Darwin their opportunity of making an attack upon his theory which should tell with the public. The first was on Thursday, June 28. Dr Daubeny of

Oxford made a communication to the Section, 'On the final causes of the sexuality of plants, with particular reference to Mr Darwin's work on the *Origin of Species*.' Huxley was called upon to speak by the President, but tried to avoid a discussion, on the ground 'that a general audience, in which sentiment would unduly interfere with intellect, was not the public before which such a discussion should be carried on.'

This consideration, however, did not stop the discussion; it was continued by Owen. He said he 'wished to approach the subject in the spirit of the philosopher,' and declared his 'conviction that there were facts by which the public could come to some conclusion with regard to the probabilities of the truth of Mr Darwin's theory.' As one of these facts, he stated that the brain of the gorilla 'presented more differences, as compared with the brain of man, than it did when compared with the brains of the very lowest and most problematical of the Quadrumana.'[a][4]

Now this was the very point, as said above, upon which Huxley had made special investigations during the last two years, with precisely opposite results, such as, indeed, had been arrived at by previous investigators. Hereupon he replied, giving these assertions a 'direct and unqualified contradiction,' and pledging himself to 'justify that unusual procedure elsewhere,' – a pledge which was amply fulfilled in the pages of the *Natural History Review* for 1861.

Accordingly it was to him, thus marked out as the champion of the most debatable thesis of evolution, that, two days later, the Bishop addressed his sarcasms, only to meet with a withering retort. For on the Friday there was peace; but on the Saturday came a yet fiercer battle over the 'Origin,' which loomed all the larger in the public eye, because it was not merely the contradiction of one anatomist by another, but the open clash between Science and the Church. It was, moreover, not a contest of bare fact or abstract assertion, but a combat of wit between two individuals, spiced with the personal element which appeals to one of the strongest instincts of every large audience.

It was the merest chance, as I have already said, that Huxley attended the meeting of the section that morning. Dr Draper of New York was to read a paper on the 'Intellectual Development of Europe considered with reference to the views of Mr Darwin.'[5] 'I can still hear,' writes one who was present, 'the American accents of Dr Draper's opening address when he asked "Air we a fortuitous

a. The primates; literally, 'four hands'.

concourse of atoms?"' However, it was not to hear him, but the eloquence of the Bishop, that the members of the Association crowded in such numbers into the Lecture Room of the Museum, that this, the appointed meeting-place of the section, had to be abandoned for the long west room, since cut in two by a partition for the purposes of the library. It was not term time, nor were the general public admitted; nevertheless the room was crowded to suffocation long before the protagonists appeared on the scene, 700 persons or more managing to find places. The very windows by which the room was lighted down the length of its west side were packed with ladies, whose white handkerchiefs, waving and fluttering in the air at the end of the Bishop's speech, were an unforgettable factor in the acclamation of the crowd.

On the east side between the two doors was the platform. Professor Henslow, the President of the section, took his seat in the centre; upon his right was the Bishop, and beyond him again Dr Draper; on his extreme left was Mr Dingle, a clergyman from Lanchester, near Durham, with Sir J. Hooker and Sir J. Lubbock in front of him, and nearer the centre, Professor Beale of King's College, London, and Huxley.

The clergy, who shouted lustily for the Bishop, were massed in the middle of the room; behind them in the north-west corner a knot of undergraduates (one of these was T. H. Green, who listened but took no part in the cheering) had gathered together beside Professor Brodie, ready to lift their voices, poor minority though they were, for the opposite party. Close to them stood one of the few men among the audience already in Holy orders, who joined in – and indeed led – the cheers for the Darwinians.

So 'Dr Draper droned out his paper, turning first to the right hand and then to the left, of course bringing in a reference to the Origin of Species which set the ball rolling.'

An hour or more that paper lasted, and then discussion began. The President 'wisely announced *in limine* that none who had not valid arguments to bring forward on one side or the other would be allowed to address the meeting; a caution that proved necessary, for no fewer than four combatants had their utterances burked by him, because of their indulgence in vague declamation.'[6]

First spoke (writes Professor Farrar) a layman from Brompton, who gave his name as being one of the Committee of the (newly-formed) Economic section of the Association. He, in a stentorian voice, let off his theological venom. Then jumped up Richard Greswell with a thin voice, saying much the same, but speaking as a scholar; but we did not merely want any theological discussion, so we shouted them down. Then a Mr Dingle got up and tried to show that Darwin would have done much better if he had taken him into consultation. He used the blackboard and began a mathematical demonstration on the question – 'Let this point A be man, and let that point B be the mawnkey.' He got no further; he was shouted down with cries of 'mawnkey.' None of these had spoken more than three minutes. It was when these were shouted down that Henslow said he must demand that the discussion should rest on *scientific* grounds only.

Then there were calls for the Bishop, but he rose and said he understood his friend Professor Beale had something to say first. Beale, who was an excellent histologist,[a] spoke to the effect that the new theory ought to meet with fair discussion, but added, with great modesty, that he himself had not sufficient knowledge to discuss the subject adequately. Then the Bishop spoke the speech that you know, and the question about his mother being an ape, or his grandmother.

From the scientific point of view, the speech was of small value. It was evident from his mode of handling the subject that he had been 'crammed up to the throat,' and knew nothing at first hand; he used no argument beyond those to be found in his *Quarterly* article, which appeared a few days later, and is now admitted to have been inspired by Owen. 'He ridiculed Darwin badly[7] and Huxley savagely; but,' confesses one of his strongest opponents, 'all in such dulcet tones, so persuasive a manner, and in such well-turned periods, that I who had been inclined to blame the President for allowing a discussion that could serve no scientific purpose, now forgave him from the bottom of my heart.'[8]

The Bishop spoke thus 'for full half an hour with inimitable spirit, emptiness and unfairness.' 'In a light, scoffing tone, florid and fluent, he assured us there was nothing in the idea of evolution; rock-pigeons were what rock-pigeons had always been. Then, turning to his antagonist with a smiling insolence, he begged to know, was it through his grandfather or his grandmother that he claimed his descent from a monkey?'[9]

This was the fatal mistake of his speech. Huxley instantly grasped the tactical advantage which the descent to personalities gave him. He turned to Sir Benjamin Brodie, who was sitting beside him, and emphatically striking his hand upon his knee, exclaimed, 'The Lord hath delivered him into mine hands.' The bearing of the exclamation did not dawn upon Sir Benjamin until after Huxley had completed his 'forcible and eloquent' answer to the scientific part of the Bishop's argument, and proceeded to make his famous retort.[10]

On this (continues the writer in *Macmillan's Magazine*) Mr Huxley slowly and deliberately arose. A slight tall figure, stern and pale, very quiet and very grave, he stood

---

a. Histology is the science of organic tissue.

before us and spoke those tremendous words – words which no one seems sure of now, nor, I think, could remember just after they were spoken, for their meaning took away our breath, though it left us in no doubt as to what it was. He was not ashamed to have a monkey for his ancestor; but he would be ashamed to be connected with a man who used great gifts to obscure the truth. No one doubted his meaning, and the effect was tremendous. One lady fainted and had to be carried out; I, for one, jumped out of my seat.

The fullest and probably most accurate account of these concluding words is the following, from a letter of the late John Richard Green, then an undergraduate, to his friend, afterwards Professor Boyd Dawkins:–

I asserted – and I repeat – that a man has no reason to be ashamed of having an ape for his grandfather. If there were an ancestor whom I should feel shame in recalling it would rather be a *man* – a man of restless and versatile intellect – who, not content with an equivocal success in his own sphere of activity, plunges into scientific questions with which he has no real acquaintance, only to obscure them by an aimless rhetoric, and distract the attention of his hearers from the real point at issue by eloquent digressions and skilled appeals to religious prejudice.

Further, Mr A. G. Vernon-Harcourt, FRS, Reader in Chemistry at the University of Oxford, writes to me:–

The Bishop had rallied your father as to the descent from a monkey, asking as a sort of joke how recent this had been, whether it was his grandfather or further back. Your father, in replying on this point, first explained that the suggestion was of descent through thousands of generations from a common ancestor, and then went on to this effect – 'But if this question is treated, not as a matter for the calm investigation of science, but as a matter of sentiment, and if I am asked whether I would choose to be descended from the poor animal of low intelligence and stooping gait, who grins and chatters as we pass, or from a man, endowed with great ability and a splendid position, who should use these gifts' [here, as the point became clear, there was a great outburst of applause, which mostly drowned the end of the sentence] 'to discredit and crush humble seekers after truth, I hesitate what answer to make.'

No doubt your father's words were better than these, and they gained effect from his clear, deliberate utterance, but in outline and in *scale* this represents truly what was said.

After the commotion was over, 'some voices called for Hooker, and his name having been handed up, the President invited him to give his view of the theory from the Botanical side. This he did, demonstrating that the Bishop, by his own showing, had never grasped the principles of the "Origin," and that he was absolutely ignorant of the elements of botanical science. The Bishop made no reply, and the meeting broke up.'[11]

ACCOUNT OF THE OXFORD MEETING by the REV W. H. FREMANTLE (in *Charles Darwin, his Life Told*, &c., 1892, p. 238).

The Debate with Wilberforce

The Bishop of Oxford attacked Darwin, at first playfully, but at last in grim earnest. It was known that the Bishop had written an article against Darwin in the last *Quarterly Review*; it was also rumoured that Professor Owen had been staying at Cuddesdon and had primed the Bishop, who was to act as mouthpiece to the great Palæontologist, who did not himself dare to enter the lists. The Bishop, however, did not show himself master of the facts, and made one serious blunder. A fact which had been much dwelt on as confirmatory of Darwin's idea of variation, was that a sheep had been born shortly before in a flock in the North of England, having an addition of one to the vertebræ of the spine. The Bishop was declaring with rhetorical exaggeration that there was hardly any evidence on Darwin's side. 'What have they to bring forward?' he exclaimed. 'Some rumoured statement about a long-legged sheep.' But he passed on to banter: 'I should like to ask Professor Huxley, who is sitting by me, and is about to tear me to pieces when I have sat down, as to his belief in being descended from an ape. Is it on his grandfather's or his grandmother's side that the ape ancestry comes in?' And then taking a graver tone, he asserted, in a solemn peroration, that Darwin's views were contrary to the revelation of God in the Scriptures. Professor Huxley was unwilling to respond: but he was called for, and spoke with his usual incisiveness and with some scorn: 'I am here only in the interests of science,' he said, 'and I have not heard anything which can prejudice the case of my august client.' Then after showing how little competent the Bishop was to enter upon the discussion, he touched on the question of Creation. 'You say that development drives out the Creator; but you assert that God made you: and yet you know that you yourself were originally a little piece of matter, no bigger than the end of this gold pencil-case.' Lastly as to the descent from a monkey, he said: 'I should feel it no shame to have risen from such an origin; but I should feel it a shame to have sprung from one who prostituted the gifts of culture and eloquence to the service of prejudice and of falsehood.'

Many others spoke. Mr Gresley, an old Oxford don, pointed out that in human nature at least orderly development was not the necessary rule: Homer was the greatest of poets, but he lived 3000 years ago, and has not produced his like.

Admiral FitzRoy was present, and said he had often expostulated with his old comrade of the *Beagle* for entertaining views which were contradictory to the First Chapter of Genesis.

Sir John Lubbock declared that many of the arguments by which the permanence of species was supported came to nothing, and instanced some wheat which was said to have come off an Egyptian mummy, and was sent to him to prove that wheat had not changed since the time of the Pharaohs; but which proved to be made of French chocolate. Sir Joseph (then Dr) Hooker, spoke shortly, saying that he had found the hypothesis of Natural Selection so helpful in explaining the phenomena of his own subject of Botany, that he had been constrained to accept it. After a few words from Darwin's old friend, Professor Henslow, who occupied the chair, the meeting broke up, leaving the impression that those most capable of estimating the arguments of Darwin in detail saw their way to accept his conclusions.

Note. – Sir John Lubbock also insisted on the embryological evidence for evolution.   F.D.

T. H. Huxley to Francis Darwin (*ibid.*)   June 27, 1891

I should say that Fremantle's account is substantially correct, but that Green has the substance of my speech more accurately. However, I am certain I did not use the word 'equivocal.'

Thomas Henry Huxley (1825–1895)

The odd part of the business is, that I should not have been present except for Robert Chambers. I had heard of the Bishop's intention to utilise the occasion. I knew he had the reputation of being a first-class controversialist, and I was quite aware that if he played his cards properly, we should have little chance, with such an audience, of making an efficient defence. Moreover, I was very tired, and wanted to join my wife at her brother-in-law's country house near Reading, on the Saturday. On the Friday I met Chambers in the street, and in reply to some remark of his, about his going to the meeting, I said that I did not mean to attend it – did not see the good of giving up peace and quietness to be episcopally pounded. Chambers broke out into vehement remonstrances, and talked about my deserting them. So I said, 'Oh! if you are going to take it that way, I'll come and have my share of what is going on.'

So I came, and chanced to sit near old Sir Benjamin Brodie. The Bishop began his speech, and to my astonishment very soon showed that he was so ignorant that he did not know how to manage his own case. My spirits rose proportionately, and when he turned to me with his insolent question, I said to Sir Benjamin, in an undertone, 'The Lord hath delivered him into mine hands.'

That sagacious old gentleman stared at me as if I had lost my senses. But, in fact, the Bishop had justified the severest retort I could devise, and I made up my mind to let him have it. I was careful, however, not to rise to reply until the meeting called for me – then I let myself go.

In justice to the Bishop, I am bound to say he bore no malice, but was always courtesy itself when we occasionally met in after years. Hooker and I walked away from the meeting together, and I remember saying to him that this experience had changed my opinion as to the practical value of the art of public speaking, and that from that time forth I should carefully cultivate it, and try to leave off hating it. I did the former, but never quite succeeded in the latter effort.

I did not mean to trouble you with such a long scrawl when I began about this piece of ancient history. – Ever yours very faithfully,   T. H. HUXLEY.

In the evening there was a crowded conversazione in Dr Daubeny's rooms, and here, continues the writer in *Macmillan's*, 'every one was eager to congratulate the hero of the day. I remember that some naïve person wished "it could come over again"; Mr Huxley, with the look on his face of the victor who feels the cost of victory, put us aside saying, "Once in a lifetime is enough, if not too much."'

In a letter to me the same writer remarks –

I gathered from Mr Huxley's look when I spoke to him at Dr Daubeny's that he was not quite satisfied to have been forced to take so personal a tone – it a little jarred upon his fine taste. But it was the Bishop who first struck the insolent note of personal attack.

Again, with reference to the state of feeling at the meeting:–

I never saw such a display of fierce party spirit, the looks of bitter hatred which the audience bestowed (I mean the majority) on us who were on your father's side; as we passed through the crowd we felt that we were expected to say 'how abominably the Bishop was treated'– or to be considered outcasts and detestable.

It was very different, however, at Dr Daubeny's, 'where,' says the writer of the account in *Darwin's Life*, 'the almost sole topic was the battle of the "Origin," and I was much struck with the fair and unprejudiced way in which the black coats and white cravats of Oxford discussed the question, and the frankness with which they offered their congratulations to the winners in the combat.'

The result of this encounter, though a check to the other side, cannot, of course, be represented as an immediate and complete triumph for evolutionary doctrine. This was precluded by the character and temper of the audience, most of whom were less capable of being convinced by the arguments than shocked by the boldness of the retort, although, being gentlefolk, as Professor Farrar remarks, they were disposed to admit on reflection that the Bishop had erred on the score of taste and good manners. Nevertheless, it was a noticeable feature of the occasion, Sir M. Foster tells me, that when Huxley rose he was received coldly, just a cheer of encouragement from his friends, the audience as a whole not joining in it. But as he made his points the applause grew and widened, until, when he sat down, the cheering was not very much less than that given to the Bishop. To that extent he carried an unwilling audience with him by the force of his speech. The debate on the ape question, however, was continued elsewhere during the next two years, and the evidence was completed by the unanswerable demonstrations of Sir W. H. Flower at the Cambridge meeting of the Association in 1862.

The importance of the Oxford meeting lay in the open resistance that was made to authority, at a moment when even a drawn battle was hardly less effectual than acknowledged victory. Instead of being crushed under ridicule, the new theories secured a hearing, all the wider, indeed, for the startling nature of their defence.

7. Charles Darwin, The Descent of Man and Selection in Relation to Sex (1871), Chapter 21, 'General Summary and Conclusion'

pp. 385-405

As we have seen, the *Origin* hinted at man's inclusion in Darwin's evolutionary theory, and both critics and supporters were not slow to seize on the hint. But Darwin waited until 1871 to make public his views on the matter. He had in a sense been anticipated by the publications of his friends Huxley and Lyell. Huxley's *Man's Place in Nature* and Lyell's *Antiquity of Man* both came out in 1863. Huxley, continuing and developing his argument with Wilberforce and Owen, had shown the near physical resemblance between man and the apes: 'the proposition holds good, that the differences between Man and the Gorilla are of smaller value than those between the Gorilla and some other Apes' (*Collected Essays* (1893–4), vol. 7, p. III). Lyell had established that fossil remains of men were deposited at the same time as those of some extinct animals, thus disposing of the theory that man had only been created after the last 'catastrophe'. He had also given rather half-hearted and tentative support to Darwin's hypothesis. It was now up to Darwin to apply his theory of natural selection to the evolution of man. But this is just where the difficulty lay: to start with, Darwin himself had come increasingly to doubt the unaided power of natural selection, and a large part of the *Descent* is devoted to discussing a quite different mechanism, *sexual* selection. Sexual selection means the selection of mates by individual animals: the preference for particular variations could cause them to become inherited, at the expense of characteristics that were not attractive to the other sex. This process would account for characteristics that were of no use or survival value to the species – such characteristics could not be accounted for under natural selection. Darwin also placed increasing emphasis on Lamarckian causes – the effects of use and disuse, and the direct action of the environment. Especially in relation to man, natural selection seemed an inadequate cause. While most educated people had by now accepted that man was *physically* descended from the animals, difficulties arose in accounting for his mental, moral and religious faculties, as well as the particular problem of his immortal soul.

These problems had exercised Wallace, the co-discoverer of natural selection, and he concluded that natural selection *could not* account for man's development. Particular arguments used by Wallace were the fact that the size and capabilities of the human brain would have been of no use to man's savage ancestors, just as they were not used by present-day savages; and the fact that artistic talents were of no survival value, so how had they developed? Wallace maintained that 'Neither natural selection nor the more general theory of evolution can give any account whatever of the origin of sensational or conscious life . . . we may go even further, and maintain that there are certain purely physical characteristics of the human race which are not explicable on the theory of variation and survival of the fittest' (*Quarterly Review* (1869), pp. 391–3). In Wallace's view, some special guiding power was needed to account for man's evolution. Wallace became a spiritualist, joining the number of Victorians who were converted away from a purely scientific view of the world because of its inability to explain psychic and spiritual phenomena. Another important critic of the extension of Darwin's theory to include man, was St George Mivart, the Catholic biologist, who reviewed the *Descent* unfavourably in the *Quarterly*. He accepted man's physical evolution from the animals, but insisted that God must have intervened for the creation of man's soul. He was also a perceptive critic of natural selection as an adequate explanation for evolution – in his book, *On the Genesis of Species* (1871) he had put forward his own theory, involving an 'internal innate force', which produced new species suddenly as a whole.

Not only were the mental, moral and spiritual faculties of man difficulties for any evolutionary explanation of his origin, but they were of course extremely sensitive issues as far as religion was concerned. The way that Darwin dealt with these issues in the *Descent* could not but give offence to the religious. He took a reductive approach, arguing that these 'higher' faculties were evolved from animal instincts, from which they were only different in degree, not in kind. Thus for instance religious feelings were derived from the sort of feelings a dog has towards his master. To support this contention, Darwin put forward many quaint incidents of animals displaying 'moral' or 'intellectual' qualities – heroic monkeys, self-sacrificing gorillas, and intelligent dogs. Such instincts would become inherited and would develop if they possessed survival value for the species in any way. Thus Darwin derives morality from the social instinct, which helped to preserve the tribe as a whole. Not only does this approach close the gap between man and the other animals, depriving him of the special status of being made in God's image, it also reduces the absolute authority of moral and religious beliefs. Such beliefs are only valid in so far as they contributed to the survival of particular groups: to do this, they need not be in any way perfect, nor need they correspond with any objective reality. The fact that they are innate does not prove that they are true, only that they were useful in the past. Darwin himself saw this relativistic view as subversive of his own religious belief: having said in his *Autobiography* that he sometimes feels 'compelled to look to a First Cause having an intelligent mind', he goes on,

> But then arises the doubt – can the mind of man, which has, as I fully believe, been developed from a mind as low as that possessed by the lowest animal, be trusted when it draws such grand conclusions? May not these be the result of the connection between cause and effect which strikes us as a necessary one, but probably depends merely on inherited experience? Nor must we overlook the probability of the constant inculcation of a belief in God on the minds of children producing so strong and perhaps an inherited effect on their brains, not as yet fully developed, that it would be as difficult for them to throw off their belief in God, as for a monkey to throw off its instinctive fear and hatred of a snake. I cannot pretend to throw the least light on such abstruse problems. The mystery of the beginning of all things is insoluble by us; and I for one am content to remain an agnostic. (p. 54)

The revulsion felt by religious people to Darwin's argument in the *Descent* is well expressed by a writer in the *British and Foreign Evangelical Review*:

> We do not see how to reconcile with our Christian faith the hypothesis . . . that our moral sense is no better than an instinct like that which rules the beaver or the bee; that He whom we have been accustomed to regard as the Creator of all things, is a creature of our imagination, and that our religious ideas are a devel-

opment from the dreams and fears of anthropomorphous apes. (21 (1872), p. 31)

Chapter XXI
General Summary and Conclusion

Main conclusion that man is descended from some lower form – Manner of development – Genealogy of man – Intellectual and moral faculties – Sexual selection – Concluding remarks.

A brief summary will here be sufficient to recall to the reader's mind the more salient points in this work. Many of the views which have been advanced are highly speculative, and some no doubt will prove erroneous; but I have in every case given the reasons which have led me to one view rather than to another. It seemed worth while to try how far the principle of evolution would throw light on some of the more complex problems in the natural history of man. False facts are highly injurious to the progress of science, for they often long endure; but false views, if supported by some evidence, do little harm, as every one takes a salutary pleasure in proving their falseness; and when this is done, one path towards error is closed and the road to truth is often at the same time opened.[1]

The main conclusion arrived at in this work, and now held by many naturalists who are well competent to form a sound judgment, is that man is descended from some less highly organised form. The grounds upon which this conclusion rests will never be shaken, for the close similarity between man and the lower animals in embryonic development, as well as in innumerable points of structure and constitution, both of high and of the most trifling importance, – the rudiments which he retains, and the abnormal reversions to which he is occasionally liable, – are facts which cannot be disputed. They have long been known, but until recently they told us nothing with respect to the origin of man. Now when viewed by the light of our knowledge of the whole organic world, their meaning is unmistakeable. The great principle of evolution stands up clear and firm, when these groups of facts are considered in connection with others, such as the mutual affinities of the members of the same group, their geographical distribution in past and present times, and their geological succession. It is incredible that all these facts should speak falsely. He who is not content to look, like a savage, at the phenomena of nature as disconnected, cannot any longer believe that man is the work of a separate act of creation. He will be forced to admit that the close resemblance of the embryo of man to that, for instance, of a dog – the construction of his skull, limbs, and whole frame, independently of the uses to which the parts may be put, on the same plan with that of other mammals – the occasional re-appearance of various structures, for instance of several distinct muscles, which man does not normally possess, but which are common to the Quadrumana – and a crowd of analogous facts – all point in the plainest manner to the conclusion that man is the co-descendant with other mammals of a common progenitor.

We have seen that man incessantly presents individual differences in all parts of his body and in his mental faculties. These differences or variations seem to be induced by the same general causes, and to obey the same laws as with the lower animals. In both cases similar laws of inheritance prevail. Man tends to increase at a greater rate than his means of subsistence; consequently he is occasionally subjected to a severe struggle for existence, and natural selection will have effected whatever lies within its scope. A succession of strongly-marked variations of a similar nature are by no means requisite; slight fluctuating differences in the individual suffice for the work of natural selection. We may feel assured that the inherited effects of the long-continued use or disuse of parts will have done much in the same direction with natural selection. Modifications formerly of importance, though no longer of any special use, will be long inherited. When one part is modified, other parts will change through the principle of correlation, of which we have instances in many curious cases of correlated monstrosities. Something may be attributed to the direct and definite action of the surrounding condi-tions of life, such as abundant food, heat, or moisture; and lastly, many characters of slight physiological importance, some indeed of considerable importance, have been gained through sexual selection.[2]

No doubt man, as well as every other animal, presents structures, which as far as we can judge with our little knowledge, are not now of any service to him, nor have been so during any former period of his existence, either in relation to his general conditions of life, or of one sex to the other. Such structures cannot be accounted for by any form of selection, or by the inherited effects of the use and disuse of parts. We know, however, that many strange and strongly-marked peculiarities of structure occasionally appear in our domesticated productions, and if the unknown causes which produce them were to act more uniformly, they would probably become common to all the individuals of the species. We may hope hereafter to understand something about the causes of such occasional modifications, especially through the study of monstrosities: hence the labours of experimentalists, such as those of M. Camille Dareste,[3] are full of promise for the future. In the greater number of cases we can only say that the cause of each slight variation and of each monstrosity lies much more in the nature of constitution of the organism, than in the nature of the surrounding conditions; though new and changed conditions certainly play an important part in exciting organic changes of all kinds.

Through the means just specified, aided perhaps by others as yet undiscovered, man has been raised to his present state. But since he attained to the rank of manhood, he has diverged into distinct races, or as they may be more appropriately called sub-species. Some of these, for instance the Negro and European, are so distinct that, if specimens had been brought to a naturalist without any further information, they would undoubtedly have been considered by him as good and true species. Nevertheless all the races agree in so many unimportant details of structure and in so many mental peculiarities, that these can be accounted for only through inheritance from a common progenitor; and a progenitor thus characterised would probably have deserved to rank as man.

It must not be supposed that the divergence of each race from the other races, and of all the races from a common stock, can be traced back to any one pair of progenitors. On the contrary, at every stage in the process of modification, all the individuals which were in any way best fitted for their conditions of life, though in different degrees, would have survived in greater numbers than the less well fitted. The process would have been like that followed by man, when he does not intentionally select particular individuals, but breeds from all the superior and neglects all the inferior individuals. He thus slowly but surely modifies his stock, and unconsciously forms a new strain. So with respect to modifications, acquired independently of selection, and due to variations arising from the nature of the organism and the action of the surrounding conditions, or from changed habits of life, no single pair will have been modified in a much greater degree than the other pairs which inhabit the same country, for all will have been continually blended through free intercrossing.

By considering the embryological structure of man, – the homologies which he presents with the lower animals, – the rudiments which he retains, – and the reversions to which he is liable, we can partly recall in imagination the former condition of our early progenitors; and can approximately place them in their proper position in the zoological series. We thus learn that man is descended from a hairy quadruped, furnished with a tail and pointed ears, probably arboreal in its habits, and an inhabitant of the Old World.[4] This creature, if its whole structure had been examined by a naturalist, would have been classed amongst the Quadrumana, as surely as would the common and still more ancient progenitor of the Old and New World monkeys. The Quadrumana and all the higher mammals are probably derived from an ancient marsupial animal, and this through a long line of diversified forms, either from some reptile-like or some amphibian-like creature, and this again from some fish-like animal. In the dim obscurity of the past we can see that the early progenitor of all the Vertebrata must have been an aquatic animal, provided with branchiæ, with the two sexes united in the same individual, and with the most important organs of the body (such as the brain and heart) imperfectly developed. This animal seems to have been more like the larvæ of our existing marine Ascidians than any other known form.

The greatest difficulty which presents itself, when we are driven to the above conclusion on the origin of man, is the high standard of intellectual power and of moral disposition which he has attained. But every one who admits the general principle of evolution, must see that the mental powers of the higher animals, which are the same in kind with those of mankind, though so different in degree, are capable of advancement.[5] Thus the interval between the mental powers of one of the higher apes and of a fish, or between those of an ant and scale-insect, is immense. The development of these powers in animals does not offer any special difficulty; for with our domesticated animals, the mental faculties are certainly variable, and the variations are inherited. No one doubts that these faculties are of the utmost importance to animals in a state of nature. Therefore the conditions are favourable for their development through natural selection. The same conclusion may be extended to man; the intellect must have been all-important to him, even at a very remote period, enabling him to use language, to invent and make weapons, tools, traps, &c.; by which means, in combination with his social habits, he long ago became the most dominant of all living creatures.

A great stride in the development of the intellect will have followed, as soon as, through a previous considerable advance, the half-art and half-instinct of language came into use; for the continued use of language will have reacted on the brain, and produced an inherited effect; and this again will have reacted on the improvement of language. The large size of the brain in man, in comparison with that of the lower animals, relatively to the size of their bodies, may be attributed in chief part, as Mr Chauncey Wright has well remarked,[6] to the early use of some simple form of language, – that wonderful engine which affixes signs to all sorts of objects and qualities, and excites trains of thought which would never arise from the mere impression of the senses, and if they did arise could not be followed out. The higher intellectual powers of man, such as those of ratiocination, abstraction, self-consciousness, &c., will have followed from the continued improvement of other mental faculties; but without considerable culture of the mind, both in the race and in the individual, it is doubtful whether these high powers would be exercised, and thus fully attained.

The development of the moral qualities is a more interesting and difficult problem.[7] Their foundation lies in the social instincts, including in this term the family ties. These instincts are of a highly complex nature, and in the case of the lower animals give special tendencies towards certain definite actions; but the more important elements for us are love, and the distinct emotion of sympathy. Animals endowed with the social instincts take pleasure in each other's company, warn each other of danger, defend and aid each other in many ways. These instincts are not extended to all the individuals of the species, but only to those of the same community. As they are highly beneficial to the species, they have in all probability been acquired through natural selection.

A moral being is one who is capable of comparing his past and future actions and motives, – of approving of some and disapproving of others; and the fact that man is the one being who with certainty can be thus designated makes the greatest of all distinctions between him and the lower animals. But in our third chapter I have endeavoured to shew that the moral sense follows, firstly, from the enduring and always present nature of the social instincts, in which respect man agrees with the lower animals; and secondly, from his mental faculties being highly active and his impressions of past events extremely vivid, in which respects he differs from the lower animals. Owing to this condition of mind, man cannot avoid looking backwards and comparing the impressions of past events and actions. He also continually looks forward. Hence after some temporary desire or passion has mastered his social instincts, he will reflect and compare the now weakened impression of such past impulses, with the ever present social instinct; and he will then feel that sense of dissatisfaction which all unsatisfied instincts leave behind them. Consequently he resolves to act differently for the future – and this is conscience. Any instinct which is permanently stronger or more enduring than another, gives rise to a feeling which we express by saying that it ought to be obeyed. A pointer dog, if able to reflect on his past conduct, would say to himself, I ought (as indeed we say of him) to have pointed at that hare and not have yielded to the passing temptation of hunting it.

Social animals are partly impelled by a wish to aid the members of the same community in a general manner, but more commonly to perform certain definite actions. Man is impelled by the same general wish to aid his fellows, but has few or no special instincts. He differs also from the lower animals in being able to express his desires by words, which thus become the guide to the aid required and bestowed. The motive to give aid is likewise somewhat modified in man: it no longer consists solely of a blind instinctive impulse, but is largely influenced by the praise or blame of his fellow men. Both the appreciation and the bestowal of praise and blame rest on sympathy; and this emotion, as we have seen, is one of the most important elements of the social instincts. Sympathy, though gained as an instinct, is also much strengthened by exercise or habit. As all men desire their own happiness, praise or blame is bestowed on actions and motives, according as they lead to this end; and as happiness is an essential part of the general good, the greatest-happiness principle indirectly serves as a nearly safe standard of right and wrong. As the reasoning powers advance and experience is gained, the more remote effects of certain lines of conduct on the character of the individual, and on the general good, are perceived; and then the self-regarding virtues, from coming within the scope of public opinion, receive praise, and their opposites receive blame. But with the less civilised nations reason often errs, and many bad customs and base superstitions come within the same scope, and consequently are esteemed as high virtues, and their breach as heavy crimes.

The moral faculties are generally esteemed, and with justice, as of higher value than the intellectual powers. But we should always bear in mind that the activity of the mind in vividly recalling past impressions is one of the fundamental though secondary bases of conscience. This fact affords the strongest argument for educating and stimulating in all possible ways the intellectual faculties of every human being. No doubt a man with a torpid mind, if his social affections and sympathies are well developed, will be led to good actions, and may have a fairly sensitive conscience. But whatever renders the imagination of men more vivid and strengthens the habit of recalling and comparing past impressions, will make the conscience more sensitive, and may even compensate to a certain extent for weak social affections and sympathies.

The moral nature of man has reached the highest standard as yet attained, partly through the advancement of the reasoning powers and consequently of a just public opinion, but especially through the sympathies being rendered more tender and widely diffused through the effects of habit, example, instruction, and reflection. It is not improbable that virtuous tendencies may through long practice be inherited. With the more civilised races, the conviction of the existence of an all-seeing Deity has had a potent influence on the advancement of morality. Ultimately man no longer accepts the praise or blame of his fellows as his chief guide, though few escape this influence, but his habitual convictions controlled by reason afford him the safest rule. His conscience then becomes his supreme judge and monitor. Nevertheless the first foundation or origin of the moral sense lies in the social instincts, including sympathy; and these instincts no doubt were primarily gained, as in the case of the lower animals, through natural selection.

The belief in God has often been advanced as not only the greatest, but the most complete of all the distinctions between man and the lower animals. It is however impossible, as we have seen, to maintain that this belief is innate or instinctive in man. On the other hand a belief in all-pervading spiritual agencies seems to be universal; and apparently follows from a considerable advance in the reasoning powers of man, and from a still greater advance in his faculties of imagination, curiosity and wonder. I am aware that the assumed instinctive belief in God has been used by many persons as an argument for His existence. But this is a rash argument, as we should thus be compelled to believe in the existence of many cruel and malignant spirits, possessing only a little more power than man; for the belief in them is far more general than of a beneficent Deity. The idea of a universal and beneficent Creator of the universe does not seem to arise in the mind of man, until he has been elevated by long-continued culture.

He who believes in the advancement of man from some lowly-organised form, will naturally ask how does this bear on the belief in the immortality of the soul. The barbarous races of man, as Sir J.

Lubbock[8] has shewn, possess no clear belief of this kind; but arguments derived from the primeval beliefs of savages are, as we have just seen, of little or no avail. Few persons feel any anxiety from the impossibility of determining at what precise period in the development of the individual, from the first trace of the minute germinal vesicle to the child either before or after birth, man becomes an immortal being; and there is no greater cause for anxiety because the period in the gradually ascending organic scale cannot possibly be determined.

I am aware that the conclusions arrived at in this work will be denounced by some as highly irreligious; but he who thus denounces them is bound to shew why it is more irreligious to explain the origin of man as a distinct species by descent from some lower form, through the laws of variation and natural selection, than to explain the birth of the individual through the laws of ordinary reproduction. The birth both of the species and of the individual are equally parts of that grand sequence of events, which our minds refuse to accept as the result of blind chance. The understanding revolts at such a conclusion, whether or not we are able to believe that every slight variation of structure, – the union of each pair in marriage, – the dissemination of each seed, – and other such events, have all been ordained for some special purpose.

Sexual selection has been treated at great length in these volumes; for, as I have attempted to shew, it has played an important part in the history of the organic world. As summaries have been given to each chapter, it would be superfluous here to add a detailed summary. I am aware that much remains doubtful, but I have endeavoured to give a fair view of the whole case. In the lower divisions of the animal kingdom, sexual selection seems to have done nothing: such animals are often affixed for life to the same spot, or have the two sexes combined in the same individual, or what is still more important, their perceptive and intellectual facilities are not sufficiently advanced to allow of the feelings of love and jealousy, or of the exertion of choice. When, however, we come to the Arthropoda and Vertebrata, even to the lowest classes in these two great Sub-Kingdoms, sexual selection has effected much; and it deserves notice that we here find the intellectual faculties developed, but in two very distinct lines, to the highest standard, namely in the Hymenoptera (ants, bees, &c.) amongst the Arthropoda, and in the Mammalia, including man, amongst the Vertebrata.

In the most distinct classes of the animal kingdom, with mammals, birds, reptiles, fishes, insects, and even crustaceans, the differences between the sexes follow almost exactly the same rules. The males are almost always the wooers; and they alone are armed with special weapons for fighting with their rivals. They are generally stronger and larger than the females, and are endowed with the requisite qualities of courage and pugnacity. They are provided, either exclusively or in a much higher degree than the females, with organs for producing vocal or instrumental music, and with odoriferous glands. They are ornamented with infinitely diversified appendages, and with the most brilliant or conspicuous colours, often arranged in elegant patterns, whilst the females are left unadorned. When the sexes differ in more important structures, it is the male which is provided with special sense-organs for discovering the female, with locomotive organs for reaching her, and often with prehensile organs for holding her. These various structures for securing or charming the female are often developed in the male during only part of the year, namely the breeding season. They have in many cases been transferred in a greater or less degree to the females; and in the latter case they appear in her as mere rudiments. They are lost by the males after emasculation. Generally they are not developed in the male during early youth, but appear a short time before the age for reproduction. Hence in most cases the young of both sexes resemble each other; and the female resembles her young offspring throughout life. In almost every great class a few anomalous cases occur in which there has been an almost complete transposition of the characters proper to the two sexes; the females assuming characters which properly belong to the males. This surprising uniformity in the laws regulating the differences between the sexes in so many and such widely separated classes, is intelligible if we admit the action throughout all the higher divisions of the animal kingdom of one common cause, namely sexual selection.

Sexual selection depends on the success of certain individuals over others of the same sex in relation to the propagation of the species; whilst natural selection depends on the success of both sexes, at all ages, in relation to the general conditions of life. The sexual struggle is of two kinds; in the one it is between the individuals of the same sex, generally the male sex, in order to drive away or kill their rivals, the females remaining passive; whilst in the other, the struggle is likewise between the individuals of the same sex, in order to excite or charm those of the opposite sex, generally the females, which no longer remain passive, but select the more agreeable partners. This latter kind of selection is closely analogous to that which man unin-

tentionally, yet effectually, brings to bear on his domesticated productions, when he continues for a long time choosing the most
pleasing or useful individuals, without any wish to modify the
breed.

The laws of inheritance determine whether characters gained
through sexual selection by either sex shall be transmitted to the
same sex, or to both sexes; as well as the age at which they shall be
developed. It appears that variations which arise late in life are
commonly transmitted to one and the same sex. Variability is the
necessary basis for the action of selection, and is wholly independent
of it. It follows from this, that variations of the same general nature
have often been taken advantage of and accumulated through sexual
selection in relation to the propagation of the species, and through
natural selection in relation to the general purposes of life. Hence
secondary sexual characters, when equally transmitted to both sexes,
can be distinguished from ordinary specific characters only by the
light of analogy. The modifications acquired through sexual selection are often so strongly pronounced that the two sexes have frequently been ranked as distinct species, or even as distinct genera.
Such strongly-marked differences must be in some manner highly
important; and we know that they have been acquired in some
instances at the cost not only of inconvenience, but of exposure to
actual danger.

The belief in the power of sexual selection rests chiefly on the
following considerations. The characters which we have the best
reason for supposing to have been thus acquired are confined to one
sex; and this alone renders it probable that they are in some way
connected with the act of reproduction. These characters in innumerable instances are fully developed only at maturity; and often
during only a part of the year, which is always the breeding-season.
The males (passing over a few exceptional cases) are the most active
in courtship; they are the best armed, and are rendered the most
attractive in various ways. It is to be especially observed that the
males display their attractions with elaborate care in the presence of
the females; and that they rarely or never display them excepting
during the season of love. It is incredible that all this display should
be purposeless. Lastly we have distinct evidence with some
quadrupeds and birds that the individuals of the one sex are capable
of feeling a strong antipathy or preference for certain individuals of
the opposite sex.

Bearing these facts in mind, and not forgetting the marked results
of man's unconscious selection, it seems to me almost certain that if

the individuals of one sex were during a long series of generations to prefer pairing with certain individuals of the other sex, characterised in some peculiar manner, the offspring would slowly but surely become modified in this same manner. I have not attempted to conceal that, excepting when the males are more numerous than the females, or when polygamy prevails, it is doubtful how the more attractive males succeed in leaving a larger number of offspring to inherit their superiority in ornaments or other charms than the less attractive males; but I have shewn that this would probably follow from the females, – especially the more vigorous females which would be the first to breed, preferring not only the more attractive but at the same time the more vigorous and victorious males.

Although we have some positive evidence that birds appreciate bright and beautiful objects, as with the Bower-birds of Australia, and although they certainly appreciate the power of song, yet I fully admit that it is an astonishing fact that the females of many birds and some mammals should be endowed with sufficient taste for what has apparently been effected through sexual selection; and this is even more astonishing in the case of reptiles, fish, and insects. But we really know very little about the minds of the lower animals. It cannot be supposed that male Birds of Paradise or Peacocks, for instance, should take so much pains in erecting, spreading, and vibrating their beautiful plumes before the females for no purpose. We should remember the fact given on excellent authority in a former chapter, namely that several peahens, when debarred from an admired male, remained widows during a whole season rather than pair with another bird.

Nevertheless I know of no fact in natural history more wonderful than that the female Argus pheasant should be able to appreciate the exquisite shading of the ball-and-socket ornaments and the elegant patterns on the wing-feathers of the male. He who thinks that the male was created as he now exists must admit that the great plumes, which prevent the wings from being used for flight, and which, as well as the primary feathers, are displayed in a manner quite peculiar to this one species during the act of courtship, and at no other time, were given to him as an ornament. If so, he must likewise admit that the female was created and endowed with the capacity of appreciating such ornaments. I differ only in the conviction that the male Argus pheasant acquired his beauty gradually, through the females having preferred during many generations the more highly ornamented males; the æsthetic capacity of the females having been advanced through exercise or habit in the same manner as our own taste is gradually improved. In the male, through the fortunate chance of a few feathers not having been modified, we can distinctly see how simple spots with a little fulvous shading on one side might have been developed by small and graduated steps into the wonderful ball-and-socket ornaments; and it is probable that they were actually thus developed.

Everyone who admits the principle of evolution, and yet feels great difficulty in admitting that female mammals, birds, reptiles, and fish, could have acquired the high standard of taste which is implied by the beauty of males, and which generally coincides with our own standard, should reflect that in each member of the vertebrates series the nerve-cells of the brain are the direct offshoots of those possessed by the common progenitor of the whole group. It thus becomes intelligible that the brain and mental faculties should be capable under similar conditions of nearly the same course of development, and consequently of performing nearly the same functions.

The reader who has taken the trouble to go through the several chapters devoted to sexual selection, will be able to judge how far the conclusions at which I have arrived are supported by sufficient evidence. If he accepts these conclusions, he may, I think, safely extend them to mankind; but it would be superfluous here to repeat what I have so lately said on the manner in which sexual selection has apparently acted on both the male and female side, causing the two sexes of man to differ in body and mind, and the several races to differ from each other in various characters, as well as from their ancient and lowly-organised progenitors.

He who admits the principle of sexual selection will be led to the remarkable conclusion that the cerebral system not only regulates most of the existing functions of the body, but has indirectly influenced the progressive development of various bodily structures and of certain mental qualities. Courage, pugnacity, perseverance, strength and size of body, weapons of all kinds, musical organs, both vocal and instrumental, bright colours, stripes and marks, and ornamental appendages, have all been indirectly gained by the one sex or the other, through the influence of love and jealousy, through the appreciation of the beautiful in sound, colour or form, and through the exertion of a choice; and these powers of the mind manifestly depend on the development of the cerebral system.

Man scans with scrupulous care the character and pedigree of his horses, cattle, and dogs before he matches them; but when he comes to his own marriage he rarely, or never, takes any such care. He is impelled by nearly the same motives as are the lower animals when left to their own free choice, though he is in so far superior to them that he highly values mental charms and virtues. On the other hand he is strongly attracted by mere wealth or rank. Yet he might by selection do something not only for the bodily constitution and frame of his offspring, but for their intellectual and moral qualities. Both sexes ought to refrain from marriage if in any marked degree inferior in body or mind; but such hopes are Utopian and will never be even partially realised until the laws of inheritance are thoroughly known. All do good service who aid towards this end. When the principles of breeding and of inheritance are better-understood, we shall not hear ignorant members of our legislature rejecting with scorn a plan for ascertaining by an easy method whether or not consanguineous marriages are injurious to man.

The advancement of the welfare of mankind is a most intricate problem: all ought to refrain from marriage who cannot avoid abject poverty for their children;[9] for poverty is not only a great evil, but tends to its own increase by leading to recklessness in marriage. On the other hand, as Mr Galton[10] has remarked, if the prudent avoid marriage, whilst the reckless marry, the inferior members will tend to supplant the better members of society. Man, like every other animal, has no doubt advanced to his present high condition through a struggle for existence consequent on his rapid multiplication; and if he is to advance still higher he must remain subject to a severe struggle. Otherwise he would soon sink into indolence, and the more highly-gifted men would not be more successful in the battle of life than the less gifted. Hence our natural rate of increase, though leading to many and obvious evils, must not be greatly diminished by any means. There should be open competition for all men; and the most able should not be prevented by laws or customs from succeeding best and rearing the largest number of offspring. Important as the struggle for existence has been and even still is, yet as far as the highest part of man's nature is concerned there are other agencies more important. For the moral qualities are advanced, either directly or indirectly, much more through the effects of habit, the reasoning powers, instruction, religion, &c., than through natural selection;[11] though to this latter agency the social instincts, which afforded the basis for the development of the moral sense, may be safely attributed.

The main conclusion arrived at in this work, namely that man is descended from some lowly-organised form, will, I regret to think, be highly distasteful to many persons. But there can hardly be a doubt that we are descended from barbarians. The astonishment which I felt on first seeing a party of Fuegians on a wild and broken shore will never be forgotten by me, for the reflection at once rushed into my mind – such were our ancestors. These men were absolutely naked and bedaubed with paint, their long hair was tangled, their mouths frothed with excitement, and their expression was wild, startled, and distrustful. They possessed hardly any arts, and like wild animals lived on what they could catch; they had no government, and were merciless to every one not of their own small tribe. He who has seen a savage in his native land will not feel much shame, if forced to acknowledge that the blood of some more humble creature flows in his veins. For my own part I would as soon be descended from that heroic little monkey, who braved his dreaded enemy in order to save the life of his keeper; or from that old baboon, who, descending from the mountains, carried away in triumph his young comrade from a crowd of astonished dogs[12] – as from a savage who delights to torture his enemies, offers up bloody sacrifices, practices infanticide without remorse, treats his wives like slaves, knows no decency, and is haunted by the grossest superstitions.

Man may be excused for feeling some pride at having risen, though not through his own exertions, to the very summit of the organic scale; and the fact of his having thus risen, instead of having been aboriginally placed there, may give him hopes for a still higher destiny in the distant future. But we are not here concerned with hopes or fears, only with the truth as far as our reason allows us to discover it. I have given the evidence to the best of my ability; and we must acknowledge, as it seems to me, that man with all his noble qualities, with sympathy which feels for the most debased, with benevolence which extends not only to other men but to the humblest living creature, with his god-like intellect which has penetrated into the movements and constitution of the solar system – with all these exalted powers – Man still bears in his bodily frame the indelible stamp of his lowly origin.

8. John Tyndall, 'The Belfast Address', Nature, 20 August 1874

pp. 315–19

Tyndall's Presidential Address to the British Association meeting in Belfast in 1874 is in many ways more important than the Huxley/Wilberforce clash in 1860. Huxley was merely trying to secure a fair hearing for Darwin's theory, from churchmen and scientists who were opposed to it. Tyndall was making sweeping claims for science as such, which he presents as providing a complete 'materialistic' explanation of the whole physical world and its origins. In the first half of the Address, Tyndall had set up a 'conflict' model of the relations between science and religion. He surveys the history of science as he sees it, starting promisingly with the Greeks, but later stifled by theology:

> It was a time when thought had become abject, and when the acceptance of mere authority led, as it always does in science, to intellectual death. Natural events, instead of being traced to physical, were referred to moral causes; while an exercise of the phantasy, almost as degrading as the spiritualism of the present day, took the place of scientific speculation. (p. 310)

Religious thought is seen as retarding scientific thought, completely ignoring the huge debt that nineteenth-century science owed to natural theology. Tyndall presents intellectual history as a battle between the dark and the light, theology and science: in this he was influenced by Draper's *The Intellectual Development of Europe* (1862), one of the sources of the 'warfare' myth of the relations between science and religion (see endnote 5, p. 234).

Tyndall's large claims for science rest partly on Darwin's theory, but he also introduces other theories to make the area of scientific explanation more complete: atomic theory, the conservation of energy, and Herbert Spencer's theories of psychology. Spencer had developed and strengthened the mechanical 'associationist' psychology of Hartley, by accounting for 'innate' ideas on an evolutionary theory of inherited instinct. Thus Tyndall's science can present a continuous material process from the smallest atoms up to human mental activity. There are of course two areas of difficulty in this continuum: the leap from inorganic to organic matter, and the leap from matter to consciousness. Though Tyndall had performed many experiments to disprove spontaneous generation, nevertheless he insists on tracing the origin of life beyond the 'primordial form' that Darwin spoke of, to inorganic matter, in which he finds 'the promise and potency of every form and quality of life'. As to the evolution of consciousness, and its connection to matter, here Tyndall concedes there is an insoluble mystery, though he insists that mind *depends* on matter. In the first half of the Address, he had set up an imaginary debate between the eighteenth-century natural theologian Bishop Butler, and a disciple of the materialist philosopher Lucretius, which the Bishop won, declaring that 'You cannot satisfy the human understanding in its demand for logical continuity between molecular processes and the phenomena of consciousness. This is a rock on which materialism must inevitably split' (p. 313).

So in this sense, Tyndall is not a materialist; and in 'reducing' life to a material explanation his aim is often not to degrade life, but to upgrade our estimate of matter. At times he shows an almost mystical reverence for the powers of matter, an attitude parodied by W. H. Mallock like this:

> Who knows what the future may have in store for us? And then, on the other hand, when the awe-struck eye gazes, guided by science, through the 'dark backward and abysm of time', and sees that all that is has unfolded itself, unmoved and unbidden (astounding thought!), from a brainless, senseless, life-less gas – the cosmic vapour, as we call it – and that it may, for aught we know, one day return to it – I say, when we realise, when we truly make our own, this stupendous truth, must not our feelings . . . at such moments be religious? Are they not Religion? (*The New Republic* (1908), p. 156)

Tyndall's sense of wonder and awe at the essential mystery of the universe was partly derived from the writings of Thomas Carlyle, who became a great friend of his, and who is mentioned in the closing pages of the Address. Tyndall appreciated Carlyle's fears that science tends to destroy 'transcendent wonder', but he countered by insisting that 'preoccupation alone could close the eyes of the student of natural science to the fact that the long line of his researches is, in reality, a line of wonders . . . It was the illegitimate science which, in its claims, overstepped its warrant – profess-ing to explain everything, and to sweep the universe clear of mystery – that was really repugnant to Carlyle' (*Personal Recollections of Carlyle* (1890); *New Fragments* (1892), pp. 387–8). Carlyle was also an influence on Huxley, who learnt from him 'that a deep sense of religion was compatible with the entire absence of theology' (*Life and Letters*, vol. 1, p. 220). This is what Carlyle offered these Victorian scientific agnostics: the possibility of a religious and moral attitude divorced from any theological doctrine. They were emphatically not atheists, and pursued their scientific missions with a religious earnestness and enthusiasm.

Nevertheless, this is not how they appeared to the more conservatively religious. A letter written to the Home Secretary in 1874, by C. W. Stokes, a London merchant, suggested that Tyndall, in his Belfast Address, may have made himself liable to the 'penalty of persons expressing blasphemous opinions' (A. S. Eve and C. H. Creasey, *The Life and Works of John Tyndall* (1945), p. 187). By expressing his ideas in a Presidential Address at a meeting of the British Association, Tyndall had ensured maximum publicity: in 1863, the *Manchester Guardian* had written that 'The presi-dential address finds as many readers as a statement from Lord Palmerston or a budget speech from Mr Gladstone' (Alvar Ellegård, *Darwin and the General Reader* (Göteborg, 1958), p. 65). And Tyndall did have a particular clerical target in mind, connected with the venue of the meeting at Belfast: the Irish Catholic hierarchy had just thrown out a plan to include physical science in the curriculum of the Catholic University (see Frank M. Turner, 'John Tyndall and Victorian scientific naturalism', in *John Tyndall*, ed. W. H. Brock *et al.* (Dublin, 1981), p. 173). This seemed to Tyndall like a continuation, or revival, of the repressive theology of the Middle Ages: like Huxley, he saw himself as doing battle for scientific ideas and scientific education against a primarily clerical establishment.

However, Tyndall's style is not as aggressive as Huxley's: he relies more on per-suasion. His argument does not appeal to facts, so much as to the power of irresistably advancing ideas and theories. He brings in Darwin and Spencer as examples of powerful scientific minds, who push the scientific argument further into the area of religion. Rather than explaining Darwin's theory in detail, Tyndall uses a witty, if somewhat heavily ironic, metaphor from his own researches to convey the over-powering force of Darwin's intellect: 'He moves over the subject with the passionless strength of a glacier; and the grinding of the rocks is not always without a counterpart in the logical pulverisation of the objector.' Elsewhere in the Address, it is not particular scientific minds, but the scientific ideas and theories themselves that are the subject – they are inexorably 'reached' or 'recognised'; and, actively, they 'bind', 'extend' and 'embrace' great areas of knowledge, asserting their 'dominion'. Like the 'glacier' of Darwin's thought, Tyndall's style gives the impression of an over-whelming accumulation and advance of forceful ideas – 'the environment which, with or without your consent, is rapidly surrounding you'. Tyndall's tone is one of high authority, and his style is sometimes almost overweighted with learned allu-sions, scientific, historical and classical. The historical allusions to scientific 'heroes' such as Bruno or Lucretius, establish Tyndall's authority to speak as one who has an overview of the whole development of scientific thought; other allusions demon-strate his breadth of culture. He is concerned to show that the scientific frame of mind is not just narrowly factual or rational, it also contains emotion, imagination, and general culture. At times his style becomes over-emotional, or too solemn and por-tentous, as if he is straining to show that science, like religion, is a passionate and deeply serious human endeavour.

If Darwin, like Bruno,[1] rejects the notion of creative power acting after human fashion, it certainly is not because he is unacquainted with the numberless exquisite adaptations on which this notion of a supernatural artificer was founded. His book is a repository of the most startling facts of this description. Take the marvellous observa-tion which he cites from Dr Crüger,[2] where a bucket with an aper-ture, serving as a spout, is formed in an orchid. Bees visit the flower: in eager search of material for their combs they push each other into the bucket, the drenched ones escaping from their involuntary bath by the spout. Here they rub their backs against the viscid stigma of the flower and obtain glue; then against the pollen-masses, which are thus stuck to the back of the bee and carried away. 'When the bee, thus provided, flies to another flower, or to the same flower a second time, and is pushed by its comrades into the bucket, and then crawls out by the passage, the pollen-mass upon its back necessarily comes first into contact with the viscid stigma,' which takes up the pollen; and this is how that orchid is fertilised. Or take this other case of the *Catasetum*. 'Bees visit these flowers in order to gnaw the labellum[a]; on doing this they inevitably touch a long, tapering, sensitive pro-jection. This, when touched, transmits a sensation or vibration to a certain membrane, which is instantly ruptured, setting free a spring, by which the pollen-mass is shot forth like an arrow in the right direction, and adheres by its viscid extremity to the back of the bee.' In this way the fertilising pollen is spread abroad.

It is the mind thus stored with the choicest materials of the tele-

a. The lower division or 'lip' of an orchidaceous corolla, often enlarged or curiously shaped.

ologist that rejects teleology, seeking to refer these wonders to natural causes. They illustrate, according to him, the method of nature, not the 'technic' of a man-like artificer.[3] The beauty of flowers is due to natural selection. Those that distinguish themselves by vividly contrasting colours from the surrounding green leaves are most readily seen, most frequently visited by insects, most often fertilised, and hence most favoured by natural selection. Coloured berries also readily attract the attention of birds and beasts, which feed upon them, spread their manured seeds abroad, thus giving trees and shrubs possessing such berries a greater chance in the struggle for existence.

With profound analytic and synthetic skill, Mr Darwin investigates the cell-making instinct of the hive-bee. His method of dealing with it is representative. He falls back from the more perfectly to the less perfectly developed instinct – from the hive-bee to the humble-bee, which uses its own cocoon as a comb, and to classes of bees of intermediate skill, endeavouring to show how the passage might be gradually made from the lowest to the highest. The saving of wax is the most important point in the economy of bees. Twelve to fifteen pounds of dry sugar are said to be needed for the secretion of a single pound of wax. The quantities of nectar necessary for the wax must therefore be vast; and every improvement of constructive instinct which results in the saving of wax is a direct profit to the insect's life. The time that would otherwise be devoted to the making of wax is now devoted to the gathering and storing of honey for winter food. He passes from the humble-bee with its rude cells, through the Melipona with its more artistic cells, to the hive-bee with its astonishing architecture. The bees place themselves at equal distance apart upon the wax, sweep and excavate equal spheres round the selected points. The spheres intersect, and the planes of intersection are built up with thin laminæ. Hexagonal cells are thus formed. This mode of treating such questions is, as I have said, representative. He habitually retires from the more perfect and complex, to the less perfect and simple, and carries you with him through stages of *perfecting*, adds increment to increment of infinitesimal change, and in this way gradually breaks down your reluctance to admit that the exquisite climax of the whole could be a result of natural selection.

Mr Darwin shirks no difficulty; and, saturated as the subject was with his own thought, he must have known, better than his critics, the weakness as well as the strength of his theory. This of course would be of little avail were his object a temporary dialectic victory instead of the establishment of a truth which he means to be everlasting. But he takes no pains to disguise the weakness he has discerned; nay, he takes every pains to bring it into the strongest light. His vast resources enable him to cope with objections started by himself and others, so as to leave the final impression upon the reader's mind that if they be not completely answered they certainly are not fatal. Their negative force being thus destroyed, you are free to be influenced by the vast positive mass of evidence he is able to bring before you. This largeness of knowledge and readiness of resource render Mr Darwin the most terrible of antagonists. Accomplished naturalists have levelled heavy and sustained criticisms against him – not always with the view of fairly weighing his theory, but with the express intention of exposing its weak points only. This does not irritate him. He treats every objection with a soberness and thoroughness which even Bishop Butler[4] might be proud to imitate, surrounding each fact with its appropriate detail, placing it in its proper relations, and usually giving it a significance which, as long as it was kept isolated, failed to appear. This is done without a trace of ill-temper. He moves over the subject with the passionless strength of a glacier; and the grinding of the rocks is not always without a counterpart in the logical pulverisation of the objector. But though in handling this mighty theme all passion has been stilled, there is an emotion of the intellect incident to the discernment of new truth which often colours and warms the pages of Mr Darwin. His success has been great; and this implies not only the solidity of his work, but the preparedness of the public mind for such a revelation. On this head a remark of Agassiz impressed me more than anything else. Sprung from a race of theologians, this celebrated man combated to the last the theory of natural selection. One of the many times I had the pleasure of meeting him in the United States was at Mr Winthrop's[5] beautiful residence at Brookline, near Boston. Rising from luncheon, we all halted as if by a common impulse in front of a window, and continued there a discussion which had been started at table. The maple was in its autumn glory; and the exquisite beauty of the scene outside seemed, in my case, to interpenetrate without disturbance the intellectual action. Earnestly, almost sadly, Agassiz turned and said to the gentlemen standing round, 'I confess that I was not prepared to see this theory received as it has been by the best intellects of our time. Its success is greater than I could have thought possible.'

In our day great generalisations have been reached. The theory of the origin of species is but one of them. Another, of still wider grasp and more radical significance, is the doctrine of the Conservation of

Energy,[6] the ultimate philosophical issues of which are as yet but dimly seen – that doctrine which 'binds nature fast in fate' to an extent not hitherto recognised, exacting from every antecedent its equivalent consequent, from every consequent its equivalent antecedent, and bringing vital as well as physical phenomena under the dominion of that law of causal connection which, as far as the human understanding had yet pierced, asserts itself everywhere in nature. Long in advance of all definite experiment upon the subject, the constancy and indestructibility of matter had been affirmed; and all subsequent experience justified the affirmation. Later researches extended the attribute of indestructibility to force. This idea, applied in the first instance to inorganic, rapidly embraced organic nature. The vegetable world, though drawing almost all its nutriment from invisible sources, was proved incompetent to generate anew either matter or force. Its matter is for the most part transmuted air; its force transformed solar force. The animal world was proved to be equally uncreative, all its motive energies being referred to the combustion of its food.[7] The activity of each animal as a whole was proved to be the transferred activities of its molecules. The muscles were shown to be stores of mechanical force, potential until unlocked by the nerves, and then resulting in muscular contractions. The speed at which messages fly to and fro along the nerves was determined, and found to be, not as had been previously supposed, equal to that of light or electricity, but less than the speed of a flying eagle.

This was the work of the physicist: then came the conquests of the comparative anatomist and physiologist, revealing the structure of every animal, and the function of every organ in the whole biological series, from the lowest zoophyte up to man. The nervous system had been made the object of profound and continued study, the wonderful and, at bottom, entirely mysterious controlling power which it exercises over the whole organism, physical and mental, being recognised more and more. Thought could not be kept back from a subject so profoundly suggestive. Besides the physical life dealt with by Mr Darwin, there is a psychical life presenting similar gradations, and asking equally for a solution. How are the different grades and orders of mind to be accounted for? What is the principle of growth of that mysterious power which on our planet culminates in Reason? These are questions which, though not thrusting themselves so forcibly upon the attention of the general public, had not only occupied many reflecting minds, but had been formally broached by one of them before the 'Origin of Species' appeared.

With the mass of materials furnished by the physicist and

physiologist in his hands, Mr Herbert Spencer,[8] twenty years ago, sought to graft upon this basis a system of psychology; and two years ago a second and greatly amplified edition of his work appeared. Those who have occupied themselves with the beautiful experiments of Plateau,[9] will remember that when two spherules of olive-oil suspended in a mixture of alcohol and water of the same density as the oil, are brought together they do not immediately unite. Something like a pellicle[a] appears to be formed around the drops, the rupture of which is immediately followed by the coalescence of the globules into one. There are organisms whose vital actions are almost as purely physical as that of these drops of oil. They come into contact and fuse themselves thus together. From such organisms to others a shade higher, and from these to others a shade higher still, and on through an ever-ascending series, Mr Spencer conducts his argument. There are two obvious factors to be here taken into account – the creature and the medium in which it lives, or, as it is often expressed, the organism and its environment. Mr Spencer's fundamental principle is, that between these two factors there is incessant interaction. The organism is played upon by the environment, and is modified to meet the requirements of the environment. Life he defines to be 'a continuous adjustment of internal relations to external relations.'

In the lowest organisms we have a kind of tactual sense diffused over the entire body; then, through impressions from without and their corresponding adjustments, special portions of the surface become more responsive to stimuli than others. The senses are nascent, the basis of all of them being that simple tactual sense which the sage Democritus[10] recognised 2,300 years ago as their common progenitor. The action of light, in the first instance, appears to be a mere disturbance of the chemical processes in the animal organism, similar to that which occurs in the leaves of plants. By degrees the action becomes localised in a few pigment-cells, more sensitive to light than the surrounding tissue. The eye is here incipient. At first it is merely capable of revealing differences of light and shade produced by bodies close at hand. Followed as the interception of the light is in almost all cases by the contact of the closely adjacent opaque body, sight in this condition becomes a kind of 'anticipatory touch.' The adjustment continues; a slight bulging out of the epidermis over the pigment-granules supervenes. A lens is incipient, and, through the operation of infinite adjustments, at length reaches

a. Thin skin or membrane.

the perfection that it displays in the hawk and the eagle. So of the other senses; they are special differentiations of a tissue which was originally vaguely sensitive all over.

With the development of the senses the adjustments between the organism and its environment gradually extend in *space*, a multiplication of experiences and a corresponding modification of conduct being the result. The adjustments also extend in *time*, covering continually greater intervals. Along with this extension in space and time, the adjustments also increase in speciality and complexity, passing through the various grades of brute life and prolonging themselves into the domain of reason. Very striking are Mr Spencer's remarks regarding the influence of the sense of touch upon the development of intelligence. This is, so to say, the mother-tongue of all the senses, into which they must be translated to be of service to the organism. Hence its importance. The parrot is the most intelligent of birds, and its tactual power is also greatest. From this sense it gets knowledge unattainable by birds which cannot employ their feet as hands. The elephant is the most sagacious of quadrupeds – its tactual range and skill, and the consequent multiplication of experiences, which it owes to its wonderfully adaptable trunk, being the basis of its sagacity. Feline animals, for a similar cause, are more sagacious than hoofed animals – atonement being to some extent made, in the case of the horse, by the possession of sensitive prehensile lips. In the *Primates* the evolution of intellect and the evolution of tactual appendages go hand in hand. In the most intelligent anthropoid apes we find the tactual range and delicacy greatly augmented, new avenues of knowledge being thus opened to the animal. Man crowns the edifice here, not only in virtue of his own manipulatory power, but through the enormous extension of his range of experience, by the invention of instruments of precision, which serve as supplemental senses and supplemental limbs. The reciprocal action of these is finely described and illustrated. That chastened intellectual emotion to which I have referred in connection with Mr Darwin is, I should say, not absent in Mr Spencer. His illustrations possess at times exceeding vividness and force, and from his style on such occasion it is to be inferred that the ganglia[a] of this apostle of the understanding are sometimes the seat of a nascent poetic thrill.

It is a fact of supreme importance that actions, the performance of which at first requires even painful effort and deliberation, may by habit be rendered automatic. Witness the slow learning of its letters

---

a. Centres of the nervous system.

by a child, and the subsequent facility of reading in a man, when each group of letters which forms a word is instantly and without effort fused to a single perception. Instance the billiard-player, whose muscles of hand and eye, when he reaches the perfection of his art, are unconsciously co-ordinated. Instance the musician, who by practice is enabled to fuse a multitude of arrangements, auditory, tactual, and muscular, into a process of automatic manipulation. Combining such facts with the doctrine of hereditary transmission, we reach a theory of instinct. A chick, after coming out of the egg, balances itself correctly, runs about, picks up food, thus showing that it possesses a power of directing its movements to definite ends. How did the chick learn this very complex co-ordination of eye, muscles, and beak? It has not been individually taught; its personal experience is *nil*; but it has the benefit of ancestral experience. In its inherited organisation are registered all the powers which it displays at birth. So also as regards the instinct of the hive-bee, already referred to. The distance at which the insects stand apart when they sweep their hemispheres and build their cells is 'organically remembered.' Man also carries with him the physical texture of his ancestry, as well as the inherited intellect bound up with it. The defects of intelligence during infancy and youth are probably less due to a lack of individual experience than to the fact that in early life the cerebral organisation is still incomplete. The period necessary for completion varies with the race and with the individual. As a round shot outstrips a rifled one on quitting the muzzle of the gun, so the lower race in childhood may outstrip the higher. But the higher eventually overtakes the lower, and surpasses it in range. As regards individuals, we do not always find the precocity of youth prolonged to mental power in maturity, while the dullness of boyhood is sometimes strikingly contrasted with the intellectual energy of after years. Newton, when a boy, was weakly, and he showed no particular aptitude at school; but in his eighteenth year he went to Cambridge, and soon afterwards astonished his teachers by his power of dealing with geometrical problems. During his quiet youth his brain was slowly preparing itself to be the organ of those energies which he subsequently displayed.

By myriad blows (to use a Lucretian[11] phrase) the image and superscription of the external world are stamped as states of consciousness upon the organism, the depth of the impression depending upon the number of the blows. When two or more phenomena occur in the environment invariably together, they are stamped to the same depth or to the same relief, and are indissolubly connected.

And here we come to the threshold of a great question. Seeing that he could in no way rid himself of the consciousness of space and time, Kant assumed them to be necessary 'forms of thought,' the moulds and shapes into which our intuitions are thrown, belonging to ourselves solely and without objective existence. With unexpected power and success Mr Spencer brings the hereditary experience theory, as he holds it, to bear upon this question. 'If there exist certain external relations which are experienced by all organisms at all instants of their waking lives – relations which are absolutely constant and universal – there will be established answering internal relations that are absolutely constant and universal. Such relations we have in those of space and time. As the substratum of all other relations of the Non-Ego, they must be responded to by conceptions that are the substrata of all other relations in the Ego. Being the constant and infinitely repeated elements of thought, they must become the automatic elements of thought – the elements of thought which it is impossible to get rid of – the "forms of intuition."'

Throughout this application and extension of the 'law of inseparable association,' Mr Spencer stands on totally different ground from Mr John Stuart Mill,[12] invoking the registered experiences of the race instead of the experiences of the individual. His overthrow of Mr Mill's restriction of experience is, I think, complete. That restriction ignores the power of organising experience furnished at the outset to each individual; it ignores the different degrees of this power possessed by different races and by different individuals of the same race. Were there not in the human brain a potency antecedent to all experience, a dog or cat ought to be as capable of education as a man. These predetermined internal relations are independent of the experiences of the individual. The human brain is the 'organised register of infinitely numerous experiences received during the evolution of life, or rather during the evolution of that series of organisms through which the human organism has been reached. The effects of the most uniform and frequent of these experiences have been successively bequeathed, principal and interest, and have slowly mounted to that high intelligence which lies latent in the brain of the infant. Thus it happens that the European inherits from twenty to thirty cubic inches more of brain than the Papuan. Thus it happens that faculties, as of music, which scarcely exist in some inferior races, become congenital in superior ones. Thus it happens that out of savages unable to count up to the number of their fingers, and speaking a language containing only nouns and verbs, arise at length our Newtons and Shakespeares.'

John Tyndall (1820–1893)

At the outset of this address it was stated that physical theories which lie beyond experience are derived by a process of abstraction from experience.[13] It is instructive to note from this point of view the successive introduction of new conceptions. The idea of the attraction of gravitation was preceded by the observation of the attraction of iron by a magnet, and of light bodies by rubbed amber. The polarity of magnetism and electricity appealed to the senses; and thus became the substratum of the conception that atoms and molecules[14] are endowed with definite, attractive, and repellent poles, by the play of which definite forms of crystalline architecture are produced. Thus molecular force becomes *structural*. It required no great boldness of thought to extend its play into organic nature, and to recognise in molecular force the agency by which both plants and animals are built up. In this way out of experience arise conceptions which are wholly ultra-experiential.

The *origination* of life is a point lightly touched upon, if at all, by Mr Darwin and Mr Spencer. Diminishing gradually the number of progenitors, Mr Darwin comes at length to one 'primordial form;' but he does not say, as far as I remember, how he supposes this form to have been introduced. He quotes with satisfaction the words of a celebrated author and divine who had 'gradually learnt to see that it is just as noble a conception of the Deity to believe He created a few original forms, capable of self-development into other and needful forms, as to believe that He required a fresh act of creation to supply the voids caused by the action of His laws.'[15] What Mr Darwin thinks of this view of the introduction of life I do not know. Whether he does or does not introduce his 'primordial form' by a creative act, I do not know. But the question will inevitably be asked, 'How came the form there?' With regard to the diminution of the number of created forms, one does not see that much advantage is gained by it. The anthropomorphism, which it seemed the object of Mr Darwin to set aside, is as firmly associated with the creation of a few forms as with the creation of a multitude. We need clearness and thoroughness here. Two courses, and two only, are possible. Either let us open our doors freely to the conception of creative acts, or, abandoning them, let us radically change our notions of matters. If we look at matter as pictured by Democritus, and as defined for generations in our scientific text-books, the absolute impossibility of any form of life coming out of it would be sufficient to render any other hypothesis preferable; but the definitions of matter given in our text-books were intended to cover its purely physical and mechanical properties. And taught as we have been to regard these definitions as complete, we naturally and rightly reject the monstrous notion that out of *such* matter any form of life could possibly arise. But are the definitions complete? Everything depends on the answer to be given to this question. Trace the line of life backwards, and see it approaching more and more to what we call the purely physical condition. We reach at length those organisms which I have compared to drops of oil suspended in a mixture of alcohol and water. We reach the *protogenes*[a] of Haeckel,[16] in which we have 'a type distinguishable from a fragment of albumen only by its finely granular character.' Can we pause here? We break a magnet and find two poles in each of its fragments. We continue the process of breaking, but however small the parts, each carries with it, though enfeebled, the polarity of the whole. And when we can break no longer, we prolong the intellectual vision to the polar molecules. Are we not urged to do *something* similar in the case of life? Is there not a temptation to close to some extent with Lucretius, when he affirms that 'Nature is seen to do all things spontaneously of herself without the meddling of the gods?' or with Bruno, when he declares that matter is not 'that mere empty *capacity* which philosophers have pictured her to be, but the universal mother who brings forth all things as the fruit of her own womb?' The questions here raised are inevitable. They are approaching us with accelerated speed, and it is not a matter of indifference whether they are introduced with reverence or irreverence. Abandoning all disguise, the confession that I feel bound to make before you is that I prolong the vision backward across the boundary of the experimental evidence, and discern in that matter, which we in our ignorance, and notwithstanding our professed reverence for its Creator have hitherto covered with opprobrium, the promise and potency of every form and quality of life.

The 'materialism' here enunciated may be different from what you suppose, and I therefore crave your gracious patience to the end. 'The question of an external world,' says Mr J. S. Mill, 'is the great battle-ground of metaphysics.'[17] Mr Mill himself reduces external phenomena to 'possibilities of sensation.' Kant, as we have seen, made time and space 'forms' of our own intuitions. Fichte,[18] having first by the inexorable logic of his understanding proved himself to be a mere link in that chain of eternal causation which holds so rigidly in nature, violently broke the chain by making nature, and all that it inherits, an apparition of his own mind. And it is by no means easy to combat such notions. For when I say I see you, and that I have

---

a. Primitive, low-grade animals.

not the least doubt about it, the reply is, that what I am really conscious of is an affection of my own retina. And if I urge that I can check my sight of you by touching you, the retort would be that I am equally transgressing the limits of fact; for what I am really conscious of is, not that you are there, but that the nerves of my hand have undergone a change. All we hear, and see, and touch, and taste, and smell, are, it would be urged, mere variations of our own condition, beyond which, even to the extent of a hair's breadth, we cannot go. That anything answering to our impressions exists outside of ourselves is not a *fact*, but an *inference*, to which all validity would be denied by an idealist like Berkeley,[19] or by a sceptic like Hume.[20] Mr Spencer takes another line. With him, as with the uneducated man, there is no doubt or question as to the existence of an external world. But he differs from the uneducated, who think that the world really *is* what consciousness represents it to be. Our states of consciousness are mere *symbols* of an outside entity which produces them and determines the order of their succession, but the real nature of which we can never know. In fact the whole process of evolution is the manifestation of a Power absolutely inscrutable to the intellect of man. As little in our day as in the days of Job can man by searching find this Power out. Considered fundamentally, it is by the operation of an insoluble mystery that life is evolved, species differentiated, and mind unfolded from their prepotent elements in the immeasurable past. There is, you will observe, no very rank materialism here.

The strength of the doctrine of evolution consists, not in an experimental demonstration (for the subject is hardly accessible to this mode of proof), but in its general harmony with the method of nature as hitherto known.[21] From contrast, moreover, it derives enormous relative strength. On the one side we have a theory (if it could with any propriety be so called) derived, as were the theories referred to at the beginning of this address, not from the study of nature, but from the observation of men – a theory which converts the Power whose garment is seen in the visible universe into an Artificer, fashioned after the human model, and acting by broken efforts as man is seen to act. On the other side we have the conception that all we see around us, and all we feel within us – the phenomena of physical nature as well as those of the human mind – have their unsearchable roots in a cosmical life, if I dare apply the term, an infinitesimal span of which only is offered to the investigation of man. And even this span is only knowable in part. We can trace the development of a nervous system, and correlate with it the

parallel phenomena of sensation and thought. We see with undoubt-
ing certainty that they go hand in hand. But we try to soar in a
vacuum the moment we seek to comprehend the connection between
them.[22] An Archimedean fulcrum[23] is here required which the
human mind cannot command; and the effort to solve the problem,
to borrow an illustration from an illustrious friend of mine, is like
the effort of a man trying to lift himself by his own waistband. All
that has been here said is to be taken in connection with this fundamental truth. When 'nascent senses' are spoken of, when 'the
differentiation of a tissue at first vaguely sensitive all over' is spoken
of, and when these processes are associated with 'the modification of
an organism by its environment,' the same parallelism, without
contact, or even approach to contact, is implied. There is no fusion
possible between the two classes of facts – no motor energy in the
intellect of man to carry it without logical rupture from the one to
the other.

Further, the doctrine of evolution derives man, in his totality,
from the interaction of organism and environment through countless ages past. The human understanding, for example – the faculty
which Mr Spencer has turned so skilfully round upon its own antecedents – is itself a result of the play between organism and environment through cosmic ranges of time. Never surely did prescription
plead so irresistible a claim. But then it comes to pass that, over and
above his understanding, there are many other things appertaining
to man whose prescriptive rights are quite as strong as that of the
understanding itself. It is a result, for example, of the play of
organism and environment that sugar is sweet and that aloes are
bitter, that the smell of henbane differs from the perfume of a rose.
Such facts of consciousness (for which, by the way, no adequate
reason has ever yet been rendered) are quite as old as the understanding itself; and many other things can boast an equally ancient origin.
Mr Spencer at one place refers to that most powerful of passions –
the amatory passion – as one which, when it first occurs, is antecedent to all relative experience whatever; and we may pass its claim
as being at least as ancient and as valid as that of the understanding
itself. Then there are such things woven into the texture of man as
the feeling of awe, reverence, wonder – and not alone the sexual love
just referred to, but the love of the beautiful, physical and moral, in
nature, poetry, and art. There is also that deep-set feeling which,
since the earliest dawn of history, and probably for ages prior to all
history, incorporated itself in the religions of the world. You who
have escaped from these religions in the high-and-dry light of the

understanding may deride them; but in so doing you deride accidents of form merely, and fail to touch the immovable basis of the religious sentiment in the emotional nature of man. To yield this sentiment reasonable satisfaction is the problem of problems at the present hour. And grotesque in relation to scientific culture as many of the religions of the world have been and are – dangerous, nay, destructive, to the dearest privileges of freemen as some of them undoubtedly have been, and would, if they could, be again – it will be wise to recognise them as the forms of force, mischievous, if permitted to intrude on the region of *knowledge*, over which it holds no command, but capable of being guided by liberal thought to noble issues in the region of *emotion*, which is its proper sphere.[24] It is vain to oppose this force with a view to its extirpation. What we should oppose, to the death if necessary, is every attempt to found upon this elemental bias of man's nature a system which should exercise despotic sway over his intellect. I do not fear any such consummation. Science has already to some extent leavened the world, and it will leaven it more and more. I should look upon the mild light of science breaking in upon the minds of the youth of Ireland, and strengthening gradually to the perfect day, as a surer check to any intellectual or spiritual tyranny which might threaten this island, than the laws of princes or the swords of emperors. Where is the cause of fear? We fought and won our battle even in the Middle Ages: why should we doubt the issue of a conflict now?

The impregnable position of science may be described in a few words. All religious theories, schemes, and systems, which embrace notions of cosmogony, or which otherwise reach into its domain, must, in so far as they do this, submit to the control of science, and relinquish all thought of controlling it. Acting otherwise proved disastrous in the past, and it is simply fatuous to-day. Every system which would escape the fate of an organism too rigid to adjust itself to its environment, must be plastic to the extent that the growth of knowledge demands. When this truth has been thoroughly taken in, rigidity will be relaxed, exclusiveness diminished, things now deemed essential will be dropped, and elements now rejected will be assimilated. The lifting of the life is the essential point; and as long as dogmatism, fanaticism, and intolerance are kept out, various modes of leverage may be employed to raise life to a higher level. Science itself not unfrequently derives motive power from an ultra-scientific source. Whewell[25] speaks of enthusiasm of temper as a hindrance to science; but he means the enthusiasm of weak heads. There is a strong and resolute enthusiasm in which science finds an ally; and it is to the lowering of this fire, rather than to a diminution of intellectual insight, that the lessening productiveness of men of science in their mature years is to be ascribed. Mr Buckle[26] sought to detach intellectual achievement from moral force. He gravely erred; for without moral force to whip it into action, the achievements of the intellect would be poor indeed.

It has been said that science divorces itself from literature: The statement, like so many others, arises from lack of knowledge. A glance at the less technical writings of its leaders – of its Hehmholtz, its Huxley, and its Du Bois-Reymond[27] – would show what breadth of literary culture they command. Where among modern writers can you find their superiors in clearness and vigour of literary style? Science desires no isolation, but freely combines with every effort towards the bettering of man's estate. Single-handed,[28] and supported not by outward sympathy, but by inward force, it has built at least one great wing of the many-mansioned home which man in his totality demands. And if rough walls and protruding rafter-ends indicate that on one side the edifice is still incomplete, it is only by wise combination of the parts required with those already irrevocably built that we can hope for completeness. There is no necessary incongruity between what has been accomplished and what remains to be done. The moral glow of Socrates, which we all feel by ignition, has in it nothing incompatible with the physics of Anaxagoras[29] which he so much scorned, but which he would hardly scorn to-day. And here I am reminded of one amongst us,[a] hoary, but still strong, whose prophet-voice some thirty years ago, far more than any other of this age, unlocked whatever of life and nobleness lay latent in its most gifted minds – one fit to stand beside Socrates or the Maccabean Eleazar,[30] and to dare and suffer all that they suffered and dared – fit, as he once said of Fichte, 'to have been the teacher of the Stoa,[b] and to have discoursed of beauty and virtue in the groves of Academe.'[c] With a capacity to grasp physical principles which his friend Goethe did not possess, and which even total lack of exercise has not been able to reduce to atrophy, it is the world's loss that he, in the vigour of his years, did not open his mind and sympathies to science, and make its conclusions a portion of his message to mankind. Marvellously endowed as he was – equally equipped on the side of the heart and of the understanding – he might have done much towards teaching us how to reconcile the claims of both, and

a. Thomas Carlyle.
b. Greek portico or roofed colonnade, where the philosopher Zeno taught Stoicism.
c. Garden near Athens where Plato taught.

John Tyndall (1820–1893)

to enable them in coming times to dwell together in unity of spirit and in the bond of peace.

And now the end is come. With more time, or greater strength and knowledge, what has been here said might have been better said, while worthy matters here omitted might have received fit expression. But there would have been no material deviation from the views set forth. As regards myself, they are not the growth of a day; and as regards you, I thought you ought to know the environment which, with or without your consent, is rapidly surrounding you, and in relation to which some adjustment on your part may be necessary. A hint of Hamlet's, however, teaches us all how the troubles of common life may be ended; and it is perfectly possible for you and me to purchase intellectual peace at the price of intellectual death. The world is not without refuges of this description; nor is it wanting in persons who seek their shelter and try to persuade others to do the same. I would exhort you to refuse such shelter, and to scorn such base repose – to accept, if the choice be forced upon you, commotion before stagnation, the leap of the torrent before the stillness of the swamp. In the one there is at all events life, and therefore hope; in the other, none. I have touched on debatable questions, and led you over dangerous ground – and this partly with the view of telling you, and through you the world, that as regards these questions science claims unrestricted right of search. It is not to the point to say that the views of Lucretius and Bruno, of Darwin and Spencer, may be wrong. Here I should agree with you, deeming it indeed certain that these views will undergo modification. But the point is, that, whether right or wrong, we claim the freedom to discuss them. The ground which they cover is scientific ground; and the right claimed is one made good through tribulation and anguish, inflicted and endured in darker times than ours, but resulting in the immortal victories which science has won for the human race. I would set forth equally the inexorable advance of man's understanding in the path of knowledge, and the unquenchable claims of his emotional nature which the understanding can never satisfy. The world embraces not only a Newton, but a Shakespeare – not only a Boyle, but a Raphael – not only a Kant, but a Beethoven – not only a Darwin, but a Carlyle. Not in each of these, but in all, is human nature whole. They are not opposed, but supplementary – not mutually exclusive, but reconcilable. And if, still unsatisfied, the human mind, with the yearning of a pilgrim for his distant home, will turn to the mystery from which it has emerged, seeking so to fashion it as to give unity to thought and faith, so long as this is done, not only without intolerance or bigotry of any kind, but with the enlightened recognition that ultimate fixity of conception is here unattainable, and that each succeeding age must be held free to fashion the mystery in accordance with its own needs – then, in opposition to all the restrictions of Materialism, I would affirm this to be a field for the noblest exercise of what, in contrast with the *knowing* faculties, may be called the *creative* faculties of man. Here, however, I must quit a theme too great for me to handle, but which will be handled by the loftiest minds ages after you and I, like streaks of morning cloud, shall have melted into the infinite azure of the past.

9. Frederick Temple, The Relations between Religion and Science (1884), Lecture VI, 'Apparent Collision between Religion and the Doctrine of Evolution'; and Lecture VIII, 'The Conclusion of the Argument'

pp. 161–89, 225–52

Frederick Temple had been one of the contributors to *Essays and Reviews* in 1860, and there was great opposition to his appointment as Bishop of Exeter in 1869. But, like the attempts to prosecute some of the other Essayists, the opposition was not successful and he was consecrated. In 1896, he became Archbishop of Canterbury with hardly a protest, and Owen Chadwick, in *The Victorian Church* (1966), sees this as marking 'the final acceptance of the doctrine of evolution among the divines, clergy and leading laity of the established church, at least as a doctrine permissible and respectable in an eminent clergyman' (Part II, p. 23). Temple had made his acceptance of evolution clear in his Bampton Lectures of 1884, on 'The Relations between Religion and Science', and even then his message was generally welcomed, in marked contrast to the reaction to his contribution to *Essays and Reviews*. The editor of the *Memoirs of Archbishop Temple* (1906) comments on this change of attitude to Temple's views:

> The *Bampton Lectures*, in a sense, are the sequel to the contribution to *Essays and Reviews*. The lectures, indeed, followed the line of all that he had previously said or written as to the interpretation of the Bible in relation to modern thought. Why, then, was it that former utterances had been judged unsound, and that the Bampton Lectures were recognised as aids to faith? Mainly, no doubt, because during the fourteen years which had intervened between the publication of *Essays and Reviews* and the delivery of Bishop Temple's Bampton Lectures, not a little of the teaching for which the former had been condemned had come to be regarded as compatible with belief in the Bible as God's revelation. The volume had, at any rate, rendered this service, that men could be owned as believers without being called upon to accept every incident in the Old Testament as literally true ... (vol. 2, p. 635)

Notice that the main controversial point in the Lectures, and what links them to *Essays and Reviews*, is taken to be the attitude to the interpretation of the Bible, rather than specifically Temple's acceptance of the scientific theory of evolution, though obviously his reinterpretation of Genesis makes his acceptance of Darwin much easier.

Relations between Religion and Science

In the Lectures, Temple's attitude to Genesis is not in fact as reductive as Goodwin's in his Essay (see pp. 110–44). Temple takes the story in Genesis as not intended on any level to teach scientific truth, but rather as symbol or allegory, designed to teach moral and spiritual truth. He is concerned to separate out the realms of science and faith, basing faith firmly, in the first instance, on inner conviction, entirely independent of the external evidence of Revelation *or* of Nature. However, once this faith is granted, he finds no difficulty in reconciling the doctrine of evolution with natural theology. In Lecture IV, he even extends Paley's 'watch' analogy to cover evolutionary development:

> But Paley has supplied the clue to the answer. In his well-known illustration of the watch picked up on the heath by the passing traveller, he points out that the evidence of design is certainly not lessened if it be found that the watch was so constructed that, in course of time, it produced another watch like itself. He was thinking not of Evolution, but of the ordinary production of each generation of animals from the preceding. But his answer can be pushed a step further, and we may with equal justice remark that we should certainly not believe it a proof that the watch had come into existence if we found that it produced in the course of time not merely another watch but a better. It would become more marvellous than ever if we found provision thus made not merely for the continuance of the species, but for the perpetual improvement of the species. (pp. 111–12)

Thus Temple seems to be left with a remote Creator, rather like that in *Vestiges*, whose 'design was entertained at the very beginning and impressed on every particle of created matter' (p. 208 below). But Temple is more interested in evidence of miraculous *intervention* than of *design*. He surveys the claims of modern evolutionary science to provide a complete explanation of the world, and finds them incomplete and wanting at crucial points. He warns us against the tendency of the scientific mind to push for a completeness which is not in accord with experience. The 'gaps' in the scientific world-picture, according to Temple, are at the point where the inorganic becomes the organic, and where the organic becomes the moral and spiritual. These are of course the same gaps recognised by Tyndall in his Belfast Address, but while the scientist imaginatively pushed his belief in 'the continuity of nature' to cover the first, even though the factual evidence against spontaneous generation did not confirm his hypothesis, and relegated the second to an area of inexplicable 'mystery', the bishop sees both 'gaps' as opportunities for miraculous divine intervention. Moreover, he rejects any suggestion that man's moral and spiritual intuitions may have originated by evolution from the instincts of lower animals – the moral law is absolute and universal, though our understanding of it may be developing.

It is on our spiritual intuition that Temple bases his religious faith – he recognises that natural theology and miraculous explanations only convince those ready to be convinced. Scientists can be blind to spiritual truth, because of their excessive reliance on tangible physical evidence: Temple sees a 'difference of spirit and temper' unnecessarily dividing students of science and of religion. But this division was in fact both recent and growing: it would have been incomprehensible to most scientists and theologians up to about 1860. Though Temple is concerned to effect a reconciliation, his Lectures also epitomise the split that was taking place between these two ways of knowing. Temple from the religious side, as much as Tyndall from the scientific side, is concerned to separate out the spheres of science and of faith, assigning them to the external and the internal worlds respectively. The doctrine of evolution may have been accepted by the Church, but only at the price of relinquishing an ancient claim of religion to provide truth about the external world; science may have won its freedom, but only at the price of losing its traditional connection with inner values.

Frederick Temple (1821–1902)

Temple's tone in the Lectures is calm and factual. He presents himself as clearing up some annoying but simple misunderstandings, not as conducting a passionate or complex argument. He begins with a simple and bold assertion of the immovable spiritual ground of his faith; from here, he can proceed, unalarmed, to a dispassionate consideration of the scientific evidence, and to all manner of concession to the 'probable' truth of scientific argument. His lucid and factual account of Darwin's theory quickly exposes the holes in the 'evidence', that Tyndall carried us over with his evocations of the power of scientific thought. Just as Tyndall seemed concerned to demonstrate his emotional and imaginative credentials, through a rather florid style, so Temple seems concerned to demonstrate his scientific credentials: reasonableness, objectivity, grasp of fact, through a plain, unadorned style. From this vantage point, he can present the *scientists* as irrational, like little boys refusing to admit the inadequacy of their simplistic theories to explain a complex world. Temple's attitude to religion is also dispassionate and factual – a miracle is a possible factual explanation of the unexplained; his spiritual 'axioms' rest on spiritual experience, and have the same validity as the axioms of mathematics; the evidence of God's presence in the world is the good effects that His Revelation has 'in fact' (a phrase that recurs) had. Unlike Tyndall, Temple avoids all alarmist and extremist language – he clearly does not accept the 'conflict' metaphor for the relations of religion and science, and regrets that the 'duty to be patient, to enquire carefully, to study the other side, to wait for light' has often been swamped by 'a somewhat unreasoning impulse to resist an assault on faith'. However, Temple's dispassionate tone disappears at the end of the last lecture, and gives way to an emotional exhortation to love and follow Jesus Christ.

Lecture VI

Apparent Collision between Religion and the Doctrine of Evolution

'Know ye that the Lord He is God: it is He that hath made us, and not we ourselves.'   *Psalm* c.3.

Religion is rooted in our spiritual nature and its fundamental truths are as independent of experience for their hold on our consciences as the truths of mathematics for their hold on our reason.[1]

But as a matter of fact Religion has taken the form of a revelation. And this introduces a new contact between Religion and Science, and of necessity a new possibility of collision. There is not only possible opposition or apparent opposition of Science in what is revealed, in what we may call the actual substance of the revelation; but also in the accessories and evidences of the revelation, which may be no actual part of the revelation itself, but nevertheless are, to all appearance, inseparably bound up with it. It is therefore no more than might have been expected that the general postulate of the uniformity of nature should appear to be contravened by the claim to supernatural power made on behalf of revelation, and that the special, but just at present leading scientific doctrine, the doctrine of Evolution,[2] should be found inconsistent with parts, or what appear to be parts, of the revelation itself. And we have to consider the two questions, What has Revelation to say concerning Evolution? and what has Science to say concerning Miracles?

Concerning Evolution, we have first to consider how much in this direction has been made fairly probable, and what still remains to be determined.

It cannot then be well denied that the astronomers and geologists have made it exceedingly probable that this earth on which we live has been brought to its present condition by passing through a succession of changes from an original state of great heat and fluidity, perhaps even from a mixture mainly consisting of gases; that such a body as the planet Jupiter represents one of the stages through which it has passed, that such a body as the moon represents a stage toward which it is tending; that it has shrunk as it cooled, and as it shrank has formed the elevations which we call mountains, and the depressions which contain the seas and oceans; that it has been worn by the action of heat from within and water from without, and in consequence of this action presents the appearance when examined below the surface of successive strata or layers; that different kinds of animal and vegetable life have followed one another on the surface, and that some of their remains are found in these strata now; and that all this has taken enormous periods of time. All this is exceedingly probable, because it is the way in which, as Laplace[3] first pointed out, under well-established scientific laws of matter, particularly the law of gravitation and the law of the radiation of heat, a great fluid mass would necessarily change. And the whole solar system may and probably did come into its present condition in this way. It certainly could have been so formed, and there is no reason for supposing that it was formed in any other way.

Once more, if we begin, as it were, at the other end, and trace things backwards from the present, instead of forwards from the remote past, it cannot be denied that Darwin's investigations have made it exceedingly probable that the vast variety of plants and animals have sprung from a much smaller number of original forms.

In the first place, the unity of plan which can be found pervading any great class of animals or plants seems to point to unity of ancestry. Why, for instance, should the vertebrate animals be formed on a common plan, the parts of the framework being varied from species to species, but the framework as a whole always exhibiting the same fundamental type? If they all descended from a common ancestor, and the variations were introduced in the course of that descent, this remarkable fact is at once accounted for. But, in the second place, observation shows that slight variations ARE perpetually being introduced with every successive generation, and many of these variations are transmitted to the generations that follow. In the course of time, therefore, from any one parent stock would descend a very large variety of kinds. But if, in the third place, it be asked why this variety does not range by imperceptible degrees from extreme forms in one direction to extreme forms in the other, the answer is to be found in the enormous prodigality and the equally enormous waste of life and living creatures. Plants and animals produce far more descendants than ever come even to such maturity as to reproduce their kind. And this is particularly the case with the lower forms of life. Eggs and seeds and germs are destroyed by millions, and so in a less but still enormous proportion are the young that come from those that have not been destroyed. There is no waste like the waste of life that is to be seen in nature. Living creatures are destroyed by lack of fit nourishment, by lack of means of reproduction, by accidents, by enemies. The inevitable operation of this waste, as Darwin's investigation showed, has been to destroy all those varieties which were not well fitted to their surroundings, and to keep those that were. One species of animal has been preserved by length of neck, which enabled it to reach high-growing fruits and leaves; another by a thicker skin, which made it difficult for enemies to devour; another by a colour which made it easier to hide. One plant has been preserved by a bright flower which attracted insects to carry its pollen to other flowers of its kind; another by a sweet fruit which attracted birds to scatter its seed. Meanwhile other animals and plants that had not these advantages perished for the lack of them. The result would be to maintain, and perpetually, though with exceeding slowness, more and more to adapt to the conditions of their life, those species whose peculiarities gave them some advantage in the great struggle for existence.

Here again we have the working of known laws of life, capable of accounting for what we see. And the high probability cannot be denied that by evolution of this kind the present races of living creatures have been formed. And to these arguments the strongest corroboration is given by the frequent occurrence, both in plants and animals, of useless parts which still remain as indications of organs that once were useful and have long become useless. Animals that now live permanently in the dark have abortive eyes which cannot see, but indicate an ancestor with eyes that could see. Animals that never walk have abortive legs hidden under their skin, useless now but indicating what was useful once. Our knowledge no doubt in this as in any other province of nature is but the merest fraction of what may be known therein. But there is no evidence whatever to show that what we have observed is not a fair sample of the whole. And so taking it, we find that the mass of evidence in favour of the evolution of plants and animals is enormously great and increasing daily.

Granting then the high probability of the two theories of Evolution, that which begins with Laplace and explains the way in which the earth was fitted to be the habitation of living creatures, and that which owes its name to Darwin and gives an account of the formation of the living creatures now existing, we have to see what limitations and modifications are necessarily attached to our complete acceptance of both.

First, then, at the very meeting point of these two evolutions we have the important fact that all the evidence that we possess up to the present day negatives the opinion that life is a mere evolution from inorganic matter. We know perfectly well the constituents of all living substances. We know that the fundamental material of all plants and all animals is a compound called protoplasm, or that, in other words, organic matter in all its immense variety of forms is nothing but protoplasm variously modified.[4] And we know the constituent elements of this protoplasm, and their proportions, and the temperatures within which protoplasm as such can exist. But we are quite powerless to make it, or to show how it is made, or to detect nature in the act of making it. All the evidence we have points to one conclusion only, that life is the result of antecedent life, and is producible on no other conditions. Repeatedly have scientific observers believed that they have come on instances of spontaneous generation, but further examination has invariably shown that they have been mistaken. We can put the necessary elements together, but we cannot supply the necessary bond by which they are to be made to live. Nay, we cannot even recall that bond when it has once been dissolved. We can take living protoplasm and we can kill it. It will be protoplasm still, so far as our best chemistry can discover, but it will be dead protoplasm, and we cannot make it live again; and as far as we know nature can no more make it live than we can. It can be used as food for living creatures, animals or plants, and so its substance can be taken up by living protoplasm and made to share in the life which thus consumes it; but life of its own it cannot obtain. Now here, as it seems, the acceptance of the two evolutions lands us in acceptance of a miracle. The creation of life is unaccounted for. And it much more exactly answers to what we mean by a miracle than it did under the old theory of creation before Evolution was made a scientific doctrine. For under that old theory the creation of living creatures stood on the same footing as the creation of metals or other inorganic substances. It was part of that beginning which had to be taken for granted, and which for that reason lay outside of the domain of Science altogether. But if we accept the two evolutions, the creation of life, if unaccounted for, presents itself as a direct interference in the actual history of the world. There could have been no life when the earth was nothing but a mass of intensely heated fluid. There came a time when the earth became ready for life to exist upon it. And the life came, and no laws of inorganic matter can account for its coming. As it stands this is a great miracle. And from this conclusion the only escape that has been suggested is to suppose that life came in on a meteoric stone from some already formed habitable world; a supposition which transfers the miracle to another scene, but leaves it as great a miracle as before.

Nor, if it was a miracle, can we deny that there was a purpose in it worthy of miraculous interference. For what purpose can rank side by side with the existence and development of life, the primary condition of all moral and spiritual existence and action in this world? In the introduction of life was wrapped up all that we value and all that we venerate in the whole creation. The infinite superiority, not in degree only, but in kind, of the living to the lifeless, of a man to a stone, justifies us in believing that the main purpose of the creation that we see was to supply a dwelling-place and a scene of action for living beings. We cannot say that the dignity of the Moral Law requires that creatures to be made partakers in the knowledge of it, and even creatures of a lower nature but akin to them, must have been the results of a separate and miraculous act of creation. But we can say that there is a congruity in such a miracle, with the moral purpose of all the world, of which we are a part, that removes all difficulty in believing it. Science, as such, cannot admit a miracle, and can only say, 'Here is a puzzle yet unsolved.' Nor can the most religious scientific man be blamed as undutiful to religion if he persists in endeavouring to solve the puzzle. But he has no right to insist beforehand that the puzzle is certainly soluble; for that he cannot know, and the evidence is against him.

Secondly, if we look at the Darwinian theory by itself we see at once that it is incomplete, and the consideration of this incompleteness gravely modifies the conclusion which would otherwise be rightly drawn from it, and which, indeed, Darwin himself seems disposed to draw. For the theory rests on two main pillars, the transmission of characteristics from progenitor to progeny, and the introduction of minute variations in the progeny with each successive generation. Now, the former of these may be said to be well established, and we recognise it as a law of life that all plants and animals propagate their own kind. But the latter has, as yet, been hardly examined at all. Each new generation shows special slight variations. But what causes these variations? and what determines what they shall be? In Darwin's investigations these questions are not touched. The variations are treated as if they were quite indefinite in number and in nature. He concerns himself only with the effect of these variations after they have appeared. Some have the effect of giving the plant or animal an advantage in the struggle of life; some give no such advantage; some are hurtful. And hence follows the permanent preservation or speedy destruction of the plants and animals themselves. But we are bound to look not only to their effects but to their causes, if the theory is to be completed. And then we cannot fail to see that these variations in the progeny cannot be due to something in the progenitors, or otherwise the variations would be all alike, which they certainly are not. They must, therefore, be due to external circumstances. These slight variations are produced by the action of the surroundings, by the food, by the temperature, by the various accidents of life in the progenitors. Now, when we see this, we see also how gravely it modifies the conclusions which we have to draw concerning the ancestry of any species now existing. Let us take, for instance, the great order of vertebrate animals. At first sight the Darwinian theory seems to indicate that all these animals are descended from one pair or one individual, and that their unity of construction is due to that fact; but if we go back in thought to the time at which the special peculiarities were introduced which really constituted the order and separated it from other animals, we see that it is by no means clear that it originated with one pair or with one individual, and that, on the contrary, the probabilities are the other way. Although the separation of this order from the rest must have taken place very early, it cannot well have taken place until millions of animals had already come into existence. The prodigality of nature in multiplying animal life is fully acknowledged by Darwin, and that prodigality is apparently greatest in the lowest and most formless type of animal. There being, then, these many millions of living creatures in existence, the external surroundings introduce into them many variations, and among these the special variations to which the vertebrate type is due. It is quite clear that wherever the external surroundings were the same or nearly the same, the variations introduced would be the same or nearly the same. Now, it is far more probable that external surroundings should be the same or nearly the same in many places than that each spot should be absolutely unlike every other spot in these particulars. The beginnings of the vertebrate order would show themselves simultaneously, or at any rate independently, in many places wherever external conditions were sufficiently similar. And the unity of the plan in the vertebrata would be due, not to absolute unity of ancestry, but to unity of external conditions at a particular epoch in the descent of life. Hence it follows that the separation of animals into orders and genera and even into species took place, if not for the most part yet very largely, at a very early period in the history of organic evolution. Of course the descendants of any one of the original vertebrata might, and probably in not a few cases did, branch off into new subdivisions and yet again into further subdivisions, and we are always justified in looking for unity of ancestry among all the species. But it is also quite possible that any species may be regularly descended, without branching off at all, from one of the originals,[5] and that other species that resemble it may owe the resemblance simply to very great similarity of external conditions. To find, for instance, the unity of ancestry between man and the other animals, it will certainly be necessary to go back to a point in the history of life when living creatures were as yet formless, undeveloped – the materials, as we may call them, of the animal creation as we now see it, and not in any but a strictly scientific sense, what we mean when we ordinarily speak of animals. The true settlement of such questions as these can only be obtained when long and patient study shall have completed Darwin's investigations by determining under what laws and within what limits the slight variations which characterise each individual animal or plant are congenitally introduced into its structure. As things stand the probabilities certainly are that a creature with such especial characteristics as man has had a history altogether of his own, if not from the beginning of all life upon the globe, yet from a very early period in the development of that life. He resembles certain other animals very closely in the structure of his body; but the part which external conditions had to play in the earliest stages of evolution of life must have been so exceedingly large that identity or close similarity in these external conditions may well account for these resemblances. And the enormous gap which separates his nature from that of all other creatures known, indicates an exceedingly early difference of origin.

Lastly, it is quite impossible to evolve the Moral Law out of anything but itself. Attempts have been made, and many more will no doubt be made, to trace the origin of the spiritual faculty to a development of the other faculties. And it is to be expected that great success will ultimately attend the endeavours to show the growth of all the subordinate powers of the soul. That our emotions, that our impulses, that our affections should have had a history, and that their present working should be the result of that history, has nothing in it improbable. There can be no question that we inherit these things very largely, and that they are also very largely due to special peculiarities of constitution in each individual. That large part of us which is rightly assigned to our nature as distinct from our own will and our own free action, it is perfectly reasonable to find subject to laws of Evolution. Much of this nature, indeed, we share with the lower animals. They, too, can love; can be angry or pleased; can put affection above appetite; can show generosity and nobility of spirit; can be patient, persevering, tender, self-sacrificing; can take delight in society: and some can even organise it, and thus enter on a kind of civilisation. The dog and the horse, man's faithful servants and companions, show emotions and affections rising as far as mere emotions and affections can rise to the human level. Ants show an advance in the arts of life well comparable to our own. If the bare animal nature is thus capable of such high attainments by the mere working of natural forces, it is to be expected that similar forces in mankind should be found to work under similar laws. We are not spiritual beings only, we are animals, and whatever nature has done for other animals we may expect it to have done and to be doing for us. And if their nature is capable of evolution, so too should ours be. And the study of such evolution of our own nature is likely to be of the greatest value. This nature is the main instrument, put into the grasp as it were of that spiritual faculty which is our inmost essence, to be used in making our whole life an offering to God. It is good to know what can be done with this instrument and what cannot; how it has been formed in the past, and may be still further formed for the future. It is good to study the evolution of humanity. But all this does not touch the spiritual faculty itself, nor the Moral Law which that faculty proclaims to us. The essence of that law is its universality; and out of all this development, when carried to its very perfection, the conception of such universality cannot be obtained. Nothing in this evolution ever rises to the height of a law which shall bind even God Himself, and enable Abraham to say, 'Shall not the Judge of all the earth do right?'[6] The very word right in this, its fulness of meaning, cannot be used.

Evolution may lead the creature to say what is hateful and what is loveable, what is painful and what is delightful, what is to be feared and what is to be sought; it may develop the sentiment which comes nearest of all to the sentiment of reverence, namely, the sentiment of shame; but it cannot reveal the eternal character of the distinction between right and wrong. Nay, there may be, as was pointed out in the last Lecture, an evolution in our knowledge even of the Moral Law, just as there is an evolution in our knowledge of mathematics. The fulness of its meaning can become clearer and ever clearer as generation learns from generation. But the principle of the Moral Law, its universality, its supremacy, cannot come out of any development of human nature any more than the necessity of mathematical truth can so come. It stands not on experience, and is its own evidence. Nor indeed have any of the attempts to show that everything in man (religion included) is the product of Evolution ever touched the question how this conception of universal supremacy comes in. It is treated as if it were an unauthorised extension from our own experience to what lies beyond all experience. This, however, is to deny the essence of the Moral Law altogether: that Law is universal or it is nothing.

Now, when we compare the account of the creation and of man given by the doctrine of Evolution with that given in the Bible, we see at once that the two are in different regions. The purpose of giving the accounts is different; the spirit and character of the accounts is different; the details are altogether different. The comparison must take note of the difference of spirit and aim before it can proceed at all.

It is then quite certain, and even those who contend for the literal interpretation of this part of the Bible will generally admit, that the purpose of the revelation is not to teach Science at all. It is to teach great spiritual and moral lessons, and it takes the facts of nature as they appear to ordinary people. When the creation of man is mentioned there is clearly no intention to say by what processes this creation was effected, or how much time it took to work out those processes. The narrative is not touched by the question, Was this a single act done in a moment, or a process lasting through millions of years? The writer of the Book of Genesis sees the earth peopled, as we may say, by many varieties of plants and animals. He asserts that God made them all, and made them resemble each other and differ from each other. He knows nothing and says nothing of the means used to produce their resemblances or their differences. He takes them as he sees them, and speaks of their creation as God's work. Had he been commissioned to teach his people the science of the matter, he would have had to put a most serious obstacle in the way of their faith. They would have found it almost impossible to believe in a process of creation so utterly unlike all their own experience. And it would have been quite useless to them besides, since their science was not in such a condition as to enable them to coordinate this doctrine with any other. As science it would have been dead; and as spiritual truth it would have been a hindrance.

But he had, nevertheless, great ideas to communicate, and we can read them still.

He had to teach that the world as we see it, and all therein contained, was created out of nothing; and that the spiritual, and not the material, was the source of all existence. He had to teach that the creation was not merely orderly, but progressive; going from the formless to the formed; from the orderless to the ordered; from the inanimate to the animate; from the plant to the animal; from the lower animal to the higher; from the beast to the man; ending with the rest of the Sabbath, the type of the highest, the spiritual, life. Nothing, certainly, could more exactly match the doctrine of Evolution than this. It is, in fact, the same thing said from a different point of view. All this is done by casting the account into the form of a week of work with the Sabbath at the end. In so constructing his account, the writer made use of a mode of teaching used commonly enough in the Bible. The symbolical use of the number seven is common in other inspired writers. The symbolical use of periods of time is not without example. That the purpose of the account was not to teach great truths, but to give men information upon scientific questions, is incredible. And, in fact, if we look in this account for literal history, it becomes very difficult to give any meaning to what is said of the seventh day, or to reconcile the interpretation of it with our Lord's words concerning the Sabbath, 'My Father worketh hitherto, and I work.'[7] There is no more reason for setting aside Geology, because it does not agree in detail with Genesis, than there is for setting aside Astronomy because all through the Old Testament the sun is spoken of as going round the earth.

And when the writer of Genesis passes from creation in general to man in particular, it is still clear that he has no mission to tell those for whom he was writing by what processes man was formed, or how long those processes lasted. This was as alien from his purpose as it would have been to tell what every physiologist now knows of the processes by which every individual man is developed from a small germ to a breathing and living infant. He takes men – and he could not but take men as he sees them – with their sinful nature, with their moral and spiritual capacity, with their relations of sex, with their relations of family. He has to teach the essential supremacy of man among creatures, the subordination in position but equality in nature of woman to man, the original declension of man's will from the divine path, the dim and distant but sure hope of man's restoration. These are not, and cannot be, lessons of science. They are worked out into the allegory of the Garden of Eden. But in this allegory there is nothing whatever that crosses the path of science, nor is it for reasons of science that so many great Christian thinkers from the earliest age of the Church downwards have pronounced it an allegory. The spiritual truth contained in it is certainly the purpose for which it is told; and evolution such as science has rendered probable had done its work in forming man such as he is before the narrative begins.

It may be said that it seems inconsistent with the dignity of man's nature as described in the Bible to believe that his formation was effected by any process of evolution, still more by any such process of evolution as would represent him to have been an animal before he became a man.

But, in the first place, it is to be observed that Science does not yet assert, and there is no reason to believe that it ever will assert, that man became a fully developed animal, with the brute instincts and inclinations, appetites and passions, fully formed, an animal such as we see other animals now, before he passed on into a man such as man is now. His body may have been developed according to the theory of Evolution, yet along a parallel but independent line of its own; but at any rate it branched off from other animals at a very early point in the descent of animal life. And, further, as Science cannot yet assert that life was not introduced into the world when made habitable by a direct creative act, so too Science cannot yet assert, and it is tolerably certain will never assert, that the higher and added life, the spiritual faculty, which is man's characteristic prerogative, was not given to man by a direct creative act as soon as the body which was to be the seat and the instrument of that spiritual faculty had been sufficiently developed to receive it. That the body should have been first prepared, and that when it was prepared the soul should either have been then given, or then first made to live in the image of God, – this is a supposition which is inconsistent neither with what the Bible tells nor with what Science has up to this time proved.

And to this must be added that it is out of place for us to define what is consistent or inconsistent with the dignity of man in the process or method by which he was created to be what he is. His dignity consists in his possession of the spiritual faculty, and not in the method by which he became possessed of it. We cannot tell, we never can tell, and the Bible never professes to tell, what powers or gifts are wrapped up in matter itself, or in that living matter of which we are made. How absolutely nothing we know of the mode by which any single soul is created! The germ which is to become a man can be traced by the physiologist through all the changes that it has to undergo before it comes to life. Is the future soul wrapped up in it from the first, and dormant till the hour of awakening comes? or is it given at some moment in the development?[8] We see in the infant how its powers expand, and we know that the spiritual faculty, the very essence of its being, has a development like the other faculties. It has in it the gift of speech, and yet it cannot speak. Judgment, and taste, and power of thought; self-sacrifice and unswerving truth; science and art, and spiritual understanding, all may be there in abundant measure and yet may show no sign. All this we know; and because it is common and well known we see nothing inconsistent with the dignity of our nature in this concealment of all that dignity, helpless and powerless, within the form of an infant in arms. With this before us it is impossible to say that anything which Science has yet proved, or ever has any chance of proving, is inconsistent with the place given to man in Creation by the teaching of the Bible.

In conclusion, we cannot find that Science, in teaching Evolution, has yet asserted anything that is inconsistent with Revelation, unless we assume that Revelation was intended not to teach spiritual truth only, but physical truth also. Here, as in all similar cases, we find that the writer of the Book of Genesis, like all the other writers in the Bible, took nature as he saw it, and expressed his teaching in language corresponding to what he saw. And the doctrine of Evolution, in so far as it has been shown to be true, does but fill out in detail the declaration that we are 'fearfully and wonderfully made; marvellous are Thy works; and that my soul knoweth right well.' There is nothing in all that Science has yet taught, or is on the way to teach, which conflicts with the doctrine that we are made in the

Divine Image, rulers of the creation around us by a Divine superiority, the recipients of a Revelation from a Father in Heaven, and responsible to judgment by His Law. We know not how the first human soul was made, just as we know not how any human soul has been made since; but we know that we are, in a sense in which no other creatures living with us are, the children of His special care.

Lecture VIII

The Conclusion of the Argument

'No man can say that Jesus is the Lord, but by the Holy Ghost.' I *Cor.* xii. 3.

It is now the proper time to review the argument of these Lectures, and to endeavour to trace, if possible, the source of the estrangement which just at present separates Religion and Science.

The postulate of Science is admitted on all hands to be the uniformity of nature, and the proof of this postulate has been found to consist in an induction from the facts which nature presents and our senses observe. Uniformity is quickly noticed, and after it has been noticed for some time it is instinctively used as a working hypothesis. So used it accumulates perpetually increasing evidence of its truth, and if we except two great classes of facts, we never find any instance of its failure. The two classes of facts which are thus excepted are the acts of the human will and the miraculous element in Revelation, both of them instances of one thing, namely, the interference of the moral with the physical. To complete the induction and to deprive the denial of universal uniformity of all evidence to rest on, all that is necessary is to get rid of these two exceptions. If Science could get rid of these exceptions, though it could not be said that the fundamental postulate was demonstrated, it could be said that all the evidence was in its favour and absolutely no evidence against it. And although scientific belief would then still rank below mathematical belief, it would nevertheless have a cogency quite irresistible. Science would not thereby gain in power of progress, in practical acceptance, or in utility to man. But men are so constituted that completeness gives a special kind of satisfaction not to be got in any other way. If Science could but be complete it would seem to gain in dignity, if it gained in nothing else. And it is easy to foster a kind of passion for this completeness until every attempt to question it is resented. I have seen a boy first learning mechanics show a dislike to consider the effect of friction as marring the symmetry and beauty of mechanical problems; too vague, too uncertain, too irregular to be allowed any entrance into a system which is so rounded and so precise without it. And something of the same temper can sometimes be seen in students of Science at the very thought of there being anything in the world not under the dominion of the great scientific postulate. The world which thus contains something which Science cannot deal with is pronounced forthwith to be not the world that we know, not the world with which we are concerned; a conceivable world if we choose to indulge our imagination in such dreams, but not a real world either now or at any time before or after. And yet the freedom of the human will and the sense which cannot be eradicated of the responsibility attaching to all human conduct, perpetually retorts that this world in which we live contains an element which cannot be subdued to obedience to the scientific law, but will have a course of its own. The sense of responsibility is a rock which no demand for completeness in Science can crush. All attempts at reconciling the mechanical firmness of an unbroken law of uniformity with the voice within that cannot be silenced telling us that we must answer for our action, have failed, and we know that they will for ever fail.

If indeed it could be said that the progress of Science was really barred by this inability to make the induction complete, and to assert the unbroken uniformity of all nature; if it could be said that any uncertainty was thus cast over scientific conclusions, or any false or misleading lights thus held up to draw inquirers from the true path, it would undoubtedly become a duty to examine, and to examine anxiously, whether indeed it could be true that our faculties were thus hopelessly at variance with each other, the scientific faculty imposing on us one belief, and the spiritual faculty another, and the two practically irreconcileable. But there is no reason whatever for thinking this. Newton's investigations were unquestionably pursued, as all true scientific investigations must ever be pursued, in reliance on the truth of the uniformity of nature, and yet he never felt it the slightest hindrance to his progress that he always tacitly and often expressly acknowledged that God had reserved to Himself the power of setting this uniformity aside, and indeed believed that He had used this power. The believer who asserts the universality of a law except when God works a miracle to set it aside is certainly at no real disadvantage in comparison with an unbeliever who makes the same assertion with no qualification at all. It is granted on all hands that miracles are, and ever have been, exceedingly rare, and for that reason need not be taken into account in the investigation of nature. It is granted that the freedom of the human will works within narrow limits, and very slowly and slightly affects the great mass of human conduct and what depends on human conduct. And Science has often to deal with approximations when nothing but approximations can be obtained. We perpetually meet in nature with quantities and relations that cannot be accurately expressed nor accurately ascertained, and we have to be content with approximations, and we know how to use them in Science. Many chemical properties can only be so expressed; many primary facts, such as the distances, the volumes, the weights of heavenly bodies; and yet the approximations serve our purpose. And so too, if there be a reserve still uncovered by the scientific postulate, that will not in any degree affect our investigation of what is so covered.

In short, the unity of all things which Science is for ever seeking will be found not in the physical world alone, but in the physical and spiritual united. That unity embraces both. And the uniformity which is the expression of that unity is not a uniformity complete in nature, taken by itself, but complete when the two worlds are taken together. And this Science ought to recognise.

Let us turn from the physical to the spiritual.

The voice within us which demands our acceptance of religion makes no direct appeal to the evidence supplied by the senses. We are called on to believe in a supreme law of duty on pain of being lowered before our own consciences. And this law of duty goes on to assert its own supremacy over all things that exist, and that not as an accidental fact, but as inherent in its essence. And this supremacy cannot be other than an accidental fact unless it be not only actual but intended. And intention implies personality; and the law thus shows itself to be a Supreme Being, claiming our reverence, and asserting Himself to be the Creator, the Ruler, and the Judge of all things that are. And this same voice within us asserts that we are responsible to Him for all our conduct, and are capable of that responsibility because free to choose what that conduct shall be. We are to believe not because the truth of this voice is proved independently of itself, but simply because we are commanded. Corroborative evidence may be looked for elsewhere, but the main, the primary evidence is within the soul.

Hence the strength of this belief depends on ourselves and on our own character. To every man the voice speaks. But its authority is felt in proportion to the spirituality of each who hears. Its acceptance is bound up in some way with our own wills. How far it is a matter of choice to believe or to disbelieve it is not possible to define. The will lies hidden as it were behind the emotions, the affections, the nobler impulses. The conscience shades off into the other faculties, and we cannot always isolate it from the rest. But though it be impossible to say precisely how the will is concerned in the spiritual belief, there can be no doubt that it always takes its part in such belief. It is the keen conscience, it is the will that can be moved to its depths by the conscience, that grasp most strongly the certainty of the law of duty. It is the man with the strongest and noblest aspirations, the man who sees the beauty of humility, the man who feels most strongly the deep peace of self-sacrifice, *that* is the man who finds the voice within most irresistible. It is not by any means always the man who lives the most correct life; correctness of life may be due to natural and not to spiritual causes. And the man whom we should find faultless in point of morals may yet be wanting in spiritual depth, and not have as yet, and perhaps may not have to the last, the spiritual faculty strong within him. But the man, even if he have many and grievous faults, who nevertheless is keenly suscep- tible of higher things, is the one to whom the voice within speaks with authority not to be gainsaid, and to him that voice is final.

It is this fact that the perception of things spiritual varies from man to man, and depends on character, and involves action of the will, that makes it always possible to represent our knowledge of the law of duty as in itself standing on a less sure foundation than our knowledge of scientific truth. Whether a man has or has not the necessary power of mind to comprehend scientific reasoning is tested with comparative ease. And if he have that power, the reasoning is certain in course of time to be understood, and when it is understood it compels assent so long as it keeps within its own proper domain. But the perception of spiritual truth depends on a faculty whose power or weakness it is far more difficult to test; and it involves the will which may be exerted on either side. And for this reason men sometimes dismiss this truth as being no more than an imagination, needed by some men to satisfy an emotional nature, but having no substance that can be brought to an external test. The believer in God knows that the truth which he holds is as certain as the axioms of mathematics; but he cannot make others know this whose spiritual faculty is not awake; and he is liable to be asked for proof not of the spiritual but of the physical kind.

Now this much must be acknowledged, that we cannot but expect the claim to supremacy over all things to show itself in some way in the creation which has come from Him who makes that claim. It would, no doubt, be a serious difficulty if things physical and things spiritual were cut off from one another by an absolute gulf; if we were required to believe that God had created and now ruled everything, and yet we could trace not the slightest evidence of His hand either in the creation or in the history of the world.

There are then two ways in which we are able to recognise Him even in this world of phenomena. For in the first place, the creation in its order and its beauty and its marvellous adaptation of means to ends, confirms the assertion of the spiritual faculty that it owes its origin to an intelligent and benevolent purpose, exhibited in the form in which purpose is always exhibited. It works towards ends which we should expect a holy and benevolent Creator to have in view, and it accomplishes those ends in so large a proportion that, making allowance for the limited range of our knowledge, the general aim of the whole is seen with sufficient clearness. The argument is not strong enough to compel assent from those who have no ears for the inward spiritual voice, but it is abundantly sufficient to answer those who argue that there cannot be a Creator because they cannot trace His action. And the scientific doctrine of Evolution, which at first seemed to take away the force of this argument, is found on examination to confirm it and expand it. The doctrine of Evolution shows that with whatever design the world was formed, that design was entertained at the very beginning[9] and impressed on every particle of created matter, and that the appearances of failure are not only to be accounted for by the limitation of our knowledge, but also by the fact that we are contemplating the work before it has been completed.

And in the second place, while the creation, the more closely it is examined the more distinctly shows the marks of the wisdom and goodness of the Creator, so the history of the world exhibits in the Revelation made to man clear proofs of that heavenly love which corresponds to the character of Him who has put love at the head of all the requirements of His law. The Revelation given to us has undeniably made a real mark on the world. It has upheld millions of men in a holiness of life corresponding in a very real degree to the holiness required by the law of duty. It has perpetually more and more cleared up the true teaching of that law. It is still continuing the same process, and generation after generation is better able to understand that teaching. Its fruits have been a harvest of saints and martyrs, some known and reverenced, some quite unnoticed. It has leavened all literature and all legislation. It has changed the customs of mankind and is still changing them. And if it be replied that all this is nothing but one form of the development of humanity and shows no proof of a Divine Ruler, we have a right to ask what then could be the source of such a development, and how is it that so great a power should always have worked in the name of God and should have always referred everything to His command? That fanaticism should plead God's authority without any right to do so is intelligible. But is it intelligible that all this truth and justice and purity and self-sacrificing love, all this obedience to the Supreme Law, should be the fruit of believing a lie? If there be a God, it is to be expected that He would communicate with His creatures if those creatures were capable of receiving the communication; and if He did communicate with His creatures it is to be expected that His communication would be such as we find in the Bible. The purpose of the Bible, the form of it, the gradual formation of it, the steadily-growing Revelation contained in it,[10] these harmonise with the moral law revealed originally in the conscience. And the effect which the Revelation has produced on human history is real and great. The power which God's Revelation has exerted on the world is an undeniable fact among phenomena. It is not a demonstration of His existence; but it is a full answer to those who say, 'If God made and rules the world why do we find no signs of His hand in its course?'

And thirdly, this Revelation has not merely taken the form of a message or a series of messages, but has culminated in the appearance of a person who has always satisfied and still satisfies the conception formed by our spiritual faculty of a human representation of the divine law. Our Lord's life is that law translated into human action, and all the more because human faculties had not first framed the conception which He then came to fulfil, but He exhibited the ideal, and our conception rose as it were to correspond to it. And, as He includes in Himself all the teaching, so does He give from Himself all the power of the Revelation which He came to crown. And every true disciple of Christ can bear witness to the reality of that power in sustaining the soul.

Thus has the God, whom our spiritual faculty commands us to worship and to reverence, shown Himself in the world of phenomena. And He has given proofs of His existence and His character precisely corresponding to the conception which He has enabled, and indeed commanded, us to form of Him. And it is because the proofs that He has given are of this nature that we are tempted to ask for more proofs of a different kind.

For it is undeniable that believers and unbelievers alike are perpetually asking for proofs that shall have more of the scientific and less of the religious character, proofs that shall more distinctly appeal to the senses. Believers in all ages have longed for external support to their faith; unbelievers have refused to believe unless supplied with more physical evidence. Believers shrink from being thrown inwards on themselves; they fear the wavering of their own faith; they are alarmed at the prospect of the buttresses of their belief being taken from them. They find it easier to believe the spiritual evidence, if they can first find much physical evidence. They wish (to use the Apostle's words) to walk by sight and not by faith.[11] And unbelievers want a tangible proof that shall compel their understanding before it awakes their conscience. They demand a Revelation, not only confirmed by miracles at the time, but confirmed again and again by repeated miracles to every succeeding generation. They want miracles in every age adapted to the science of the age, miracles which no hardness of heart would be able to deny, which would convince the scientific man through his Science independently of his having any will to make holiness his aim when he had been convinced. This kind of evidence it has not pleased God to give. It is not the scientific man that God seeks as such, any more than it is the ignorant man that He seeks as such. And the proofs that He gives are plainly in all cases conditioned by the rule that the spiritually minded shall most easily and most keenly perceive their force.

And, as far as unbelievers are concerned, I do not see that more need be said except to tell them that this rule is inflexible, and that it is by another way that they must look to find God, and not by the way that they insist on choosing. But believers who are in the same case need to be warned of some very real dangers that always attend a faith which makes too much of things not spiritual.

For, first, there is a real and great danger that the spiritual may be altogether obscured by the literal and the physical. We look back with astonishment on the Rabbinical interpretations of the Old Testament, and all the more because of the really great and true thoughts that are sometimes to be found in the midst of their fanciful conceits. We can trace the mischief they did to true Religion by the perverted reverence with which they regarded the words and even the letters, and the very shapes of the letters, in which their sacred books were written. Their perversions of the law of God, their subtle refinements of interpretation, their trivial conceits, their false and misleading comments and inferences, all certainly tended to encourage the hypocrisy which our Lord rebuked, and against which St Paul contended. But we still see something of the same spirit in the attempt to maintain a verbal and even literal inspiration of the whole Bible, filling it not with the breath of a Divine Spirit, but with minute details of doctrine and precept often questionable, and, whenever separated from the principles of the eternal law, valueless or even mischievous. God's Word, instead of leading us to Him, is made to stand between and hide His face.

But, secondly, there is a serious risk that if the mind be fastened on things external in some way connected with, but yet distinct from the substance of Revelation, it may turn out that these external things cannot hold the ground on which they have been placed. They have to be given up by force at last, when they ought to have been given up long before. And when given up they too often tear away with them part of the strength of that faith of which they had previously been not only the buttress outside but a part of the living framework. It is distinctly the fault of religions, not of scientific men, that there was once a great contest between the Bible and Astronomy, that there has since been a great contest between the Bible and Geology, that there is still a great contest between the Bible and Evolution. In no one of these cases was the Revelation contained in the Bible in danger, but only the interpretation commonly put on the Bible. It is easy long afterwards to condemn the opponents of Galileo and speak of their treatment of him and his teaching as fanaticism and bigotry; and such condemnation has not unfrequently been heard from the very lips that nevertheless denounced the teaching of the geologists. But in all these cases the principle has been the same, and believers have insisted that the Bible itself was gone unless their interpretation of it was upheld. And the mischief is double. For many believers, and more especially unlearned believers, instead of gently helping one another to form the necessary modification of their view of the Bible teaching, instead of endeavouring to find the way out of the perplexity and to disentangle the true spiritual lesson from the accessories which are no part of itself, insisted that it must be all or nothing, and prepared for themselves a very severe trial. There was no doctrine involved whatever; there was nothing at stake on which the spiritual life depended. The duty to be patient, to enquire carefully, to study the other side, to wait for light, was as plain as any duty could be. But all this was forgotten in a somewhat unreasoning impulse to resist an assault on the faith. And there cannot be a doubt that on all these occasions many believers have been seriously shaken by slowly finding out that the position they have taken is untenable. When men have to give up in such circumstances they generally give up far more than they need, and in some cases an unreasonable resistance has

has been followed by an equally unreasonable surrender. And while believers have thus prepared a stumblingblock for themselves they have put quite as great a stumblingblock before others. For students of Science, informed by instant voices all around that they must choose between their Science and the Bible, knowing as they did that their Science was true, and supposing that the lovers and defenders of the Bible best knew what its teaching was, had no choice as honest men but to hold the truth as far as they possessed it and to give up the Bible in order to maintain their Science. It was a grievous injury inflicted on them; and though some among them might deserve no sympathy, there were some whom it was a great loss to lose.

But in the third place, the result of this clinging to externals is to shut out Science and all its correlative branches of knowledge from their proper office of making perpetually clearer the true and full meaning of the Revelation itself. It is intended that Religion should use the aid of Science in clearing her own conceptions. It is intended that as men advance in knowledge of God's works and in power of handling that knowledge, they should find themselves better able to interpret the message which they have received from their Father in Heaven. Our knowledge of the true meaning of the Bible has gained, and it was intended that it should gain, by the increase of other knowledge. Science makes clearer than anything else could have made it the higher level on which the Bible puts what is spiritual over what is material. I do not hesitate to ascribe to Science a clearer knowledge of the true interpretation of the first chapter of Genesis, and to scientific history a truer knowledge of the great historical prophets.[12] The advance of secular studies, as they are called, clears up much in the Psalms, and much in the other poetical Books of Scripture. I cannot doubt that this was intended from the beginning, and that as Science has already done genuine service to Religion in this way, so will it do still better service with process of time.

On this side also, as on the scientific side, the teaching of the spiritual faculty and the teaching of Revelation indicate that the physical and the spiritual worlds are one whole, and that neither is complete without the other. Science enters into Religion, and is its counterpart, and has its share to take in the conduct of life and in the formation of opinion. And the believer is bound to recognise its value and make use of its services.

In conclusion, it is plain that the antagonism between Science and Religion arises much more from a difference of spirit and temper in the students of each than from any inherent opposition between the two. The man of Science is inclined to shut out from consideration a whole body of evidence, the moral and spiritual; the believer is inclined to shut out the physical. And each, from long looking at that evidence alone which properly belongs to his own subject, is inclined to hold the other cheap, and to charge on those who adduce it either blindness of understanding or wilful refusal to accept the truth. And when such a conflict arises it is the higher and not the lower, it is Faith and not Science that is likely to suffer. For the physical evidence is tangible, and the perception of it not much affected by the character of the man who studies it; the spiritual evidence stands unshaken in itself, but it is hid from eyes that have no spiritual perception, and that perception necessarily varies with the man.

By what means then can a man keep his spiritual perception in full activity? And is there any test by which a man may know whether his spiritual faculty is in contact with the source of all spiritual life and is deriving from that source the full flow of spiritual power? Revelation, if it tells us anything, ought to tell us this. And the answer which Revelation makes is expressed in the words of St Paul, 'No man can say that Jesus is the Lord, but by the Holy Ghost.'[13] This doctrine runs through the New Testament, and it implies that one main purpose of our Lord's appearance among men was to give them in His life, His character, His example, His teaching, at once a touchstone by which they could always try their own spirits, and judge of the real condition of their own spiritual faculty, and also a vivid presentation of the supreme spiritual law by which they could for ever more and more elevate and purify and strengthen their own spiritual power and knowledge.

Let a man study the Jesus of the Gospels. Let him put before his *conscience* the teaching that Jesus gives; the picture drawn of our Father in Heaven whose holiness cannot allow a stain upon a single soul, and whose tenderness cannot endure that a single soul should perish; Who ruleth all the universe, and yet without whom not a sparrow falleth to the ground; the picture drawn of the ideal human life, the humility, the hunger and thirst after righteousness, the utter self-sacrifice, the purity; the picture drawn of human need, the help-lessness, the hopelessness of man without God. Let him ponder on all this and on the many touching expressions, the truth, the depth, the force, the superhuman sweetness and gentleness with which all is presented. And if his conscience bows before it, and can say without reserve and in unalloyed sincerity, 'This is my Lord; He shall be my teacher; here I recognise the fulness of the eternal law; at His feet will I henceforth sit and learn; through Him will I drink of the well-springs of eternal truth; His voice will I trust to the very utmost;' then may that man be sure that his conscience is in contact with the Father of spirits, and that his study will guide him into fuller and clearer knowledge, and more certain conviction that he is grasping the truth of God.

Let a man put before his *heart* our Lord's own character. Let him think of the life of privation without complaint, of service to His kind without a thought of self; of His unfailing sympathy with the unhappy, of His tenderness to the penitent; of His royal simplicity and humility; of His unwearied perseverance in the face of angry opposition; of His deep affection for the friends of His choice even when they deserted Him in His hour of darkness; of His death on the Cross and the unearthly love that breathed in every word He uttered and everything He did. Let him read all this many times; and if his heart goes out to the Man whom he is thus beholding, if he can say with all his soul, This is my Lord; here is the supreme object of my affection; Him will I love with all my strength; from Him I will never, if I can help it, let my heart swerve; no other do I know more worthy to be loved; no other will I keep more steadily before my eyes; no other will I more earnestly desire to imitate; no other shall be my example, my trust, my strength, my Saviour; if a man can say this, it is certain that his heart is touched by God, and the heavenly fire is kindled in his soul.

Let a man put before his *will* the Lord's commands; the aims, the self-restraints, the aspirations that the Lord required in His disciples. Let him ponder on the call to heavenly courage in spite of all that earth can inflict or can take away; the call to take up the Cross and follow Him that was crucified; the warnings and the promises, the precepts and the prohibitions; let him think of the Leader who never flinched, of the Lawgiver who outdid His own law; let him think on the nobleness of the aims to which He pointed; of the promise of inward peace made to those who sacrificed themselves, made by our Lord and re-echoed from the very depths of our spiritual being; let him think of the sure help promised in return for absolute trust, tried by millions of saints and never yet known to fail. Let a man put this before his will, and if he can say with all his soul, This is my Lord; here I recognise Him who has a right to my absolute obedience; here is the Master that I mean to serve and follow; and in spite of my own weakness and blindness, in spite of my sins, in spite of stumbling and weariness of resolution, in spite of temptations and in spite of falls, I will not let my eyes swerve, nor my purpose quit my will; through death itself I will obey my Lord and trust to Him to carry me through whatever comes; that man most certainly is moving in the strength of God, and the power of the Eternal Spirit lives within him.

Our Lord is the crown, nay, the very substance of all Revelation. If He cannot convince the soul, no other can. The believer stakes all faith on His truth; all hope on His power. If the man of Science would learn what it is that makes believers so sure of what they hold, he must study with an open heart the Jesus of the Gospels; if the believer seeks to keep his faith steady in the presence of so many and sometimes so violent storms of disputation, he will read of, ponder on, pray to, the Lord Jesus Christ.

Notes

INTRODUCTORY ESSAY

1. *Autobiography*, ed. Gavin de Beer (1974), p. 109.
2. See pp. 145–6.
3. *Quarterly Review*, July 1860, p. 257.
4. Peter Bayne, *The Life and Letters of Hugh Miller* (1871), vol. 1, p. 257.
5. *Autobiography*, pp. 50–1.
6. See pp. 25–45.
7. Alvar Ellegård, *Darwin and the General Reader (Göteborg, 1958)*, p. 337; also *James R. Moore, The Post-Darwinian Controversies* (1979), p. 84; and Charles Coulston Gillispie, *Genesis and Geology* (1959), p. ix.
8. See Gillispie, *Genesis and Geology*, pp. 4–5.
9. Quoted in John H. Brooke *et al.*, *The Crisis of Evolution* (1974), p. 60.
10. See pp. 87–8 for these two responses quoted in full.
11. See pp. 81–4.
12. See p. 229.
13. 1844 – see extract 2.
14. See pp. 46–7.
15. See note, pp. 224–5.
16. See p. 64.
17. See p. 208.
18. See pp. 157, 234–6 .
19. Vol. 1, p. 200.
20. See pp. 32–3, 69–72.
21. See Gillispie, *Genesis and Geology*, p. 75.
22. For the confusion of these two ideas in Victorian science, see p. 228.
23. For more on Lyell, see pp. 67–8.
24. See p. 86.
25. See p. 87.
26. See p. 108.
27. *Life and Letters*, vol. 2, p. 312 – see also p. 229 below.
28. (1874) – see p. 184.
29. See pp. 229–30.
30. See pp. 151–3.
31. See pp. 157, 236–8.
32. *Post-Darwinian Controversies*, pp. 117–21.
33. See p. 177–81.
34. See Owen Chadwick, *The Selwyn Lectures* (Auckland, 1968), Lecture 2, pp. 20–1; Moore, *Post-Darwinian Controversies*, pp. 58–68; J. R. Lucas, 'Wilberforce and Huxley: a legendary encounter', *The Historical Journal*, 22, no. 2 (1979), p. 329;

and Frank M. Turner, 'John Tyndall and Victorian scientific naturalism', in *John Tyndall*, ed. W. H. Brock *et al.* (Dublin, 1981), pp. 169–80.

35. (1862) – see p. 234.
36. *Autobiography*, p. 109.
37. See Turner, 'John Tyndall', pp. 174–5.
38. See pp. 146–7, 173.
39. See Turner, 'John Tyndall'; and 'Victorian scientific naturalism and Thomas Carlyle', *Victorian Studies*, 18 (1975), 325–43.
40. See pp. 239–40.
41. See p. 241.
42. 'Science and Morals', *Collected Essays* (1893), vol. 9, p. 146.
43. 'On the Study of Physics', 1854, *Fragments* (1889), vol. 1, p. 291.
44. 'Science and Man', 1877, *Fragments*, vol. 2, p. 337.
45. See p. 173.
46. *Post-Darwinian Controversies*, p. ix.
47. p. 102.
48. For this argument, see W. F. Cannon, 'The bases of Darwin's achievement: a revaluation', *Victorian Studies* (Dec. 1961).
49. See pp. 220–1.
50. As quoted by Baden Powell, 'On the Study of the Evidences of Christianity', *Essays and Reviews* (1860), p. 120.
51. See W. F. Cannon, 'Scientists and Broad Churchmen: an early Victorian intellectual network', *Journal of British Studies*, 4, no. 1 (Nov. 1964), 65–88.
52. See extract 5.
53. *Quarterly Review*, Jan. 1861, pp. 248–305.
54. pp. 95, 295–6, 332.
55. Ch. 12.
56. See extract 5.
57. See p. 190.
58. *Essays and Reviews*, p. 139.
59. See pp. 111, 143.
60. 'On the Interpretation of Scripture', *Essays and Reviews*, p. 374.
61. See pp. 233.
62. *Collected Essays*, vol. 1, p. 156.
63. See Ieuan Ellis, *Seven Against Christ* (1980), p. 108.
64. See extract 9.
65. See pp. 87–8, 230.
66. Quoted by Ellegård, *Darwin and the General Reader*, p. 103.
67. ed. Clark and Hughes (1890), vol. 2, pp. 76–8.
68. 31 Aug., p. 308.
69. See p. 46.
70. See pp. 67–8.
71. *Life and Letters*, vol. 2, pp. 332–3, 334.
72. *Genesis and Geology*, p. 186.
73. *Post-Darwinian Controversies*, p. 90.
74. *Selwyn Lectures*, Lecture 2, p. 16.
75. A collection of lectures first written from 1852, and published together under this title in 1873.
76. Discourse IX, 'Duties of the Church Towards Knowledge', *The Idea of a University*, ed. I. T. Ker (1976), pp. 190–3.
77. Lecture VII, 'Christianity and Physical Science', *Idea of a University*, p. 361.

78. *ibid.*, p. 354.
79. *ibid.*, p. 355.
80. Lecture V, 'A Form of Infidelity of the Day', *Idea of a University*, pp. 324–5.
81. Discourse IX, *Idea of a University*, p. 189.
82. *Post-Darwinian Controversies*, p. 25, and pp. 230–1 below.
83. See *Post-Darwinian Controversies*, pp. 24–8.
84. See pp. 156–7.
85. Francis Darwin, *The Life and Letters of Charles Darwin* (1887), vol. 2, p. 203.

1. WILLIAM PALEY, *Natural Theology*

1. Leslie Stephen goes into the antecedents of the 'watch' as an analogy for the designed universe, in *History of English Thought in the Eighteenth Century*, p. 409, footnote. See also *New Interactions between Theology and Natural Science*, ed. John Brooke *et al.* (1974), pp. 15–17, for its use in Robert Boyle's natural theology.
2. Paley is here arguing against a totally naturalistic interpretation of Nature, which would attribute causation to 'natural laws'. He contends that a 'law' is not the same as a 'cause' – it is merely a description of what happens, rather than a reason for it to happen. It is interesting that Darwin later makes a similar criticism of Paley's own type of 'explanation': 'It is so easy to hide our ignorance under such expressions as the "plan of creation", "unity of design" &c., and to think that we give an explanation when we only restate a fact' (see p. 103). In contrast, Darwin's 'law' of 'natural selection' is not purely descriptive, it is a causal mechanism. Darwin himself was ambiguous about the entire self-sufficiency of natural law: in 1860, he wrote, 'I am inclined to look at everything as resulting from designed laws, with the details, whether good or bad, left to the working out of what we may call chance.' But in 1881 he expressed his disagreement with the idea 'that the existence of so-called natural laws implies purpose. I cannot see this' (*Life and Letters*, vol. 2, p. 312; vol. 1, p. 315).
3. This grotesque idea is Paley's means of including the reproductive powers of the organic world in his analogy. Reproduction does not imply independent self-generation.
4. Again, Paley is arguing against the self-sufficiency of Nature – however far back you trace natural causes, eventually you must come to a supernatural First Cause.
5. Here we come to the centre of Paley's argument, and also possibly one of its weak points – that is, the analogy between the works of God in Nature and the works of human contrivance. Paley's argument depends on a very anthropomorphic concept of God. Paley can be seen to be projecting his own limited, eighteenth-century, human personality onto the Creator. As Leslie Stephen says, 'God has become civilised like man; he has become scientific and ingenious; he is superior to Watt or Priestley in devising mechanical and chemical contrivances, and is, therefore, made in the image of that generation of which Watt and Priestley were conspicuous lights' (*History of English Thought in the Eighteenth Century*, p. 411). The limiting anthropomorphism of natural theology was later satirised by Browning in his poem 'Caliban upon Setebos, or Natural Theology in the Island' (1864), whose epigraph is 'Thou thoughtest that I was altogether such a one as thyself' (Psalm 1.21). In the poem, Caliban is theorising about the nature of his God, Setebos, who turns out to be remarkably similar in character to Caliban himself, in his arbitrary savagery. Browning is applying his caricature of natural theology to a Darwinian Nature, but by exposing the anthropomorphic limitations of the whole natural theological approach, he demonstrates its

irrelevance to any truly spiritual experience. Here is an example of Caliban's analogies between his own 'contrivances' and God's:

> Put case, unable to be what I wish,
> I yet could make a live bird out of clay:
> Would I not take clay, pinch my Caliban
> Able to fly? – for, there, see, he hath wings,
> And great comb like the hoopoe's to admire,
> And there, a sting to do his foes offense,
> There, and I will that he begin to live,
> Fly to yon rock-top, nip me off the horns
> Of grigs high up that made the merry din,
> Saucy through their veined wings, and mind me not.
> In which feat, if his leg snapped, brittle clay, –
> And he lay stupid-like – why, I should laugh;
> And if he, spying me, should fall to weep,
> Beseech me to be good, repair his wrong,
> Bid his poor leg smart less or grow again –
> Well, as the chance were, this might take or else
> Not take my fancy: I might hear his cry,
> And give the manikin three sound legs for one,
> Or pluck the other off, leave him like an egg,
> And lessoned he was mine and merely clay.
> Were this no pleasure, lying in the thyme,
> Drinking the mash, with brain become alive,
> Making and marring clay at will? So He.

(lines 75–97)

6. The construction of the eye as evidence of design had been used as an example as far back as Cicero, in *De Natura Deorum*. It was also used by Darwin, as a central example of the difficulties of his theory of natural selection when faced with 'organs of extreme perfection'. As Darwin also brings in the 'telescope' analogy, it seems likely he was thinking of Paley here, and demolishing what was both a lynch-pin of Paley's argument and a possible objection to his own theory. Here is Darwin's argument:

> To suppose that the eye, with all its inimitable contrivances for adjusting the focus to different distances, for admitting different amounts of light, and for the correction of spherical and chromatic aberration, could have been formed by natural selection, seems, I freely confess, absurd in the highest possible degree. Yet reason tells me, that if numerous gradations from a perfect and complex eye to one very imperfect and simple, each grade being useful to its possessor, can be shown to exist; if further, the eye does vary ever so slightly, and the variations be inherited, which is certainly the case; and if any variation or modification in the organ be ever useful to an animal under changing conditions of life, then the difficulty of believing that a perfect and complex eye could be formed by natural selection, though insuperable to our imagination, can hardly be considered real . . .
>
> It is scarcely possible to avoid comparing the eye to a telescope. We know that this instrument has been perfected by the long-continued efforts of the highest human intellects; and we naturally infer that the eye has been formed by a somewhat analogous process. But may not this inference be presumptuous? Have we any right to assume that the Creator works by

intellectual powers like those of man? If we must compare the eye to an optical instrument, we ought in imagination to take a thick layer of transparent tissue, with a nerve sensitive to light beneath, and then suppose every part of this layer to be continually changing slowly in density, so as to separate into layers of different densities and thicknesses, placed at different distances from each other, and with the surfaces of each layer slowly changing in form. Further we must suppose that there is a power always intently watching each slight accidental alteration in the transparent layers; and carefully selecting each alteration which, under varied circumstances, may in any way, or in any degree, tend to produce a distincter image. We must suppose each new state of the instrument to be multiplied by the million; and each to be preserved till a better be produced, and then the old ones to be destroyed. In living bodies, variation will cause the slight alterations, generation will multiply them almost infinitely, and natural selection will pick out with unerring skill each improvement. Let this process go on for millions on millions of years; and during each year on millions of individuals of many kinds; and may we not believe that a living optical instrument might thus be formed as superior to one of glass, as the works of the Creator are to those of man? (*Origin*, pp. 186–9)

It is interesting to find Darwin protesting against the anthropomorphism of natural theology, but at the same time using highly anthropomorphic language to describe the action of 'natural selection': 'always intently watching', 'carefully selecting', 'pick out with unerring skill'. The difference of course is that Darwin's language is purely metaphorical; and despite the pious references to 'the works of the Creator', Darwin is giving purely naturalistic causes for one of Paley's key 'evidences'.

7. John Harrison (1693–1776), horologist, invented many improvements to the construction of clocks and watches. 'To prevent the effects of heat and cold upon timekeepers, he devised in 1726 his "gridiron pendulum" which consists in having the bob suspended by a series of parallel rods, alternately of steel and brass, so arranged that the downward expansion of the steel rods from change of temperature is exactly compensated for by the upward expansion of the brass rods. This principle of compensation is now generally accepted' (*DNB*).

8. Paley does not include insects in the examples of the exquisite adaptations of the eye in each species, but we can see the connection between the sorts of examples of contrivance he gives here, and those that Tennyson gives in stanza CXXIV of *In Memoriam*, where the poet rejects natural theology as a way of finding God, in favour of direct emotional experience:

> I found Him not in world or sun,
>   Or eagle's wing, or insect's eye,
>   Nor through the questions men may try,
> The petty cobwebs we have spun.
>
> If e'er when faith had fallen asleep,
>   I heard a voice, 'believe no more,'
>   And heard an ever-breaking shore
> That tumbled in the Godless deep,
>
> A warmth within the breast would melt
>   The freezing reason's colder part,

And like a man in wrath the heart
Stood up and answered, 'I have felt.'

(lines 5–16)

Tennyson had of course like Darwin read Paley at Cambridge, if not before: there was a copy of *Natural Theology* at Somersby. At a meeting of the Apostles at Cambridge, Tennyson had voted 'No' to the question 'Is an intelligible First Cause deducible from the phenomena of the Universe?' His difficulty in accepting natural theology in *In Memoriam* comes not from any alternative scientific explanation for Paley's evidences, but from the difficulty of applying Paley's way of reasoning to the discoveries of geology. Paley's argument assumes a fixed creation, every detail of which was carefully constructed by God: the evidence of the extinction of species in geology seemed to Tennyson to indicate instead God's carelessness and destructiveness.

9. Probably Johann Sturm (1607–89), a religious thinker and educationalist, supporter of Zwingli against Luther.

10. *Memoirs for natural history of animals, containing the anatomical description of several creatures dissected by the Royal Academy of Sciences at Paris,* Done into English [from the 'Memoires' of Claude Perrault] by a Fellow of the Royal Society [Alexander Pitfield] (1701), p. 249.

2. ROBERT CHAMBERS, *Vestiges of the Natural History of Creation*

1. Chambers used the word 'development' rather than 'evolution' – 'evolution' was hardly ever used in its modern sense at this time, and it only occurs once in Darwin's *Origin of Species*. It was usually used to refer more particularly to the growth of an embryo, rather than the development of species. Darwin himself often uses the words 'modification' and 'mutation' – unlike 'evolution' or 'development', these do not imply a *progressive* unfolding of *inherent* potential.

2. The French naturalist, Georges Cuvier (1769–1832), opponent of Lamarck.

3. Chambers' theory relies centrally on the importance of recent embryological evidence, showing the stages through which an embryo passes during its development. These seemed to correspond to the forms of lower animals, in the order in which they first appeared in the fossil record. Chambers therefore sees a parallel between species development and embryo development, which he converts into an identity of cause in *Vestiges* (see p. 53), speaking of 'the parity, or rather identity, of the laws presiding over the development of the animated tribes on the face of the earth, and that of the individual in embryo'. The theory that embryo development parallels species development came to be known as 'ontogeny recapitulates phylogeny', or 'recapitulation theory'. It became even more popular after Darwin's *Origin* had been published, in spite of insufficient detailed evidence to support it. It had its roots in the metaphysical ideas of the German *Naturphilosophen* (see extract 3, pp. 79–80), who saw Nature as the manifestation of essential archetypes (see William Coleman, *Biology in the Nineteenth Century* (1971), pp. 36, 47–54, 56, 80, 82). Tennyson makes use of 'recapitulation' in the Epilogue to *In Memoriam*, which could possibly have been influenced by *Vestiges*, when he imagines the conception of his sister's child:

A soul shall draw from out the vast
And strike his being into bounds,

And, moved through life of lower phase,
　Result in man, be born and think,
And act and love, a closer link
　Betwixt us and the crowning race . . .

(verses 31–2)

Here Tennyson combines the embryological evidence with Chambers' idea of the eventual development of a 'crowning race'.

4. Perceval Barton Lord, *Popular Physiology; being a familiar explanation of the most interesting facts connected with the structure and functions of animals and particularly of man*, 2nd ed. (1839), pp. 295–6.

5. The embryological evidence of the development of the human brain through stages resembling the brains of lower creatures was referred to by Tennyson in the 1832 version of *The Palace of Art*, as one of the presumptuous claims of the soul:

> 'From change to change four times within the womb
> 　The brain is moulded', she began,
> 'So through all phases of all thought I come
> 　Into the perfect man.

> 'All nature widens upward: evermore
> 　The simpler essence lower lies.
> More complex is more perfect, owning more
> 　Discourse, more widely wise.'

6. Sir Roderick Murchison (1792–1871) was an important member of the Geological Society, elected President in 1831. He worked closely with Lyell and with Sedgwick. He pioneered the investigation of the older layers of rock, beneath the Carboniferous formations, where he looked for evidence of the origin of life. He coined the word 'Silurian' for these earlier layers, and in 1838 he published his findings in *The Silurian System*.

7. John Phillips (1800–74) was a nephew and helper of William Smith, the founder of stratigraphy (i.e. dating strata by their fossil contents). Phillips did further work on stratigraphy. In 1844, he became Professor of Geology at Trinity College, Dublin; in 1856, he succeeded Buckland as Professor of Geology at Oxford. He had recently done some work on Palaeozoic (the oldest fossil-bearing) formations.

8. Chambers' belief in life on other planets supports his vision of *universal* natural law. There was a notable controversy on this question of 'the plurality of worlds' in the 1840s and 1850s, between William Whewell and Sir David Brewster. Both used primarily theological, as opposed to scientific, arguments. See Whewell, *Of the Plurality of Worlds* (1853) and Brewster, *More Worlds than One, the Creed of the Philosopher and the Hope of the Christian* (1854), and Charles Coulston Gillispie, *Genesis and Geology* (1959), pp. 205–7.

9. William Kirby and William Spence, *An Introduction to Entomology; or Elements of the natural history of insects* (4 vols., 1816–26), vol. 2, pp. 132–3.

10. Chambers' belief in the *Acarus Crossii* is his most outstanding scientific blunder. Edward Cross and W. H. Weekes claimed to have generated a new species of *acarus* by passing an electrical current through inorganic substances. Later, it was shown to be the common *Acarus horridus*, that had been accidentally

allowed to get into the experiment. But Chambers never removed the reference to the *acarus* in any of the later editions.

11. John Fletcher, *Rudiments of Physiology* (Edinburgh, 1835–7), pp. 8–9.

12. Carniola was formerly a duchy of Austria, but is now part of Slovenia, in Yugoslavia. Its calcareous mountains contain many caves and underground water systems, where there live animals that survived the glacial era, such as the proteus, or olm, a newt whose external gills persist throughout its life.

13. Lamarck was a deist; but the British tended to equate 'French philosopher' with 'atheist'. So Chambers stresses the deistic component of his own theory here, 'the original Divine conception'. In his caricature of Lamarck's theory, Chambers omits, though it is implied, Lamarck's theory of the inheritance of acquired characteristics. Lamarck had first put forward his theory of development in his *Philosophie Zoologique* in 1809.

14. William Macleay (1792–1865) invented a new system of biological classification, known as the 'quinary' or 'circular' system. It involved dividing each zoological group into five interlocking circular arrangements. William Swainson (1789–1855), and Nicholas Vigors (1785–1840), both zoologists, adhered to this system, and tried to apply it in their work.

15. This supposed 'degradation' is what most of Chambers' critics fixed on. Not only is Chambers reducing man to beast, as Sedgwick protested, but he is sidestepping the issue of man's immortal soul, which, in Christianity, differentiates him from the animals. This is the centre of Hugh Miller's attack on *Vestiges* in his *Footprints of the Creator* (1847):

> There are, however, beliefs, in no degree less important to the moralist or the Christian than even that in the being of a God, which seem wholly incompatible with the development hypothesis. If, during a period so vast as to be scarce expressible by figures, the creatures now human have been rising, by *almost* infinitesimals, from compound microscopic cells, – minute vital globules within globules, begot by electricity on dead gelatinous matter, – until they have at length become the men and women whom we see around us, we must hold either the monstrous belief, that all the vitalities, whether those of monads or of mites, of fishes or of reptiles, of birds or of beasts, are individually and inherently immortal and undying, or that human souls are *not* so. The difference between the dying and the undying, – between the spirit of the brute that goeth downward, and the spirit of the man that goeth upward, – is not a difference infinitesimally, or even atomically, *small*. It possesses all the breadth of the eternity to come, and is an *infinitely great* difference. It cannot, if I may so express myself, be shaded off by infinitesimals or atoms; for it is a difference which – as there can be no class of beings intermediate in their nature between the dying and the undying – admits not of gradation at all. What mind regulated by the ordinary principles of human belief can possibly hold that every one of the thousand vital points which swim in a drop of stagnant water are inherently fitted to maintain their individually throughout eternity? Or how can it be rationally held that a mere progressive step, in itself no more important than that effected by the addition of a single brick to a house in the building state, or of a single atom to a body in the growing state, could ever have produced immortality? And yet, if the *spirit* of a monad or of a mollusc be not immortal, then must there either have been a point in the history of the species at which a dying brute, – differing from its offspring merely by an inferiority of development, represented by a few atoms, mayhap by a single atom, –

produced an undying man, or man in his present state must be a mere animal, possessed of no immortal soul, and as irresponsible for his actions to the God before whose bar he is, in consequence, never to appear, as his presumed relatives and progenitors the beasts that perish. Nor will it do to attempt escaping from the difficulty, by alleging that God at some certain link in the chain *might* have converted a mortal creature into an immortal existence, by breathing into it a 'living soul;' seeing that a renunciation of any such direct interference on the part of the Deity in the work of creation forms the prominent and characteristic feature of the scheme, – nay, that it constitutes the very nucleus round which the scheme has originated. And thus, though the development theory be not atheistic, it is at least practically tantamount to atheism. For, if man be a dying creature, restricted in his existence to the present scene of things, what does it really matter to him, for any one moral purpose, whether there be a God or no? If in reality on the same religious level with the dog, wolf, and fox, that are by nature *atheists*, – a nature most properly coupled with irresponsibility, – to what one practical purpose should he know or believe in a God whom he, as certainly as they, is never to meet as his Judge? or why should he square his conduct by the requirements of the moral code, farther than a low and convenient expediency may chance to demand? (*Footprints*, 11th ed. (1869), pp. 13–14)

3. HUGH MILLER, *The Testimony of the Rocks*

1. Robert Hall (1764–1831) was a Baptist divine. In 1800, the delivery and publication of his discourse on 'Modern Infidelity considered with respect to its Influence on Society' made a great sensation. He was an admirer of the scientist, Joseph Priestley.

2. Richard Bentley, classicist and natural theologian, gave the Boyle Lecture in 1692, 'A Confutation of Atheism from the Origin and Frame of the World'. Robert Boyle, the scientist, had left money for a series of lectures 'for proving the Christian Religion, against notorious Infidels, viz. Atheists, Theists, Pagans, Jews and Mahometans, not descending lower to any Controversies, that are among the Christians themselves'.

3. Paley too had been embarrassed by this problem. His analogy of the 'chain' does not really provide a way out: 'A chain composed of an infinite number of links, can no more support itself, than a chain composed of a finite number of links' (see p. 32). There is no clear reason why the chain should need 'support'. Here Miller sees himself as improving upon natural theology, and providing empirical geological evidence as opposed to 'metaphysic' arguments to confute the atheists.

4. The names of the various geological systems and ages were still being coined and decided upon in the nineteenth century. This is the scheme that Miller seems to be working with: geological time is divided into three great eras, the Palaeozoic (the most ancient fossil-bearing strata), the Secondary, and the Tertiary. There is also the 'Recent', which includes the appearance of Man, but Miller sees this as a smooth continuation of the Tertiary, with no catastrophic break intervening. The Palaeozoic is divided into the Silurian (most ancient), the Old Red Sandstone, the Carboniferous (or Coal Measures), and the Permian. The Secondary divides into the Trias (most ancient), the Lias, the Oolite, the Cretaceous, and the Weald. The Tertiary is divided into the Eocene, the Miocene, the

Pliocene (this includes the Coraline Crag), and the Pleistocene (to which belong the Red Crag, and the Clyde-beds). See *Testimony of the Rocks*, pp. 1–191.

5. *Uncle Tom's Cabin.*

6. Miller had refuted Lamarck in *The Old Red Sandstone* (1841) and Chambers in *Footprints of the Creator* (1847). It sounds as if he is specifically mocking Chambers here, with the reference to embryological development near the end of the previous paragraph, and the theory of spontaneous generation in this paragraph. Miller presents spontaneous generation as a silly, totally unscientific, superstition.

7. Miller here takes up a strategy used by some of Chambers' critics: attacking *Vestiges* without actually *naming* it. William Whewell had done this in his *Indications of a Creator* (1845), and so had Sir John Herschel in his presidential address to the British Association in 1845. Miller had named *Vestiges* in his attack on it in *Footprints*: perhaps he felt this had only drawn attention to the book, and caused more people to buy it. Thus here he only refers darkly to modern 'Lamarckians'.

8. Joachim Barrande (1799–1883) was a French palaeontologist and stratigrapher, who worked mainly in Bohemia. He studied the Silurian system, and worked out a genealogy for the trilobites he found. He was a Cuverian catastrophist.

9. This absence of links also impressed Lyell, and was one of his reasons for rejecting Lamarck's theory in *The Principles of Geology*. However, Lyell was also very aware of the imperfection of the geological record, which was not by any means a full account of the history of species. It was this awareness that enabled him eventually to accept Darwin's evolutionary theory.

10. Miller is referring to David Hume here, who had attacked natural theology in his *Dialogues Concerning Natural Religion* (1779). Miller is using geology to refute two of Hume's arguments in particular: first, that since no one has ever experienced the creation of worlds, design cannot prove that our world was created by God. According to Hume's view of causation, *one* instance was not enough to prove a connection between a cause and an effect: it was only repeated similar experience that connected the two. Miller refutes this argument by producing exactly the *'experience* in creations' that Hume requires, from the geological evidence of successive Creations. Secondly, Hume argues that a cause must be in a proportion to its effect, so we cannot infer an infinite cause from a finite universe. Miller refutes this by showing that the Divine cause was, as it were, working 'under strength' in early Creations, as we can see from His subsequent Creations. If we had applied Hume's argument to the *first* Creation, we would have assumed a totally inadequate conception of the Divine Power as it was later to be shown.

11. Bolingbroke and Jenyns were eighteenth-century deistic thinkers. Pope's *Essay on Man*, which finds God in the order of Nature, is dedicated to Bolingbroke. Jenyns wrote the fatuously optimistic *Free Enquiry into the Nature and Origin of Evil* (1757), which was savagely attacked by Dr Johnson (see Basil Willey, *The Eighteenth Century Background* (1962), pp. 47–59). Miller refers to Johnson's critique on p. 79. Miller objects to the way these writers make man only a part of their whole ordered scheme, an insignificant link in the 'great chain of being'. He also objects to the abstract and remote nature of the God they deduce from their scheme. Miller is basing his natural theology much more on God's *intervention* in Nature than on God's *design*.

12. *Essay on Man*, Epistle I, v, lines 133–40.

13. *Essay on Man*, Epistle I, iii, lines 87–90.

14. *Essay on Man*, Epistle I, viii, lines 245–6.
15. 'The Traveller, or, A Prospect of Society' (1794), line 50.
16. *The Task*, Book V, 'The Winter Morning Walk'.
17. Lorenz Oken, German *Naturphilosophe*, proponent of a mystical 'archetypal' theory of species.
18. Sir Richard Owen, anatomist and opponent of Darwin.
19. Richard Owen, *On the Nature of the Limbs, a discourse delivered on Friday, February 9, at an evening meeting of the Royal Institution of Great Britain* (1849), p. 86.
20. Louis Agassiz, Swiss geologist, another proponent of the 'prophetic types' idea.
21. Louis Agassiz and A. A. Gould, *Outlines of Comparative Physiology* [the first part of *Principles of Zoology* – no more were published] ed. and enlarged by Thomas Wright (1851), pp. 417–18. The italics and capital letters in the quotation are Miller's.
22. Psalm 139: 16.
23. In Biblical exegesis, 'type' refers to any incident in the Old Testament which prefigures what is to happen in the New Testament. It is also a term in natural history, denoting a species or class. Miller is ingeniously bringing the two meanings together: God's earlier Creations are symbolic prophecies of His later ones, especially man, the 'antetype' who includes the whole series, and fulfils the prophecies. On this basis, rudimentary organs and 'recapitulation' – Chambers' evidence for development – can be explained away (see pp. 82–3).
24. See Virgil's Fourth Eclogue, addressed to Gaius Asinius Pollio, poet, historian, and friend of Virgil, Consul in 40 BC. In the Eclogue, Virgil predicts that a Golden Age of peace and reconciliation will begin during Pollio's Consulship: Pollio had been instrumental in bringing about a reconciliation between Octavian and Antony. Virgil also predicts the coming of a Messiah-like child, who will inaugurate the New Golden Age: it is most likely that he was referring not to Octavian himself, as Miller suggests, but to the possible birth of a son to Octavian, who had just married. Virgil's source for his Messianic ideas was probably the Sibylline Books; but some Christian readers of the poem, including Miller here, assume Virgil must have known and used the Old Testament predictions of the Messiah. The Early Church in Rome in fact interpreted the poem as predicting the birth of Christ. See E. V. Rieu, *Virgil: The Pastoral Poems, The Text of the Eclogues with a Translation* (1954), pp. 51–7, and especially translator's *Essay*, pp. 136–43.
25. Johann Gottfried Herder (1741–1803), Prussian philosopher and mystic, influenced Goethe.
26. James M'Cosh and George Dickie, *Typical Forms and Special Ends in Creation* (Edinburgh, 1856), p. 505.
27. Coleridge, *Aids to Reflection* (1825), Aphorism XXXVI, pp. 111–12. Also quoted in M'Cosh and Dickie, *Typical Forms*, p. 506.
28. Here Miller is abandoning a scientific reading of Nature, and reading it in the same way as he would read the Bible – as a book written by God, whose symbols and allegories we can decipher. This suggests that Miller was not a literalist in his reading of the Bible; but neither is he strictly scientific in his reading of Nature. Nature is another of God's attempts to communicate with us.
29. 2 Timothy, 1:10.
30. Revelation, 22:3.
31. See Argument to Epistle I, *Essay on Man*.

4. CHARLES DARWIN, *On the Origin of Species*

1. Here Darwin explicitly sets up his theory in antagonism to the 'design' theory of Paley, which assumed that God used 'means superior to, though analogous with, human reason' to perfect the organic world.

2. Darwin has a 'gradualist' preconception about the way Nature works, possibly derived from Lyell's 'uniformitarian' geology. Both Lyell and Darwin confuse *naturalism* and *gradualism* – that is, they assume that in order to account for something by natural causes they have to supply an explanation involving slow, gradual change. This confusion probably came about because both were opposing 'catastrophist' theorists, who are similarly confusing catastrophism and supernaturalism. That is, geologists like Sedgwick and Miller interpreted the geological record as evidence of a number of catastrophes which they referred to Divine intervention. But it is quite possible for there to be *natural* catastrophes. T. H. Huxley realised this, and regretted that Darwin had restricted the scope of his theory by confining himself to gradualism. As he wrote to Darwin, on first reading the *Origin*, 'you have loaded yourself with an unnecessary difficulty in adopting *Natura non facit saltum* so unreservedly' (*Life and Letters of Darwin*, vol. 2, p. 231. See also Himmelfarb, *Darwin and the Darwinian Revolution*, pp. 89–90, 265).

3. By definition, sterility is a variation that cannot be directly passed on to the next generation, so natural selection cannot have worked on individuals to preserve it. Darwin gets round this by considering the whole ant community as *one* organism, which is benefited by containing the sterile workers.

4. These last two 'laws' are Lamarckian.

5. The influence of Malthus is clear here.

6. Darwin's theory of natural selection depends on this analogy between human activity and natural processes. In a strange way, this makes him like Paley – but Darwin's aim is to show that natural selection can accomplish *unconsciously* what conscious human selection accomplishes. On p. 93, he actually stresses that man's adaptation of domestic species by selection is sometimes *unconscious*: 'He may do it unconsciously by preserving the individuals most useful to him at the time, without any thought of altering the breed.' But of course the actual selection procedure is still conscious and voluntary. Some of the difficulties of the analogy are discussed by Robert M. Young, in 'Darwin's metaphor: does nature select?', *The Monist*, 55 (1971), 442–503. Darwin often blurs the essential distinction between the two types of selection, by using highly anthropomorphic or even 'supernatural' language to describe *natural* selection: so here he describes 'this power . . . rigidly scrutinising . . . favouring the good and rejecting the bad . . . slowly and beautifully adapting each form to the most complex relations of life'. In one sense, this sort of language *strengthens* the theory, by emphasising that natural selection is quite powerful enough to accomplish all that human selection can, and more. It also strengthens natural selection's claim to rival and supersede the creative role formerly assigned to God. But on the other hand, it does blur Darwin's insistence on impersonal *natural* causation, and invite confusion and misunderstanding. For instance, a religious journal claimed that 'the action which he attributes to natural selection is clearly regulated action. Why should natural selection favour the preservation of useful varieties only? Such action cannot be referred to blind force; it can belong to mind alone'; and another periodical wrote that 'This power on the part of man to bring about changes in species such as those referred to by Mr Darwin con-

stitutes, as it appears to us, an irrefragable proof that the larger changes produced in nature were executed by and under the direction of a wise and mighty Being, who adapted fresh forms to new conditions of existence' (cited in Alvar Ellegård, *Darwin and the General Reader* (1958), pp. 125–6). These writers had clearly missed the point of natural selection. It is, however, possible to argue that Darwin's anthropomorphic language, and his whole approach via an analogy between human and natural activity, testify to the enormous influence that natural theology and its ways of thought had on him. Darwin eventually came to prefer the formulation 'survival of the fittest' (coined by Herbert Spencer), instead of 'natural selection' with its anthropomorphic connotations.

7. The only rival theory that Darwin had to contend with was that of the 'independent creation' of each species, either all at once, as in Genesis, or serially, as in the successive creations of the 'catastrophists'. Here he is massing evidence against these positions.

8. Natural selection can account for the *imperfections* of contrivance in Nature, which are inexplicable on the 'design' theory. Notice that these examples are 'imperfect' not in the sense that they do not function, but in the sense that, from a human point of view, they seem wasteful and cruel. It was his strong awareness of this sort of imperfection that led Darwin to reject belief in beneficent design – as he wrote to Asa Gray, 'I cannot persuade myself that a beneficent and omnipotent God would have designedly created the Ichneumonidae with the express intention of their feeding within the live bodies of Caterpillars, or that a cat should play with mice. Not believing this, I see no necessity in the belief that the eye was expressly designed' (Letter of 1860, *Life and Letters*, vol. 2, p. 312).

9. As described in Darwin's *Voyage of the Beagle* (1839).

10. For embryology, see endnotes to extract 2, p. 222–3.

11. Here Darwin is explicitly deriving his gradualism from Lyell. Like Lyell, he has to contend with our inability to imagine the vast amounts of time necessary for his theory to work. Archbishop Ussher (1581–1656) had fixed the creation of the world at 4004 BC, a date which was printed in the margins of the Authorised Version of the Bible throughout the nineteenth century. But geology had already undermined the credibility of this date, and 'reconcilers' like Hugh Miller had reinterpreted the Bible into harmony with the new time-span.

12. Possibly a reference to Oken's theory of archetypes, as used by Owen and Agassiz (see extract 3, p. 80).

13. Darwin could be referring here to the theory of Philip Gosse, as expressed in *Omphalos* (1857). Gosse was a marine biologist, and a member of the Plymouth Brethren. Darwin had informed him of his theory in 1857; Gosse's book was designed to refute any such theory. He argues ingeniously that whenever God created the world, it would necessarily bear 'false' marks of age: the trees would have rings as if they had been growing before, and Adam would have a naval ('omphalos'), as if he had been produced by a natural mother. By analogy, the earth would be full of fossils that *seemed* to show it too had had a previous history of growth. Gosse was very cast down by the unenthusiastic reception of his theory. The whole incident is charmingly described by Edmund Gosse in *Father and Son* (1907).

14. This is Darwin's one, intentionally vague, reference to the evolution of *man* in the *Origin*. He wrote to Wallace in 1857, 'You ask me whether I shall discuss "man". I think I shall avoid the whole subject, as so surrounded with prejudices; though I fully admit that it is the highest and most interesting problem for the naturalist' (*Life and Letters*, vol. 2, p. 109). He waited until 1871 before pub-

lishing *The Descent of Man*, in which he explicitly extends his theory to include man. Nevertheless, most of his critics took the *Origin* as implying man's animal descent, and popular references to the 'ape theory' were numerous. Bishop Wilberforce, as we shall see, took up this question in his famous attack on Darwin at the British Association in 1860 (see pp. 145–55).

15. Darwin uses the optimistic language of Victorian progressivism here. As in natural theology, everything is finally seen to be for the good: but it is also interesting to remember that Malthus had produced his argument about surplus population to prove that progress towards a perfect society was *impossible*, and not part of God's plan. In Malthus' argument, suffering and death were providentially necessary in order to check the excess population: any relief for the poor was therefore a bad thing. When Darwin's theory came to be applied to human society, social Darwinists would in fact agree with Malthus here, but in the interests of free competition and the destruction of the unfit, which would allow the fittest to survive and be improved. So while Malthusianism incorporates suffering in the interest of balance, social Darwinism incorporates it in the interest of progress and improvement.

16. The way Darwin incorporates suffering as a necessary part of his scheme was seized on by optimistic teleologists trying to reintroduce natural theology into the Darwinian view of Nature. Thus Asa Gray argues,

> Darwinian teleology has the special advantage of accounting for the imperfections and failures as well as for the successes. It not only accounts for them, but turns them to practical account. It explains the seeming waste as being part and parcel of a great economical process. Without the competing multitude, no struggle for life; and without this, no natural selection and survival of the fittest, no continuous adaptation to changing surroundings, no diversifications, and improvements, leading from the lower up to higher and nobler forms. So the most puzzling things of all to the old-school teleologists are the *principia* of the Darwinian. In this system the forms and species, in all their variety, are not mere ends in themselves, but the whole a series of means and ends, in the contemplation of which we may obtain higher and more comprehensive, and perhaps worthier, as well as more consistent, views of design in Nature than heretofore. At least, it would appear that in Darwinian evolution we may have a theory that accords with if it does not explain the principal facts, and a teleology that is free from the common objections. (*Darwiniana*, ed. A. Hunter Depree (1963), pp. 310–11)

On the other hand, we must remember that Darwin himself found these 'imperfections and failures' in Nature compelling evidence *against* Design (see p. 229).

5. CHARLES GOODWIN, 'On the Mosaic Cosmogony'

1. Nicholas Copernicus, who put forward the theory that the earth moved round the sun.

2. Galileo Galilei was persecuted by the Inquisition for supporting Copernicus' views in the first half of the seventeenth century.

3. In fact, in 1864, the encyclical *Quanta Cura*, in its 'Syllabus of errors' condemned, among others, the propositions that 'public institutions generally which are devoted to teaching literature and science and providing for the education of youth, be exempted from all authority of the Church', and that 'the Roman Pontiff can and ought to reconcile and harmonize himself with progress,

with liberalism, and with modern civilisation' (see James R. Moore, *The Post-Darwinian Controversies* (1979), p. 25). In the 'Belfast Address' in 1874 (see pp. 172–89), the scientist Tyndall is so aggressive towards religion partly because of a particular battle he is having with the Catholic Church in Ireland about the teaching of science. Goodwin goes on to make an important distinction between Catholic and Protestant attitudes to science.

4. This is the idea that the words of the Bible are literally and directly the words of the Holy Spirit, 'inspiring', in the sense of speaking through, the prophets and evangelists. Biblical scholars had discovered that this was not in fact an original Hebrew idea, it was a Greek idea adopted by the early Church; but most Christians still believed in it in the nineteenth century. The idea that the writers of Genesis were fallible human historians is central to Goodwin's argument: he keeps calling the Bible 'the Hebrew records' to stress this, and to place it in its historical context.

5. Psalm 93:1.

6. This refers to Archbishop Ussher's chronology, according to which the world was created in 4004 BC (see endnote 11, p. 229).

7. Thomas Hartwell Horne, *An Introduction to the Critical Study and Knowledge of the Holy Scriptures*, 10th ed. (1956).

8. Goodwin is referring to the 'nebular hypothesis' which P. S. Laplace (1749–1827), the French astronomer, put forward in 1796. The theory was very popular, and was an important part of Robert Chambers' cosmogony in *Vestiges*, though some doubts had been cast on it by further astronomical observations. Tennyson had also been imaginatively attracted by the theory; this is how he describes it in *The Princess*:

> This world was once a fluid haze of light,
> Till towards the centre set the starry tides
> And eddied into suns, that wheeling cast
> The planets;

> (Book II)

9. Goodwin does not come out in favour of evolutionary theory: the Essayists are by no means solidly behind Darwin.

10. This picture of a methodical and ordered introduction of new species, culminating in man, is very similar to the message of the rocks as read by Hugh Miller (see pp. 81–5), except that Goodwin favours a gradualist, not a catastrophist framework: 'the slowly continued work of ages' (p. 118). He thus accepts that man is the most recent species, and he sees both progression and design in the plan of creation.

11. Jeremiah, 4:23.

12. St Ambrose (340–97), one of the doctors of the early Church, contemporary of St Augustine.

13. 'It is in the second narrative of creation that the formation of a single man out of the dust of the earth, is described, and the omission to create a female at the same time, is stated to have been repaired by the subsequent formation of one from the side of the man' (Goodwin's footnote).

14. 'The common arrangement of the Bible in chapters is of comparatively modern origin, and is admitted, on all hands, to have no authority or philosophical worth whatever. In many cases, the division is most preposterous, and interferes greatly with an intelligent perusal of the text' (Goodwin's footnote).

15. A contemporary of Christ, a Christian and a Platonist, whose work showed the Church Fathers how to reconcile Greek philosophy with the Bible.

16. The Rev Dr Thomas Chalmers, professor of moral philosophy, geologist, and friend of Hugh Miller. He gave the first *Bridgewater Treatise* in 1833, 'On the Power, Wisdom, and Goodness of God as Manifested in the Adaptation of External Nature to the Moral and Intellectual Constitution of Man'. In 1814, he had put forward his scheme to reconcile Genesis and geology in 'A Review of Cuvier's Theory of the Earth'.

17. Goodwin is supporting the gradualist and uniformitarian geological theory of Lyell's *Principles of Geology* (1830–3), as opposed to Buckland's catastrophism.

18. Hugh Miller, *Testimony of the Rocks* (1857), p. 10.

19. St Augustine (d. 430), Church Father, whose special theory about Genesis was that God is a Creator, not an 'artificer', so the world was not created out of matter, but out of nothing, and God therefore is outside of matter.

20. Bishop of Cyrrhus (*c.* 313–*c.* 458), early theologian and expositor of the Bible.

21. See Pusey's note, Buckland's *Bridgewater Treatise* (1836), pp. 24, 25.

22. The 'recent writer of mathematical eminence' is John Henry Pratt, who was Third Wrangler at Cambridge in 1833. In 1850, he became Archdeacon of Calcutta. Goodwin quotes from his work *Science and Scripture not at Variance*, 3rd ed. (1859), p. 34.

23. Flavius Josephus (37–100), Jewish historian, soldier, Pharisee, who wrote *Antiquities of the Jews*.

24. *Bridgewater Treatise*, p. 17.

25. For Pratt, see endnote 22. The reference here is to *Science and Scripture not at Variance*, p. 40, note.

26. Rev Donald Macdonald, *Creation and the Fall: a defense and exposition of the first three Chapters of Genesis* (Edinburgh, 1856).

27. Dionysius Lardner (ed.), *The Museum of Science and Art* (1854–6).

28. Alcide Charles Victor Desalines D'Orbigny (1802–57) was a French palaeontologist, who published his *Prodrome de paleontologie stratigraphique universelle* in 1850–2. It consisted of lists of all the invertebrate fossils, arranged according to their distribution in successive geological strata. D'Orbigny divided the strata into twenty-seven stages, representing twenty-seven successive sets of extinct animals, to each of which he gave a name based on a locality, and ending in '-ian' (e.g. 'Cambrian'). His interpretation of this series was catastrophist, not evolutionary.

29. John Lindley (1799–1865) was a botanist, who specialised in the study of orchids. He campaigned for what he called 'the Natural System' of botanical classification, which had been proposed by A. L. Jussieu and A. P. de Candolle, and improved by Robert Brown. This 'natural system' was based on more characteristics than the system of Linnaeus, which was based only on sexual characteristics. In 1830, Lindley published his *Introduction to the Natural System of Botany*, and in 1853, *The Vegetable Kingdom*. The accuracy of his system was limited by his lack of evolutionary theory. He was also interested in palaeobotany, and Lindley and Hutton's *Fossil Flora of Great Britain* came out 1831–7.

30. The French naturalist, Georges Cuvier, opponent of Lamarck.

31. *The Testimony of the Rocks*, p. 133.

32. See endnote 22.

33. James Parkinson, British geologist and palaeontologist, founder member of the Geological Society in 1807.

34. Benjamin Silliman, American geologist.
35. 'The expression, Gen. 2:4, "In the day that the Lord God created the earth and heaven," to which Hugh Miller here refers, may possibly mean "at the time when," meaning a week, year, or other limited time. But there is not the smallest reason for understanding it to mean "a *lengthened* period," *i.e.*, an immense lapse of time. Such a construction would be inadmissable in the Hebrew, or any other language. It is difficult to acquit Hugh Miller of an equivocation here. In real truth, the second narrative is, as we have before observed, of distinct origin from the first, and we incline to the belief that, in this case also, "day" is to be taken in its proper signification' (Goodwin's footnote).
36. *Testimony of the Rocks*, p. 134.
37. 'A very inadmissable assertion. Any one, be he geologist, astronomer, theologian, or philologist, who attempts to explain the Hebrew narrative, is bound to take it with all that really belongs to it. And in truth, if the fourth day really represented an epoch of creative activity, geology would be able to give some account of it. There is no reason to suppose that any intermission has taken place' (Goodwin's footnote).
38. Though he treats the Bible as history, and the natural world as the realm of natural law, Goodwin preserves a religious attitude to both, by seeing 'Providence' as having *made use* of the human historians of 'the Hebrew records' to begin the religious education of mankind, and by seeing beneficent *design* in Nature. The Essayists were attacked from both sides for the *minimal* nature of their religion. Frederic Harrison, the positivist, attacked them in the *Westminster Review* for not pursuing their beliefs to what he saw as their logical conclusion, and abandoning religion altogether. Here is part of his attack:

> What becomes of the Christian scheme when the origin of mankind is handed over to Mr. Darwin; and Adam and Eve take their seats beside Deucalion and Pyrrha? . . . in a word, from one end of this book to the other the same process is continued; facts are idealised, dogmas are transformed, creeds are discredited as human and provisional; the authority of the Church and of the Bible to establish any doctrine is discarded; the moral teaching of the Gospel remains; the moral sense of each must decide upon its meaning and its application . . . It may be that this is a *true* view of Christianity, but we insist in the name of common sense that it is a *new* view. . . . Religion, to regain the world, must not only be not contrary to science but it must be in entire and close harmony with science . . . That end will not be attained by our authors, by subliming religion into an emotion, and making an armistice with science. (October 1860, pp. 293–332)

The 'scientific' religion that Harrison advocates here is the positivist faith of Auguste Comte. Comte held that mankind had passed through the theological and the metaphysical phases of belief, and was now reaching the 'positivist' or scientific phase. Like the Essayists, he saw man as being progressively enlightened, but this involved abandoning the outmoded faith of Christianity altogether, in favour of Comte's 'Religion of Humanity'. From the other side, Bishop Wilberforce, attacking *Essays and Reviews* in the *Quarterly Review* for January 1861, partly agreed with Harrison:

> It is not indeed a 'neo-Christianity', but it is a new religion, which our Essayists would introduce; and they would act more rationally, more philosophically, and, we believe, less injuriously to religion, if they did as their brother unbelievers invite them to do, renounce their hopeless attempt at preserving Christianity without Christ, without the Holy Ghost, with-

out a Church . . . They believe too much not to believe more, and they disbelieve too much not to disbelieve everything. (pp. 248–305)

6. LEONARD HUXLEY, *Life and Letters of Thomas Henry Huxley*

1. Notice Leonard Huxley using 'warfare' terminology here: the incident has become an important part of the myth of a 'conflict' between science and theology. T. H. Huxley's skill and aggression in debate are commented on by Darwin: 'His mind is as quick as a flash of lightening and as sharp as a razor. He is the best talker whom I have known. He never says and never writes anything flat. From his conversation no one would suppose that he could cut up his opponents in so trenchant a manner as he can do and does do' (*Autobiography*, p. 62).

2. One main aim of the British Association (founded in 1831) was the popularisation of science. Large numbers of the general public attended the meetings, and it became the main public forum for the Darwinian debate. The non-scientific public were obviously more interested in the bearing of scientific theories on general human concerns, such as religion and morality, than they were in purely scientific theories. The Bishop was an eloquent and popular speaker, and not ill-informed: his speech was in the tradition of the Association.

3. See *The Life and Letters of Charles Darwin*, ed. Francis Darwin (1887), vol. 2, pp. 320–3; W. H. Freemantle, *Charles Darwin* (1892), pp. 236–8; and *Life, Letters and Journals of Sir Charles Lyell*, ed. Katherine Lyell (1881), vol. 2, p. 335.

4. Richard Owen, the anatomist, was one of Darwin's strongest opponents. He continued to battle with Huxley about the difference between the brains of the apes and of man, especially at the British Association meeting in Cambridge in 1862. This is how the poet George Meredith reported that encounter: 'Yesterday Huxley had such a tussle with Owen! The thinking men all side with the former' (*Letters* (1970), p. 165). This was the sort of conflict the public went to the Association to see. Huxley's opinions on the subject can be found in *Man's Place in Nature* (1863; *Collected Essays* (1894), vol. 7). Owen was regarded by Huxley and by Darwin (*Life and Letters*, vol. 2, p. 325) as being behind Wilberforce's attack (see pp. 151, 153). Later, Owen took up an evolutionary theory of his own, which depended on an 'internal law' of development. Thus he joined the many scientific opponents of natural selection, as distinguished from evolution.

5. John William Draper, Professor of Chemistry at the University of the City of New York, is largely responsible for the 'warfare' model of the relations between religion and science, which pervades his influential *History of the Intellectual Development of Europe* (1862). The book presents a simplistic vision of intellectual history as the progressive defeat of religious obscurantism by scientific enlightenment. Draper's influence can be seen in Tyndall's 'Belfast Address' (see pp. 172–89). In his paper to the British Association, Draper was drawing a parallel between the development of species, as shown by Darwin, and his version of the development of ideas. Darwin's theory was to be taken over and used by many such people, concerned to support their own interests with the authority of 'Darwinism'. What is interesting is that both Huxley and Hooker were extremely scornful of Draper's reasonings at the meeting (see Gertrude Himmelfarb, *Darwin and the Darwinian Revolution* (1967), p. 289; and James R. Moore, *The Post-Darwinian Controversies* (1979), pp. 19–49, for Draper's role in creating the 'warfare' model).

6. *Life and Letters of Darwin*, vol. 2, p. 321.

7. Here are some examples of the Bishop's 'ridicule' from his *Quarterly* article:
   To find that mosses, grasses, turnips, oaks, worms, and flies, mites and

elephants, infusoria and whales, tadpoles of today and venerable saurians, truffles and men, are all equally the lineal descendants of the same aboriginal common ancestor, perhaps of the nucleated cell of some primeval fungus, which alone possessed the distinguished honour of being the 'one primordial form into which life was first breathed by the Creator' – this, to say the least of it, is no common discovery – no very expected conclusion. But we are too loyal pupils of inductive philosophy to start back from any conclusion by reason of its strangeness. Newton's patient philosophy taught him to find in the falling apple the law which governs the silent movements of the stars in their courses; and if Mr Darwin can with the same correctness of reasoning demonstrate to us our fungular descent, we shall dismiss our pride, and avow, with the characteristic humility of philosophy, our unsuspected cousinship with the mushrooms, –

'Claim kindred there, and have our claim allowed,'

– only we ask leave to scrutinize carefully every step of the argument which has such an ending, and demur if at any point of it we are invited to substitute unlimited hypothesis for patient observation, or the spasmodic fluttering flight of fancy for the severe conclusions to which the logical accuracy of reasoning has led the way. (p. 231)

Notice that Wilberforce is not ridiculing *science*, he is ridiculing Darwin in the name of science. Wilberforce also ridicules Darwin by associating him with the 'evolutionary' theory of his grandfather, Erasmus Darwin, and quoting a contemporary parody of Erasmus's views (*Quarterly*, pp. 255–6). Charles Darwin thought this part of the article 'capital fun' (*Life and Letters*, p. 325, footnote). His good-humour contrasts with the rather prim and censorious attitude of Huxley and his supporters.

8. *Life and Letters of Darwin*, vol. 2, p. 321.
9. 'Reminiscences of a Grandmother', *Macmillan's Magazine*, October 1898. Leonard Huxley has a footnote at this point, quoting Professor Farrar's slightly different account of this part of the Bishop's speech: 'and then, denying *a fortiori* the derivation of the species Man from Ape, he rhetorically invoked the aid of *feeling*, and said, "If any one were to be willing to trace his descent through an ape as his *grandfather*, would he be willing to trace his descent similarly on the side of his *grandmother*?" His false humour was an attempt to arouse the antipathy about degrading *woman* to the quadrumana. Your father's reply showed there was vulgarity as well as folly in the Bishop's words; and the impression distinctly was, that the Bishop's party, as they left the room, felt abashed, and recognised that the Bishop had forgotten to behave like a perfect gentleman.' The Bishop's error turns out to have been one of good manners, rather than scientific accuracy.
10. Here Leonard Huxley's footnote refers us to the account in the *Athenaeum* of Huxley's answer to the 'scientific part' of the Bishop's speech: 'Darwin's theory was an explanation of phenomena in Natural History, as the undulatory theory was of the phenomena of light. No one objected to that theory because an undulation of light had never been arrested and measured. Darwin's theory was an explanation of facts, and his book was full of new facts, all bearing on his theory. Without asserting that every part of that theory had been confirmed, he maintained that it was the best explanation of the origin of species which had yet been offered. With regard to the psychological distinction between men and animals, man himself was once a monad – a mere atom, and nobody could say at what moment in the history of his development he became consciously intelligent. The question was not so much one of a transmutation or transition of species, as of the production of forms which became permanent.

Thus the short-legged sheep of America was not produced gradually, but originated in the birth of an original parent of the whole stock, which had been kept up by a rigid system of artificial selection.'

11. *Life and Letters of Darwin*, vol. 2, p. 322.

7. CHARLES DARWIN, *The Descent of Man*

1. Notice the extremely tentative and almost apologetic language Darwin is using in this paragraph: e.g. 'highly speculative', and 'worth while to try'. Obviously he is trying to forestall opposition, but perhaps he also feels that his theory is on rather shaky ground.

2. In the *Descent* Darwin backtracks rapidly from his previous emphasis on natural selection as the prime agent of evolution. In this paragraph, as well as sexual selection, he cites the Lamarckian theories of the inheritance of characteristics acquired through 'use and disuse of parts', and the direct action of the surroundings. Powerful attacks on the adequacy of natural selection had been made by Wallace and Mivart, among others.

3. Camille Dareste (1822–99) was a French doctor and zoologist. He worked on embryology, and especially teratology, or the science of foetal malformations and monstrosities. His research involved the experimental production of monstrosities, in an effort to determine their cause, and thus shed light on the causes of evolution.

4. Matthew Arnold seizes on this sentence in his *Literature and Science* (1883). He is arguing against Huxley's claim that natural science provides a sufficient basis for education. According to Arnold, science can only provide us with knowledge, unrelated to our essential 'sense for conduct' and 'sense for beauty':

> And one piece of natural knowledge is added to another, and others are added to that, and at last we come to propositions so interesting as Mr Darwin's famous proposition that 'our ancestor was a hairy quadruped furnished with a tail and pointed ears, probably arboreal in his habits.' Or we come to propositions of such reach and magnitude as those which Professor Huxley delivers, when he says that the notions of our forefathers about the beginning and end of the world were all wrong, and that nature is the expression of a definite order with which nothing interferes.
>
> Interesting, indeed, these results of science are, important they are, and we should all of us be acquainted with them. But what I now wish you to mark is, that we are still, when they are propounded to us and we receive them, we are still in the sphere of intellect and knowledge. And for the generality of men there will be found, I say, to arise, when they have duly taken in the proposition that their ancestor was 'a hairy quadruped furnished with a tail and pointed ears, probably arboreal in his habits,' there will be found to arise an invincible desire to relate this proposition to the sense in us for conduct, and to the sense in us for beauty. But this the men of science will not do for us, and will hardly even profess to do. (*The Essential Matthew Arnold*, ed. Lionel Trilling (1949), pp. 418–19)

It is interesting that Darwin's attempt to relate his theory to moral and social ideas, on pp. 162–3, is crude and lame in the extreme. But Arnold offers not religion but literature as the provider of the missing values.

5. It is this similarity of *kind* that Mivart disputes:

> We now come to the consideration of a subject of great importance – namely, that of man's mental powers. Are they, as Mr Darwin again and

again affirms they are, different only in degree and not in kind from the mental powers of the brutes? As is so often the case in discussions, the error to be combatted is an implied negation. Mr Darwin implies and seems to assume, that when two things have certain characters in common, there can be no fundamental difference between them.

To avoid ambiguity and obscurity, it may be well here to state plainly certain very elementary matters. The ordinary antecedents and concomitants of distinctly felt sensations may exist, with all their physical consequences, in the total absence of intellectual cognisance, as is shown by the well-known fact, that when through fracture of the spine the lower limbs of a man are utterly deprived of the power of feeling, the foot may nevertheless withdraw itself from tickling just as if a sensation was consciously felt. Amongst lower animals, a decapitated frog will join its hind feet together to push away an irritating object just as an uninjured animal will do. Here we have coadjusted actions resulting from stimuli which normally produce sensation, but occurring under conditions in which cerebral action does not take place. Did it take place, we should have sensations, but by no means necessarily intellectual action.

'Sensation' is not 'thought', and no amount of the former would constitute the most rudimentary condition of the latter, though sensations supply the conditions for the existence of 'thought' or 'knowledge'.

Mivart goes on to attack Darwin's examples that purport to show 'reason' in animals, and concludes, 'We maintain that while there is no need to abandon the received position that man is truly an animal, he is yet the only rational one known to us, and that his rationality constitutes a fundamental distinction – one of *kind* and not of *degree* (St George Mivart, *Essays and Criticisms* (1892), vol. 2, pp. 28–9, 56).

6. 'On the Limits of Natural Selection', *North American Review*, October 1870, p. 295.

7. Mivart dissents even more on this question: 'Man is not merely an intellectual animal, but he is also a free moral agent, and, as such – and with the infinite future such freedom opens out before him – differs from all the rest of the visible universe by a distinction so profound that none of those which separate other visible beings is comparable with it' (*Essays and Criticisms*, vol. 2, p. 59).

8. See headnote to extract 6, p. 147.

9. Malthus had made the same point.

10. Francis Galton, Darwin's cousin, and the inventor of eugenics.

11. Darwin does not realise that this admission contradicts his foregoing insistence on the necessity of 'struggle' and 'competition' in society. Huxley was to make this clear much later, in his famous lecture 'Evolution and Ethics' (1893). He distinguishes between the 'cosmic process' of the struggle for existence, and the antithetical 'ethical process' by which society is advanced. He points out that

> ... the practice of that which is ethically best – what we call goodness or virtue – involves a course of conduct which, in all respects, is opposed to that which leads to success in the cosmic struggle for existence. In place of ruthless self-assertion it demands self-restraint; in place of thrusting aside, or treading down, all competitors, it requires that the individual shall not merely respect, but shall help his fellows; its influence is directed, not so much to the survival of the fittest, as to the fitting of as many as possible to survive.

In the 'Prolegomena' that he wrote later to explain his meaning more clearly, he concludes that when the ethical process has advanced so far as to secure every member of the society in the possession of the means of existence, the struggle for existence, as between man and man, within that society is, *ipso facto*, at an end. And, as it is undeniable that the most highly civilised societies have substantially reached this position, it follows that, so far as they are concerned, the struggle for existence can play no important part within them.

Huxley is partly attacking thinkers like Herbert Spencer, who advocated competition and free enterprise in society on 'evolutionary' grounds, like Darwin does here, and partly attacking optimistic eugenicists like Galton, whom Darwin also mentions. Huxley insists that the 'progressive modification of civilisation which passes by the name of "the evolution of society" is, in fact, a process of an essentially different character, both from that which brings about the evolution of species, in the state of nature, and from that which gives rise to the evolution of varieties, in the state of art' (*Collected Essays*, vol. 9, pp. 81–2, 35–7). Huxley's treatment of the problem is much more profound than Darwin's rather lame and naive jumble of eugenics, social Darwinism and cultural evolution here. In fact, Huxley has been seen as coming nearer to a theological vision of fallen nature in this lecture than to the naturalistic and materialist views with which he is usually associated (see Gertrude Himmelfarb, *Darwin and the Darwinian Revolution* (1967), p. 408).

12. More of these delightful stories of moral behaviour in animals occur in Darwin's *The Expression of the Emotions in Animals and Man* (1874). As well as 'degrading' man in order to close the evolutionary gap between him and the animals, Darwin also 'elevates' the animals, by attributing moral and intellectual qualities to them. He always writes better on animals than on man, and seems to have great empathy for them. Mivart spends some time mocking Darwin's anecdotes about animal behaviour, and casting doubt on their authenticity. It is true that Darwin's evidence here is not very 'scientific'. Darwin's preference for animals over savages here was not shared by Wallace, who found the savages he had met on his travels both likeable and admirable.

8. JOHN TYNDALL, 'The Belfast Address'

1. Giordano Bruno (1547–1600) is one of Tyndall's key examples of the persecution of science by the Church. Bruno held that the earth moved round the sun, that the solar system was not the centre of the universe, that the universe was infinite, and that 'there is a common soul within the whole to which it gives being and at the same time is individual and yet is in all and every part'. Thus he eliminated the need for a Creator. He was imprisoned for seven years by the Inquisition, and finally burnt at the stake in 1600 (see Charles Singer, *A Short History of Scientific Ideas to 1900* (1959), pp. 218–20).

2. The references to Crüger's researches on orchids do not occur in the first edition of the *Origin of Species*. They appear first in the fourth edition (1866), in Chapter 6. Tyndall, however, would probably be referring to the sixth edition, recently published in 1872.

3. Tyndall has pinpointed the essential difference of Darwin from Paley, as well as their similarity in using the evidences of adaptation.

4. Eighteenth-century theologian: his influential *Analogy of Religion Natural and Revealed to the Constitution and Course of Nature* was published in 1736, and was widely held to be a decisive confutation of deism.

5. 'Mr Winthrop' was Robert Charles Winthrop (1809–94), a legislator and phil-anthropist. Tyndall visited America in 1872–3. Winthrop commented on his encounter with Tyndall like this: 'I hope you managed to hear some of Tyndall's delightful lectures. He came out here to lunch and I had Agassiz to meet him. I found him an intelligent and agreeable fellow, and I am not without hope he may one day change his notions about religion' (Letter of 29 October 1872, in Robert C. Winthrop, Jr, *A Memoir of Robert C. Winthrop* (Boston, 1897), p. 281).

6. This doctrine holds that all forms of energy (heat, motion, gravity, light) are interconvertible, and the amount of energy always stays the same. The impor-tance of this idea to Tyndall, is that it *unifies* the whole of Nature into a balanced system. As he lyrically put it: 'It is as if the body of Nature were alive, the thrill and interchange of its energies resembling those of an organism. The parts of the "stupendous whole" shift and change, augment and diminish, appear and dis-appear, while the total of which they are the parts remains quantitatively immu-table' ('Science and Man', *Fragments*, vol. 2, pp. 340–1). Notice that for Tyndall Nature is an *organism*, not a *mechanism* – this makes it more attractive, but it also does away with the need for a Divine Mechanic: his Nature is self-evolving.

7. So Tyndall sees no break between inorganic and organic Nature: 'The animal world is, so to say, a distillation through the vegetable world from inorganic nature. From this point of view all three worlds constitute a unity, in which I picture life as immanent everywhere' ('"Materialism" and Its Opponents', *Fortnightly Review*, n.s. 1, June 1867, p. 592).

8. Herbert Spencer was the 'philosopher' of evolution. He attempted to construct a complete cosmology based on science, known as the 'Synthetic Philosophy'. Spencer reduced everything to a few simple laws, such as the 'continuous adjust-ment of internal relations to external relations', or the law of development from 'homogeneity to heterogeneity'. These 'laws' were applied to psychology, sociology, and morality. Spencer's 'laws', however, were descriptive rather than explanatory. This is what Darwin thought of them:

> His fundamental generalisations (which have been compared in importance by some persons with Newton's laws!) which I daresay may be very valuable under a philosophical point of view, are of such a nature that they do not seem to me to be of any strictly scientific use. They partake more of the nature of definitions than of laws of nature. They do not aid one in predic-ting what will happen in any particular case. Anyhow they have not been of any use to me. (*Autobiography*, p. 64)

But Spencer was very influential, offering a complete 'scientific' system of belief to those who had lost their religious belief. This is what the hero of Jack Lon-don's novel *Martin Eden* felt about Spencer: 'And here was the man Spencer, organising knowledge for him, reducing everything to unity, elaborating ulti-mate realities . . . There was no caprice, no change. All was law . . .' (quoted in J. D. Y. Peel, *Herbert Spencer – The Evolution of a Sociologist* (1971), p. 2).

Spencer's psychological theories were elaborated in his *Principles of Psychology* (1855), revised and enlarged in order to take account of Darwin's theory in 1870. His main aim was to show how the human mind had developed out of elements existing in the lowest organism: as Peel puts it, he 'presents thinking as being only different from feeling, and as a response to the environment which should be compared with those of the lowest animals and the humblest plants' (*Herbert Spencer*, p. 120). This is why he is useful to Tyndall's argument here, as Tyndall is trying to establish a continuum up from matter, through organic life, to Mind. Spencer's theory does not derive from Darwin's: in 1855, he had written to Tennyson,

> I happened recently to be re-reading your Poem, 'The Two Voices', and coming to the verse
>
>> Or if thro' lower lives I came –
>> Tho' all experience past became
>> Consolidate in mind and frame –
>
> it occurred to me that you might like to glance through a book which applies to the elucidation of mental science the hypothesis to which you refer. I therefore beg your acceptance of *Psychology*, which I send you by this post. (*The Life and Letters of Herbert Spencer*, ed. David Duncan (1908), p. 78)

The Tennyson quotation also suggests how Spencer's theory depends on the inheritance of acquired experience, which then becomes innate. This is how he was able to explain away the traditional objections to 'associationist' psychology, that there *are* innate ideas, and that one individual life does not contain enough experience to build up all our ideas (see p. 181).

9. Belgian physicist and physiologist.

10. Democritus (*c.* 470-*c.* 400 BC) was a Greek contemporary of Socrates. He held that everything was composed of atoms, eternally rearranging themselves.

11. Lucretius (*c.* 95–55 BC), Roman author of *De Rerum Natura*, which expresses his materialist philosophy. Like Democritus, and like his master Epicurus, he was an atomist.

12. 'Associationism' was the 'mechanical' psychology of the eighteenth century, chiefly put forward by Joseph Priestley and David Hartley, and originally by Locke. They held that all our ideas were solely built up from direct sense-experience, by association: the mind at birth was like a blank sheet of paper. Hartley's ideas influenced Wordsworth and Coleridge, but Coleridge soon realised their mechanical limitations, and argued for a more creative role for the mind, in his *Biographia Literaria* (1817). The utilitarians, led by James Mill and Jeremy Bentham, made the associationist psychology the basis of their philosophy. John Stuart Mill tried to widen their rather narrow application of the idea, but essentially he too remained an associationist, arguing that the mind was built up entirely from the experiences of the individual. He thus championed the 'empiricist' school, as opposed to the 'intuitionists' such as William Whewell and Sir William Hamilton. In Tyndall's view, Mill is therefore less original than Spencer, who manages to reconcile the two schools of thought, by his 'evolutionary' equation of innate ideas with inherited experience.

13. Tyndall is very keen on what he calls elsewhere 'The Scientific Use of the Imagination' (1870) – that is, the power of the scientific mind to extrapolate by analogy from the experimental evidence to the unseen causes behind it. These are 'unseen' either because they are literally invisible forces, like 'energy', or because they are too small to see ('atoms'), or because they lie in the distant past (as with Darwin's theory of evolution). Tyndall becomes quite mystical about these hidden processes: 'besides the phenomena which address the senses, there are laws and principles and processes which do not address the senses at all, and which must be, and can be, spiritually discerned' ('Matter and Force', *Fragments*, vol. 2, p. 104). Tyndall is about to apply this power of imaginative extension to Darwin's theory, and 'cross the boundary of the experimental evidence' from the 'primordial form' to a material origin for life (p. 183 below).

14. The theory of elements composed of atoms was put forward by the chemist John Dalton in 1808; the idea of 'molecules' was invented by the Italian Amedeo Avogadro in 1811.

15. These are Kingsley's words (see pp. 87–8), as quoted approvingly by Darwin in the second edition of the *Origin*.

16. Ernst Haeckel, evolutionist.

17. *An Examination of Sir William Hamilton's Philosophy* (1865), p. 154.

18. Johann Gottlieb Fichte, German Romantic philosopher, follower of Kant, and influence on Coleridge. Differentiated from Kant by his subjectivism.

19. Bishop Berkeley, eighteenth-century idealist philosopher, who held that matter did not exist unless it was perceived.

20. David Hume, whose sceptical thought undermined the bases of both natural theology and scientific rationality. See endnote 10 to extract 3, p. 226.

21. This is very revealing. Tyndall is hoping to strengthen the claims of Darwin's theory, even though it cannot be 'proved' in any empirical way. It was much criticised as being merely 'hypothetical'. Its acceptance was probably largely due to its consonance with the naturalistic, materialistic and gradualist preconceptions of Victorian science. This means that its 'truth' depends on the acceptance of a particular historical 'scientific' world-view.

22. This impassable gulf between matter and mind had been conceded by Tyndall in the imaginary debate with Bishop Butler in the first half of the Address. Scientific naturalists tended to get round the problem by adopting a theory of 'parallelism' between mind and matter, as Tyndall does here. For instance, Huxley wrote that mental and physical events 'run, not in one series, but along two parallel lines', between which is an inexplicable bridge ('Scientific and Pseudo-Scientific Realism' (1887), *Collected Essays*, vol. 5, p. 62). The recognition of insoluble mystery here left the scientists free to investigate the physical side of the parallel, *as if* it 'caused' the mental. Agnostics like Huxley consider it is not worth thinking about questions unanswerable by scientific means – Herbert Spencer too has a category called 'The Unknowable', that lies behind everything. Tyndall, however, seems quite emotionally attached to the idea of ultimate Mystery (see pp. 188–9). Possibly he was influenced by Carlyle here (see headnote).

23. Archimedes (287–212 BC) of Syracuse, mathematician, to illustrate the powers of levers had said, 'Give me but a place to stand, and I will move the world.' A 'fulcrum' is the point on which a lever turns or is supported. In the case of the world, there is no such conceivable point, without getting outside the world altogether. So Tyndall claims we cannot get outside our own subjectivity in studying consciousness.

24. While allowing the 'religious sentiment' its importance in man, Tyndall reduces its relevance to the 'region of emotion' alone. He wants to warn theology off the domain of 'objective knowledge' which he claims for science, but about which religion has traditionally also claimed to speak. Theology was in fact to retreat from this area, into the area of the spiritual, if not the merely emotional. Tyndall's definition would reduce religion to the same status as poetry – it is interesting to compare it with Matthew Arnold's attempt to raise poetry to fulfil the functions of religion. Tyndall ends the Address with an appeal for reconciliation between man's 'knowledge' and his 'emotional nature' – but he has been largely responsible for setting up the split between value-free science on the one hand, and a purely subjective religion on the other.

25. William Whewell (1794–1866) was a historian and philosopher of science. He was Master of Trinity College, Cambridge, from 1841, and contributed to the

development of physics at Cambridge. In 1837, he published his *History of the Inductive Science*, to which Tyndall referred earlier in the Address (p. 310). In 1840, his four-volume *Philosophy of the Inductive Sciences* began to appear. Whewell was involved in an important controversy with J. S. Mill, about the philosophy of science. But Tyndall is probably more indebted to Whewell's history than to his philosophy – Whewell, like Tyndall in the Address, emphasised the scientific achievements of the Greeks, and saw the Middle Ages as a time of scientific decline.

26. H. T. Buckle, empirical historian, popularised the idea of applying scientific principles to history; he wrote *History of Civilisation in England* (1857–61).

27. Emil du Bois-Reymond, German physiologist, whom Tyndall had met while studying at Berlin.

28. This is a serious misrepresentation of the contribution of theology to scientific advance. It is a myth created by scientific naturalists like Tyndall, who want to detach science from its traditional association with religion.

29. Anaxagoras (488–428 BC), Greek scientist, friend of Pericles and Euripides. Socrates, who thought science a waste of time, differed strongly from him.

30. The Maccabees were a famous Jewish family of the first century BC, who fought against Roman persecution of the Jews; their exploits are recounted in the Apocryphal Books of the Maccabees.

9. FREDERICK TEMPLE, *The Relations between Religion and Science*

1. This idea of an essential religion, independent of any particular revelation was an important idea behind *Essays and Reviews*. As Dean Stanley put it, in his favourable review (*Edinburgh Review*, April 1861, pp. 461–99), the Essayists wished 'to place Christianity beyond the reach of accidents, whether of science or criticism; to rest its claims on those moral and spiritual truths, which, after all, are what have really won an entrance for it into the heart . . .'.

2. Darwin's particular theory of the origin of species has been elevated in importance and scope into 'the leading scientific doctrine' of 'Evolution'. In fact, pro-scientific writers like Huxley and Tyndall tend to use the word 'evolution' rather generally to mean 'explanation of origins by natural causes' (see endnote 9). As such, it is the lynch-pin of their scientific world-view; and it has also been elevated to a 'doctrine' by the semi-religious attitude of the scientific naturalists.

3. For Laplace and his 'nebular hypothesis' described here, see endnote 8, p. 231.

4. This theory was forcefully put over by Huxley in his lecture 'On the Physical Basis of Life' in 1868, in which he said that 'Protoplasm, simple or nucleated, is the formal basis of life. It is the clay of the potter: which, bake it and paint it as he will, remains clay, separated by artifice, and not by nature, from the commonest brick or sun-dried clod.' He then went on to show that protoplasm was composed of ordinary chemicals, 'carbonic acid, water, and nitrogenous compounds'. He sees the combination of these chemicals to form living protoplasm as no more wonderful than the combination of hydrogen and oxygen to form water: 'vitality' is no more real than 'aquosity'. He then warns his audience,

> But I bid you beware that, in accepting these conclusions, you are placing your feet on the first rung of a ladder which, in most people's estimation, is the reverse of Jacob's, and leads to the antipodes of heaven. It may seem a small thing to admit that the dull vital actions of a fungus, or a foraminifer, are the properties of their protoplasm, and are the direct results of the nature of the matter of which they are composed. But if, as I have endeavoured to

prove to you, their protoplasm is essentially identical with, and most readily converted into, that of any animal, I can discover no logical halting-place between the admission that such is the case, and the further concession that all vital action may, with equal propriety, be said to be the result of the molecular forces of the protoplasm which displays it. And if so, it must be true, in the same sense and to the same extent, that the thoughts to which I am now giving utterance, and your thoughts regarding them, are the expression of molecular changes in that matter of life which is the source of our other vital phenomena. (*Collected Essays* (1893–4), vol. I, pp. 142, 150, 152, 153–4)

Like Tyndall in the Belfast Address, Huxley is trying to establish a 'material' continuum up to and including 'mind'. He ignores the lack of evidence for spontaneous generation, which Temple goes on to mention as a weakness in this position.

5. The purpose of this strange theory seems to be to separate man off from the other animals as much as possible, by suggesting he is not *directly* descended from or related to any of them. Thus the stigma of 'ape' ancestry is removed; and God could have had man's independent evolution under His special care.

6. Genesis, 18:25.

7. John, 5:17.

8. It is interesting that this analogy between species development and embryo development was used for similar argumentative purposes by both Robert Chambers and T. H. Huxley (see pp. 65 and 153, 235). Chambers uses it to remove our prejudice that the idea of evolution impairs man's dignity; Huxley uses it to attack Bishop Wilberforce's creationist prejudice against the evolution of species. The apologetic arguments of the evolutionists are being taken over by the Church.

9. This idea that the course of evolution could have been foreseen from the beginning was, strangely, held by Huxley, as a consequence of scientific determinism: he writes that although

it is quite true that the doctrine of Evolution is the most formidable opponent of all the commoner and coarser forms of Teleology . . . it is necessary to remember that there is a wider Teleology, which is not touched by the doctrine of Evolution, but is actually based upon the fundamental proposition of Evolution. That proposition is, that the whole world, living and not living, is the result of the mutual interaction, according to definite laws, of the forces possessed by the molecules of which the primitive nebulosity of the universe was composed. If this be true, it is no less certain that the existing world lay, potentially, in the cosmic vapour; and that a sufficient intelligence could, from a knowledge of the properties of the molecules of that vapour, have predicted, say the state of the Fauna of Britain in 1869 . . .

The teleological and the mechanical views of nature are not, necessarily, mutually exclusive. On the contrary, the more purely a mechanist the spectator is, the more purely does he assume a primordial molecular arrangement, of which all the phenomena of the universe are the consequences; and the more completely is he thereby at the mercy of the teleologist, who can always defy him to disprove that this primordial molecular arrangement was not intended to evolve the phenomena of the universe. ('The Genealogy of Animals' (1869), *Collected Essays*, vol. 2, pp. 109–10, 112)

10. The 'gradualist', evolutionary language that Temple uses here to describe the progress of God's Revelation to man, echoes the argument of his contribution to *Essays and Reviews*, 'The Education of the World'. In the Essay, he had seen mankind's spiritual 'education' as a gradual development through various stages,

which paralleled the individual's growth from childhood, through adolescence, to maturity and self-responsibility:

> First come Rules, then Examples, then Principles. First comes the Law, then the Son of Man, then the Gift of the Spirit. The world was once a child under tutors and governors until the time appointed by the Father. Then, when the fit season had arrived, the Example to which all ages should turn was sent to teach men what they ought to be. Then the human race was left to itself to be guided by the teaching of the Spirit within. (p. 5)

This is the inner voice on which Temple bases his religion in the Bampton Lectures.

11. 2 Corinthians, 5:7.
12. It is interesting to find Temple linking science and 'scientific history', i.e. historical criticism of the Bible. When Victorians attribute their loss of faith to 'science', they may very well be referring to the new Biblical Criticism, with its 'scientific' approach to the Bible as a historical document, rather than to physical science and the theory of evolution.
13. Acts, 12:3.

Select booklist

(A guide to further reading, not a full bibliography of the subject)

PRIMARY SOURCES

(Bibliographical details of the main texts can be found in the headnotes.)

Arnold, Matthew, 'Literature and Science', *Discourses in America* (1883)

Ashwell, A. R., *Life of the Right Reverend Samuel Wilberforce, with Selections from his Diary and Correspondence* (1880–2)

Bayne, Peter, *Life and Letters of Hugh Miller* (1871)

Buckland, William, *Bridgewater Treatise:* 'Geology and Mineralogy considered with Reference to Natural Theology' (1836)
  Vindicae Geologicae; or, the Connection of Geology with Religion Explained (1820)

Chalmers, Thomas, *Bridgewater Treatise:* 'On the Power, Wisdom, and Goodness of God, as Manifested in the Adaptation of External Nature to the Moral and Intellectual Constitution of Man' (1833)

Clarke, John Willis, and Hughes, Thomas McKenny, *Life and Letters of the Reverend Adam Sedgwick* (1890)

Darwin, Charles, *Autobiography*, ed. Gavin de Beer (1974)
  The Expression of the Emotions (1874)
  The Voyage of the Beagle (1839)

Darwin, Francis (ed.), *The Life and Letters of Charles Darwin* (1887)

Draper, John William, *History of the Intellectual Development of Europe* (1862)

Gosse, Edmund, *Father and Son* (1907)

Gosse, Philip, *Omphalos* (1857)

Gray, Asa, *Darwiniana*, ed. A. Hunter Depree (1963)

Huxley, Thomas Henry, *Collected Essays* (1893–4)

Kingsley, Charles, *Glaucus, or, the Wonders of the Shore* (1855)
  Scientific Lectures and Essays (1880)

Lyell, Charles, *Life, Letters and Journals*, ed. Katherine Lyell (1881)
  Principles of Geology (1830–3).

Miller, Hugh, *Footprints of the Creator* (1847)
  The Old Red Sandstone (1841)

Mivart, St George, *Essays and Criticisms* (1892)

Newman, John Henry, *The Idea of a University*, ed. I. T. Ker (1976)

Sandford, E. G. (ed.), *Memoirs of Archbishop Temple* (1906)

Sedgwick, Adam, *A Discourse on the Studies of the University* (1833)

Stephen, Leslie, *History of English Thought in the Eighteenth Century* (1902)

Tyndall, John, *Fragments of Science*, 6th ed. (1879)

Wallace, Alfred Russel, *My Life: a Record of Events and Opinions* (1905)
  On Miracles and Modern Spiritualism (1875)
  The World of Life. A Manifestation of Creative Power, Directive Mind, and Ultimate Purpose (1910)

Select booklist

Whewell, William, *Bridgewater Treatise:* 'Astronomy and General Physics considered with Reference to Natural Theology' (1833)
History of the Inductive Sciences (1837)
Wilberforce, Samuel, 'Darwin's *Origin of Species*', *Quarterly Review*, July 1860
'Essays and Reviews', *Quarterly Review*, January 1861

SECONDARY MATERIAL

Modern studies

On the individual writers

Paley: M. L. Clarke, *Paley: Evidences for the Man* (1974) is a sympathetic and readable biography, which also sets Paley in his historical and intellectual context. Frederick Ferre's Introduction to his *William Paley, 'Natural Theology':* *Selections* (Indianapolis, 1963), provides a useful critical analysis of Paley's way of thought.

Chambers: Milton Millhauser's biography of Chambers, *Just Before Darwin: Robert Chambers and 'Vestiges'* (Middletown, Conn., 1959) includes studies of the climate of scientific thought at the time of *Vestiges*, and of the scientific and theological reaction to *Vestiges*.

Miller: Millhauser's book also contains a brief biography of Miller and study of his works. George Rosie, *Hugh Miller: Outrage and Order* (1981) is a fuller modern biography.

Darwin: Peter Brent, *Charles Darwin: a Man of Enlarged Curiosity* (1981) is an interesting modern biography. A simple biography, and explication of the evolution controversy, can be found in William Irvine, *Apes, Angels and Victorians: The Story of Darwin, Huxley and Evolution* (1955). A biography is also included in Gertrude Himmelfarb, *Darwin and the Darwinian Revolution* (1967), followed by a more complex study of the scientific context and contents of Darwin's thought. Howard E. Gruber, in *Darwin on Man, A Psychological Study of Scientific Creativity* (1974) provides further insight into Darwin's thought processes and his method of arriving at his theory. Stanley Edgar Hyman, *The Tangled Bank: Darwin, Marx, Frazer and Freud as Imaginative Writers* (New York, 1962), applies literary criticism to Darwin's writings, revealing their metaphoric structure. Peter J. Vorzimmer, *Charles Darwin: the Years of Controversy: The Origin of Species and its Critics, 1859–1882* (1970) discusses the purely scientific controversy over Darwin's theory. Walter F. Cannon's article, 'The bases of Darwin's achievement: a revaluation' (*Victorian Studies*, December 1961) puts forward an important argument for the essential influence of natural theological writers on Darwin's thought. Robert M. Young's article, 'Darwin's metaphor: does nature select?' (*The Monist*, 55, 1971) investigates Darwin's use of the crucial 'selection' analogy.

Goodwin: A brief biography is included in Ieuan Ellis, *Seven Against Christ, A Study of Essays and Reviews*, which traces the intellectual and theological backgrounds of all the Essayists, as well as analysing their individual contributions, and the reactions to the whole work.

246

Select booklist

Huxley: Irvine's *Apes, Angels and Victorians* (see section on Darwin) also contains a biography of Huxley, and an account of his role in the evolution controversy. Other aspects of Huxley's career are also dealt with in Cyril Bibby, *T. H. Huxley: Scientist, Humanist, and Educator* (1959). The article by J. R. Lucas, 'Wilberforce and Huxley: a legendary encounter' (*The Historical Journal*, 22, no. 2, 1979) is a crucial revaluation of the significance of the Oxford meeting.

Tyndall: The standard biography is A. S. Eve and C. H. Creasey, *The Life and Works of John Tyndall* (1945). A collection of interesting modern evaluations of Tyndall – scientific, biographical, historical, literary, intellectual, educational – can be found in *John Tyndall: Essays on a Natural Philosopher* (Dublin, 1981), edited by W. H. Brock, N. D. McMillan and R. C. Mollan.

Temple: Ieuan Ellis's book on *Essays and Reviews* (see section on Goodwin, above) provides biographical material on Temple, in fact following his career as far as the Bampton Lectures and beyond.

More general studies

The Open University publications *New Interactions between Theology and Natural Science* (1974) and *The Crisis of Evolution* (1974), both edited by John Brooke and others, and which belong to a course on 'Science and Religious Belief, 1600–1900', provide a well-informed and carefully structured account of the subject, using many extracts from primary sources, and critical studies by modern experts in the field. These course books are complemented by *Science and Religious Belief 1600–1900: A Selection of Primary Sources* (1973), edited by D. C. Goodman, and *Science and Religious Belief: A Selection of Recent Historical Studies* (1973), edited by C. A. Russell. Charles Coulston Gillispie, *Genesis and Geology: the Impact of Scientific Discoveries upon Religious Beliefs in the Decades before Darwin* (1959), impressively analyses this earlier period. Milton Millhauser's *Just Before Darwin* (see section on Chambers) also provides useful material in this area, as does Himmelfarb's book (see section on Darwin), which also describes later reactions to Darwin. Popular reactions to Darwin's theory are invaluably charted and illustrated in Alvar Ellegård, *Darwin and the General Reader, The Reception of Darwin's Theory of Evolution in the British Periodical Press, 1859–1872* (Göteborg, 1958). More complex theological reactions are covered in James Moore, *The Post-Darwinian Controversies: A Study of the Protestant Struggle to Come to Terms with Darwin in Great Britain and America, 1870–1900* (1979), which aims to demolish the influential 'warfare' model of the relations between religion and science by showing its origins in the crudely polemical historiography of certain scientific writers, and by demonstrating the harmonious adjustment to Darwinism achieved by the most orthodox Protestant thinkers. On the way, Moore gives many examples of the blurred line between the scientific and theological 'camps' in the nineteenth century. An earlier, less specialised anti-conflict argument can be found in Owen Chadwick's *The Selwyn Lectures: Religion and Science in Victorian England: Legend and Reality* (Auckland, 1968). Chadwick's *The Victorian Church* (1966) also gives valuable information on both the evolution and the Biblical Criticism controversies as they affected the Church. Ieuan Ellis's study of *Essays and Reviews* (see section on Goodwin) gives a more specialised account of the Broad Church Movement and its involvement with science and Biblical Criticism. The agnostics are discussed, unsympathetically, by A. O. J. Cockshut in *The Unbelievers: English Agnostic Thought, 1840–1890* (1964); while 'scientific naturalism' is defined and described

Select booklist

by Frank M. Turner in 'Victorian scientific naturalism and Thomas Carlyle' (*Victorian Studies*, 18, 1975). George Eliot's agnosticism and her connection with Biblical Criticism are analysed by Basil Willey in Chapters VIII and IX of *Nineteenth Century Studies* (1980), which also contains a chapter (VII) on the influential positivist thought of Auguste Comte. Willey's *More Nineteenth Century Studies: A Group of Honest Doubters* (1980) contains sympathetic studies of agnostics and 'liberal' churchmen, including Tennyson, and the Essayists. The whole subject of the growth of evolutionary science and the loss of faith is ably surveyed by John C. Green, in *The Death of Adam: Evolution and its Impact on Western Thought* (Iowa, 1959); and, from a more philosophical angle, in Alfred North Whitehead's *Science and the Modern World* (1926), which is concerned to demonstrate and deplore the growth of a mechanistic and materialistic scientific philosophy. An interesting and readable account of the purely scientific developments in nineteenth-century biology is given in William Coleman, *Biology in the Nineteenth Century: Problems of Form, Function and Transformation* (1971).

Some studies of the connections between science and literature

Beech, Joseph Warren, *The Concept of Nature in Nineteenth Century English Poetry* (New York, 1936)

Beer, Gillian, 'Plot and analogy with science in later nineteenth-century novelists', *Comparative Criticism*, 2 (1980)

Cosslett, Tess, *The 'Scientific Movement' and Victorian Literature* (1982)

Gliserman, Susan, 'Early Victorian science writers and Tennyson's *In Memoriam*' *Victorian Studies*, 18, nos. 3 and 4 (1975)

Henkin, Leo, *Darwinism in the English Novel 1860–1910, the Impact of Evolution on Victorian Fiction* (New York, 1963)

Hough, Graham, 'The natural theology of *In Memoriam*', in *Selected Essays* (1978)

Mason, Michael, '*Middlemarch* and science: problems of life and mind', *Review of English Studies*, n.s. 22, no. 86 (May 1971)

Paris, Bernard J., *Experiments in Life; George Eliot's Quest for Values* (Detroit, 1965)

Roppen, Georg, *Evolution and Poetic Belief; a Study in some Victorian and Modern Writers* (Oslo, 1956)

Stevenson, Lionel, *Darwin Among the Poets* (New York, 1963)

Webster, Harvey Curtis, *On a Darkling Plain; the Art and Thought of Thomas Hardy* (Chicago, 1947)

Wolff, R. L., *Gains and Losses: Novels of Faith and Doubt in Victorian England* (New York, 1977)

Select list of nineteenth-century novels and poems touching on the science and religion 'conflict'

Arnold, Matthew, 'Dover Beach' (1867), 'Empedocles on Etna' (1852), 'Stanzas from the Grande Chartreuse' (1855)

Browning, Robert, 'Bishop Blougram's Apology' (1855), 'Caliban upon Setebos, or, Natural Theology on the Island' (1864), 'Christmas Eve and Easter Day' (1850), 'An Epistle of Karshish the Arab Physician' (1855)

Butler, Samuel, *The Way of All Flesh* (1903)

Select booklist

Clough, Arthur Hugh, 'Easter Day, Naples, 1849' and 'Easter Day II' (1869), 'Epi-Strauss-ium' (1869)

Dickens, Charles, *Hard Times* (1854)

Eliot, George, *Middlemarch* (1871)

Hardy, Thomas, novels: *The Return of the Native* (1878), *Tess of the D'Urbervilles* (1891), *The Woodlanders* (1887). Poems: 'God's Funeral' (1908–10), 'Hap' (1866), 'The Impercipient' (1898), 'The Mother Mourns' (1901), 'Nature's Questioning' (1898), 'New Year's Eve' (1906), 'A Plaint to Man' (1909–10)

Kingsley, Charles, *The Water Babies* (1863)

Meredith, George, 'The Lark Ascending' (1881), 'Meditation Under Stars' (1888), 'Melampus' (1881), 'Ode to the Spirit of Earth in Autumn' (1862), 'The Thrush in February' (1885), 'The Woods of Westermain' (1883)

Tennyson, Alfred, 'Maud' (1864), 'In Memoriam' (1850), 'The Two Voices' (1833–4).

Ward, Mrs Humphrey, *Robert Elsmere* (1888)